ÉIRE-IRELAND

A journal of Irish Studies published quarterly by
THE IRISH AMERICAN CULTURAL INSTITUTE
Table of Contents XXIX: 4

EDITOR: *Thomas Dillon Redshaw, University of St. Thomas.*
BOOK REVIEW EDITOR: *James Rogers.*

ADVISORY EDITORS: *Architecture, Roger Conover, The Massachusetts Insitute of Technology; Arts, James MacKillop, Onondaga Community College; Ascendancy Ireland, John Greene, The University of Southwestern Louisiana; Bibliography, John B. Davenport, University of St. Thomas; Classics, Marianne McDonald, University of California-San Diego; Drama, Christopher Murray, University College Dublin; Gaelic Literature, Ruairí Ó hUiginn, Coláiste Phádraig, Má Nuad; Irish America, Charles Fanning, University of Southern Illinois; Literature, Adrian Frazier, Union College; Nineteenth-Century History, Irene Whelan, Manhattanville College; Political Science, Desmond Dinan, George Mason University; Twentieth-Century History, Lawrence W. McBride, Illinois State University; Women's Studies, Patricia Haberstroh, La Salle University.*

EDITORS EMERITI: *Eóin McKiernan (1965–86); James J. Blake (1987–89).*

EDITORS' NOTES

FOR OVER thirty years, beginning in the late 1920s, Sean O'Casey and the American critic George Jean Nathan continued a transatlantic correspondence full of theatrical enthusiasms and philosophical idiosyncracies. O'Casey spent only three months in Nathan's New York, in 1934, yet the two corresponded as if they were Broadway bon vivants or boulevardiers of the West End—though O'Casey insisted in calling both himself and Nathan "communists"! Patricia Angelin's distillation of their friendship from the letters derives from service as executrix of the Nathan estate. With Robert G. Lowery, Patricia Angelin has published *My Very Dear Sean: George Jean Nathan to Sean O'Casey, Letters and Articles* (1985).

ðà

PERHAPS it is the Dickensian esprit of O'Casey's plays and autobiographies that have led Prof. David Krause back to the sprawling tales of William Carleton. One of Carleton's least studied novels, *Fardorougha the Miser,* begun in 1837, offers a prescient portrayal of pre-Famine Ireland—its folkways, rural social structure, economic exigencies, and Catholic conscience. As Prof. Krause suggests, in *Fardorougha the Miser* Carleton mixes genres and effects so generously that his fiction anticipates the abundant variety of voices and themes characteristic of Revival fiction and drama. Our readers will recall both Prof. Krause's *The Profane Book of Irish Comedy* and his recent article on "The Conscience of Ireland" in ÉIRE-IRELAND (Summer, 1993).

ðà

DURING the Great Hunger, the Irish Constabulary often had to police evictions and clearances. More often, however, as Prof. W. J. Lowe delineates here, the Constabulary had to protect ordinary commerce and public relief efforts. Working from public records, Dr. Lowe details incidents at, for example, Corofin, Ballinlass, Dunfanaghy, and Cranagh that testify not only to the severity of the Famine, but also to the stewardship and discipline of the new police force. Prof. Lowe's articles have appeared in many journals—

including *Hermathena, Saothar,* and *Irish Historical Studies*—and he is author of *The Irish in Mid-Victorian Lancashire* (1989).

ᚥ

CURRENTLY composing a biographical study of the Irish naturalist R. L. Praeger, Seán Lysaght is the author of two collections of poems: *Noah's Irish Ark* (1989) and *Clare Island Survey* (1991). A single sequence dedicated to his father, *Clare Island Survey* records as tokens and emblems of tradition and self the poet's sightings of Clare birds—bunting, shearwater, pipit, or stonechat. These new poems, including prose poems from the sequence *Tagon,* hint at autobiography and offer sightings of Ireland's human landscape. Seán Lysaght studied at University College, Dublin, and the University of Geneva before spending a few years in Germany.

ᚥ

ECONOMETRIC and demographic statistics of all sorts depict the erratic performance of the Irish economy from the founding of the Free State up to the latest "inter-party" government, but statistics by themselves provide few explanations for the waywardness of economic life in Ireland. Here, Prof. Mary E. Daly, editor of *Irish Economic and Social History,* shows plainly that the economy of Ireland expresses the cultures of Ireland and especially the entwined ideas and assumptions of rural nationalism and Catholicism, notably Catholic social teaching of the 1930s. Economic liberalism, whether classical capitalism or moderating Keynesian policies remained suspect even through the Fianna Fáil premiership of Seán Lemass and the publication of T. K. Whitaker's famous white paper, *Economic Development* (1958). Prof. Daly is the author of, among other titles, *A Social and Economic History of Ireland since 1800* and *Dublin: The Deposed Capital, 1860–1914.*

ᚥ

MORE peripatetic than most Irish poets, Derek Mahon is known for the elegance of his film scripts and the ironies, both withering and tender, of his poetry—much of it collected in *Selected Poems* (1991). Now living in Manhattan's Greenwich Village, Mahon is a native of Belfast and it is Mahon's troubled and distant relations with a Belfast recalled from haunts in London or Dublin, that Tim Kendall examines here; but less in terms of the tangible residues of Mahon's physical Belfast, and more in terms of Mahon's turning and inevitably returning stances toward the shut pubs and the well-known places. Tim Kendall is the author of several studies of the poetry of Paul Muldoon in *Irish University Review, London Magazine, Oxford Poetry Review,* and *Verse.*

ᐳᐸ

KNOWN primarily as a didactic and moralizing author, Maria Edgeworth is often perceived as "Irish" only in the pages of *Castle Rackrent* (1800), a satire on the decline of the Protestant Nation and the Ascendancy. Clearly, Edgeworth had the Act of Union in mind as a motive for her satire and, as Prof. Marjorie Lightfoot here delineates, Edgeworth's satires extended through the realm of the courtship novel in *Belinda* (1801) to encompass both dramatic and moral irony and, moreover, subverting parodies of genres and colonial manners. Currently at work on a study of the women in the Brontë Circle, Prof. Lightfoot has lately published articles on Maxine Hong Kingston and Doris Lessing.

ᐳᐸ

FICTION sometimes supplants fact. John Eglinton became a character in Joyce's *Ulysses* only after, however, he had achieved prominence as a critic of the Revival writers and, as Prof. Mary E. Bryson shows, first-hand historian of the movement complementary to Ernest Boyd. Eglinton's *Irish Literary Portraits* (1935) epitomize his views, and a number of those "portraits" were written for the American magazine *The Dial* in the 1920s. Eglinton concerned himself chiefly with George Moore, William Butler Yeats, and A.E. in those articles, though he had the distinction of reviewing himself fictionalized when he reviewed *Ulysses* in 1922. Readers interested in Eglinton's career at *The Dial* will wish to consult Prof. Bryson's earlier study of Eglinton's philosophy in ÉIRE-IRELAND (Summer, 1975).

ᐳᐸ

SUCH journals as *The Dial* or *The Bell,* though bound on library shelves or metamorphosed into microfilm, still give documentary shape to their cultures, and that is why it is useful to reflect on their characters and on the character of their editors, as does Prof. Heather Bryant Jordan here. Of course, Sean O'Faolain is best known for his stories, novels, and critical studies, but his editorship of *The Bell* during the Great Emergency has a noble, because eccentric, value all its own, and *The Bell* established a standard for the literary periodical in Ireland that yet has influence today. Prof.

EDITOR'S NOTES

Jordan is the author of *How Will the Heart Endure: Elizabeth Bowen and the Landscape of War* (1992).

≈

WITH THE return in each issue of the "Language Report"—rendered bilingually now as "*Tuarascáil ar Theanga*"—ÉIRE-IRELAND welcomes back to its pages the enthusiasm and wit of Prof. James J. Blake, who served as editor of ÉIRE-IRELAND from 1987 through 1989. An active and able promoter of Gaelic, Prof. Blake broadcasts in Irish from Fordham University every week and, in the spring of 1995, will be offering graduate-level instruction in Irish at New York University. Here, in the main, Prof. Blake surveys the woeful effects of the "Language Freedom Movement" of the 1970s on the current state of Irish in the Republic.

≈

TWO TITLES by George Brandon Saul remain familiar to students of Yeats and of Irish literature—the two prolegomenas to the study of Yeats's plays and poems (1957, 1958)—but other than those titles and, perhaps, *Traditional Irish Literature and Its Backgrounds* (1953, 1970), Saul's scholarship is little remembered by critics today. Prof. M. Kelly Lynch's memoir and appreciation of Saul's career, accompanied by a checklist of Saul's literary publications, depicts a sensibility well attuned to the nuances of the Irish Revival and rather less attuned to the exigencies of the large, postwar American university. Saul aspired to be more than a scholar and critic, but to be a man of letters in the best turn-of-the-century style, as his volumes of poetry, novels, and plays reveal. A collection of Saul's publications and his literary papers are now housed in the Ellen Clark Research Library at Bucknell University. George Brandon Saul was one of the earliest contributors to ÉIRE-IRELAND.

COMRADES IN ARMS:
GEORGE JEAN NATHAN
AND SEAN O'CASEY

PATRICIA ANGELIN

APRIL, 1993, marked the thirty-fifth anniversary of the death of drama critic George Jean Nathan, and September, 1994, the thirtieth year after the passing of Sean O'Casey. It is a fitting time to recall the unusual friendship between this American critic and an Irish playwright. Although the two men had only one concentrated period of time together, during New York pre-production of *Within the Gates* in the 1934–35 Broadway season, their rapport ran deep. O'Casey expresses their relationship in inscriptions on two of the dozen of his works which the playwright sent to his friend.

> To George Jean Nathan, Poet-Critic Champion of the truth as it is in the Drama, from Sean O'Casey, his comrade in the fight that Drama may have life, and have it more abundantly. New York, 1934.[1]

> From Sean O'Casey to George Jean Nathan, comrade in arms for righteousness, deep sorrow, the loud, reckless laugh, the stirring dance, and the gay song in the theatre; the voice of man speaking his best, in good round terms. . . . Devon, 1945.[2]

Nathan was forty-four and O'Casey forty-six years old when they encountered each other's work on opposite sides of the Atlantic. Nathan saw an inadequate production of *Juno and Paycock* at the tiny Mayfair Theatre in New York in March, 1926. Thomas Quinn Curtiss, Nathan's biographer, says:

> Nathan had x-ray sight for theatrical value. He could detect the value of a script however shoddy the production. He was at once aware of O'Casey's skill at character delineation and in treating situations, and he perceived

---

1 Personal inscription in *Windfalls,* 1934. George Jean Nathan Collection, Olin Library, Cornell University, Ithaca, New York.

2 Personal inscription in *Drums Under the Windows,* 1945.

O'Casey's daring dovetailing of uproarious comedy and stark tragedy. He appreciated O'Casey's extraordinary ability to turn a phrase that transformed the talk of Dublin slum-dwellers into lyric speech.[3]

Later that same spring Nathan saw *The Plough and The Stars* in London. He thought that this play went beyond *Juno and the Paycock* in its deep and ruthless humanity and lyricism. He wrote in *The American Mercury* that O'Casey's play was the major event of the London season, and heralded it again when performed in New York the following year.[4] And later, in 1928, George Jean Nathan heard of and was shocked by Yeats's rejection of *The Silver Tassie* for Dublin's Abbey Theatre. He had not seen the play, but had read the published version. At the same time, O'Casey discovered the critical writings of Nathan in a second-hand bookstore along the River Liffey in Dublin, as O'Casey himself relates in his fourth volume of autobiography:

> So Sean . . . was now puzzled by the Irish critics, for, innocent gaum that he was, he didn't realize then that these fellows didn't know what they were talking about. . . . Then first began Sean's distrust of, and contempt for, the Irish critics. . . . Two critics now began to shine on his thoughts—one Irish, curiously enough, and the other American. They were George Jean Nathan and George Bernard Shaw—the two Georges.
>
> The books formed a gorgeous episode in Sean's life. . . . Comments . . . on plays which—bar Shakespeare, Wilde, and Ibsen—he had neither seen nor read, and which, now, he would never see nor read, for they were all dead, never to rise again; but the criticisms lived on, and gave Sean a candle-light view of the theatre dead, and an arc-lamp view of the theatre living. Nathan's *The Critic and the Drama,* was a book of revelations to Sean. He was becoming less of the innocent gaum every page he passed. Here was a live man of the drama. As deep in what he wrote as he was gay. A wise philosopher, an undaunted critic, a lover of the theatre with cothurnus and sock attached to the glittering costume of the harlequin who carried a torch in his right hand instead of a lath. The Irish drama critics, even those who were poets, could now go to hell for Sean.[5]

From then on O'Casey considered Nathan to be his "*Anam chara* or Soul-Friend—as we say in Irish."[6] Although the two men had not yet met

---

3   Thomas Quinn Curtiss, Introduction to *My Very Dear Sean*, ed. Robert G. Lowery and Patricia Angelin (New Jersey: Associated University Presses, 1985), p. 14.

4   *Ibid.,* p. 15.

5   Sean O'Casey, *Inishfallen, Fare Thee Well* (New York: Macmillan, 1949), pp. 247–8.

6   Sean O'Casey to George Jean Nathan, 30 January 1935. The New York Public Library.

face-to-face, as far as the Irishman was concerned, their minds and souls had met. The two men almost met in April of 1931 when Nathan was invited to London by Lord Beaverbrook to be guest critic on *The Daily Express*. O'Casey read his articles and wrote to Nathan's hotel, but the letter arrived after the critic had sailed for New York.

The following summer Nathan typically answered O'Casey not only in word but in deed—he invited the playwright to contribute to the new literary magazine he was founding and editing with Eugene O'Neill, Theodore Dreiser, James Branch Cabell, and Ernest Boyd—*The American Spectator*. This O'Casey did, soon sending an article entitled "Laurel Leaves and Silver Trumpets" and the welcome news that he was completing a new play. In his very first letters he also expressed the feeling that he already knew Nathan: "I am sorry that you hadn't time to visit London so that I could see you and talk to you for a little while; but, then you have often talked to me, long and earnestly, in the articles and book which you have written . . ."[7] and again, eight months later: "I heard of you first in the Abbey Theatre many years ago; I have read some of your books, and a great many of your articles in *The American Mercury*, so I look upon you as an old and valued friend."[8] Since he had lost the Abbey as a venue for his developing work with the rejection of *The Silver Tassie* in 1928, O'Casey was broadening his prospects instinctively. His nature needed encouragement. After Lady Gregory died in Ireland in 1932, the voluntary expatriate, living in England, reached out to America.

George Jean Nathan grasped that hand and acted the part of an old friend, arranging for O'Casey's business interests and tirelessly hawking *Within the Gates*. "I am determined to get a production for you here and shall leave no stone unturned," Nathan wrote.[9] He had a difficult time doing so. Despite its beauty, the play was risky. It was rejected by the Theatre Guild—producers of much of Shaw and O'Neill and the European avant-garde—and many others. Nathan tried to help buoy O'Casey's finances and spirits in the interim by publishing "Dramatis Personas Ibsenisensis" (July, 1933) and "A Protestant Kid Thinks of the Reformation" (July, 1934) in *The American Spectator* magazine. Finally, even after O'Casey had given it up—"Never mind; it can't be helped. I'm sorry you have given

7 Sean O'Casey to George Jean Nathan, 28 September 1932.

8 Sean O'Casey to George Jean Nathan, 30 May 1933.

9 George Jean Nathan to Sean O'Casey, 14 December 1933 and 11 January 1934. Olin Library, Cornell University.

yourself so much trouble. . . ."[10]—Nathan found two ambitious young men, John Tuerk and George Bushar Markell, who took on the responsibility of producing the play in the upcoming autumn season of 1934 under terms advantageous to the playwright. O'Casey was to come to New York to supervise rehearsals. Nathan wished to assure his comfort and welcome. Enthusiastically O'Casey wrote:

> Mr. [Richard] Madden [O'Casey's business agent] has mentioned that I am to be a guest of yours during my stay in America. If that be your personal wish, then I couldn't and wouldn't ask for a greater honour. . . . I should love to be close to you during the heat and burden of the rehearsals. It would be a decided help and a great comfort. Anyhow, I am determined to do nothing without your and Madden's advice, for, on the whole, I have some common sense left. Without your generous help. . . . there would have been no production of the play in America during my or my kid's lifetime. . . .[11]

Sean O'Casey sailed from Southampton on the Cunard ship *Majestic,* on the following September 13, arriving six days later in New York where Nathan met him at the pier. O'Casey recorded his excitement and fear in his fifth volume of autobiography, *Rose and Crown*:

> He [O'Casey] . . . had contributed a few things to *The American Spectator,* a magazine that had told him there were minds in America that were flushed with courage, with wit, and an unreluctant will to show up political hypocrisy and intellectual sin. He knew something about Nathan's American Theatre by what the critic had written about it. . . . Here thought went back to the past, and here thought stretched forth to the future. . . . During all his life Sean had spoken but to four Americans. . . . Going down the gangway, he felt very lonely. . . . Not for long, though: in the Customs' shed, George Jean Nathan, the famous drama critic, [was] waiting for him with hands outstretched.
>
> Here, Nathan stood looking at nothing, seeing everything, his luminous, wine-coloured eyes glancing at Sean, to see, maybe, if there was a chance of him being something more than a bore; and Sean thinking what in the name of God he would say to this famous critic now standing before him, a soft slouch hat on his finely formed head, set safely on a thick crop of dark hair, slightly tinged with grey, here and there; a greatcoat, so full in the shoulders that it fell round him capewise, down below his knees, a

---

10 Sean O'Casey to George Jean Nathan, 15 February 1934.
11 Sean O'Casey to George Jean Nathan, 18 August 1934.

curving wrinkle of humour, now in repose, trimming the corners of a full, sensuous, handsome mouth.

Nathan in his cape-coat . . . half a dream in the agitated crowd; almost motionless, his own wakefulness, maybe, a hope that this O'Casey will be something more than just bearable company, standing there, with the surge of two thousand years of drama forming the kingdom of heaven within him.[12]

So the playwright came down the gangway not to an "indifferent maw" but to "rest on a friendly arm."[13] His American host installed him near his own apartment in his own hotel and home of thirty years, the Royalton at 44 West 44th Street in the middle of Manhattan. He showed the Irishman all the sights of New York, introduced him to his society and literary associates and friends—Dreiser, Anderson, O'Neill. Nathan assured his acceptance in the new world. The critic also provided a calm center to O'Casey's whirlwind three-month visit during which he not only attended to his play, but earned money by speaking to groups: "a wash, a meal, an evening's chat with George Jean Nathan, a sleep, and off again. . . ."[14] Both previous affinity and mutual needs worked together to bring into flower a friendship that helped infuse both men with renewed creative vigor. The two writers had a wonderful time from that very first day of O'Casey's arrival:

> On that same calm evening, when the moon rode high, George Jean Nathan guided him towards the one hansom cab left living in the world. . . . The serious critic and the serious dramatist, the man from Indiana and the man from Dublin, climbed into the cab for a jaunt through a park in the moonlight. . . . [They were] two old children enjoying it all; a joyous jingling hour of life; a big, red berry on life's tree. A joyride: the pair of them were young again, and heaven was all around them.[15]

This "joyride" time was so intense, so special, so essential an extended moment between two men in their fifties experiencing life together, that O'Casey's children more than fifty years after the event speak of their father's trip as though they were there.

> It was the visit O'Casey never tired of describing when they were growing up in the ramshackle Victorian house in Totnes, England. . . .

---

12 Sean O'Casey, *Rose and Crown* (New York: Macmillan, 1952), pp. 240–242.
13 *Rose and Crown*, p. 241
14 *Rose and Crown*, p. 316.
15 *Rose and Crown*, p. 262-3.

COMRADES IN ARMS: GEORGE JEAN NATHAN AND SEAN O'CASEY

'I bet you $100 Sean came here with George Jean Nathan and Lillian Gish,' said Shivaun O'Casey. She gestured at the mellowing turn-of-the-century racing photos on the oak walls of Gallagher's Steak House in Manhattan's theatre district, 'this was a speak-easy, and all the notables came here.'

'Yes, George Jean Nathan took Sean everywhere,' said Breon O'Casey, her elder brother. 'And this is absolutely the kind of place he'd have come to.'[16]

Indeed, the pair visited all George Jean Nathan's haunts—the Blue Ribbon Cafe, The Colony, The Stork Club, and his private corner table at '21' Club—still marked with a discreet brass plaque.

When O'Casey returned to London just before Christmas, 1934, to attend the birth of his second child, *Within the Gates* was running well, and Nathan had firmly joined those closest to O'Casey's heart and mind. The critic could do no wrong. Aboard ship he wrote "Were New York nothing but a place of ruins, it would be a great city having you there . . . you are the one champion of the Drama, ever standing in the gap o'danger."[17] The two had spent hours upon hours taking together during the autumn of 1934, this ill-matched pair—the suave critic, splendid in custom-made suits with an extra pocket on the right side for his glasses, and the weak-eyed playwright, always informal in turtleneck and tweeds. Nathan suggested he celebrate this eccentricity with an article, and "Why I Don't Wear Evening Dress" duly appeared in the November, 1934, issue of *The American Spectator*. The two attended literary receptions together, went to the theatre, dined, and shared life in the manner to which the cosmopolitan New Yorker was accustomed. Nathan took O'Casey to meet the reclusive Eugene O'Neill in his hotel suite.[18] O'Neill deeply impressed O'Casey: "I liked the joining of the two of us together in a mystical cryptogram of George Sean Nathan, and feel inclined since to sign myself Sean Jean O'Casey. . . . Or better still, Gene [O'Neill], Jean, and Sean—trinity of the Drama."[19] The playwright had need of so deep an enthusiasm to conquer distance and time, for the two men were never to see each other again. Their friendship had been cemented by this time together and, despite the ocean sep-

---

16 Glen Collins, "Gallery Show Unites O'Casey Clan," *New York Times*, Wednesday, 12 April 1989.

17 Sean O'Casey to George Jean Nathan, 22 December 1934.

18 George Jean Nathan, *The Theatre of the Moment* (New York: Knopf, 1936), p. 199.

19 Sean O'Casey to George Jean Nathan, 10 March 1935.

arating the two, O'Casey felt less isolated: "Now, I see that George Jean Nathan stands against the world . . . and this is very comforting."[20] For his part, Nathan's letters immediately went from the salutation, "Dear Sean O'Casey" to "My very dear Sean"—much more personal, and deeply felt. He dedicated his book, *Passing Judgments* (1934), to Sean O'Casey.

In 1936, Sean O'Casey took time off from starting any new plays to produce his own book of criticism, *The Flying Wasp*, clearly inspired by his time with Nathan. Here his frustration over the unsympathetic critics of his native Ireland and of England found vent:

> We haven't a critic like Nathan in the English Theater, and it is time we had. We have only to read some of his works—*Testament of a Critic, Art of the Night, The House of Satan, Since Ibsen, The Critic and the Drama, Another Book on the Theatre, The Theater of the Moment*— to realize that in the Theater of Nathan the curtain is always going up, while in the Theater of the critics here the curtain is always coming down. The critics here are afraid to be alive. . . .[21]

One of Nathan's qualities most admired by O'Casey can be glimpsed in his appropriation of Nathan's own idea of the critical necessity sometimes to mingle "the mind of a gentleman with the emotions of a bum."[22] He exhorts English critics:

> . . . listen, now, to what Nathan has to say to ye: 'It is impossible for the true critic to be a gentleman. I use the word in its common meaning, to wit, a man who avoids offense against punctilio, who is averse to an indulgence in personalities, who is ready to sacrifice the truth to good manners and good form. The critic who is a gentleman is no critic. He is merely the dancing-master of an art.' Put that in your pipes and smoke it.[23]

And, in a letter to Nathan the following year, O'Casey calls *The Flying Wasp* his:

> . . . first and probably last, effort in 'Dramatic Criticism.' It is just that I felt something ought to be said about the way the English critics thought about the Theatre. The shots fired are mostly made from the talks and writings of a fellow called George Jean Nathan. There is, as you know

---

20 Sean O'Casey to George Jean Nathan, 30 January 1935.
21 Sean O'Casey, *The Green Crow* (New York: George Braziller, Inc., 1956), p. 85.
22 George Jean Nathan, *Autobiography of an Attitude* (New York: Knopf, 1928), p. 50.
23 *Ibid.*, p. 64.

yourself, no one here worth enough to make a patch on the seat of your trousers.[24]

There are no letters extant from Nathan to O'Casey from the year 1936, and some are clearly missing from the World War II years. Enough remains, however, to let us know of O'Casey already reminiscing about Nathan's short-lived *American Spectator* (1932–35) as he sends Nathan his first autobiography, *I Knock at the Door.*

> It contains *A Protestant Kid Thinks of the Reformation* and there are many more that would have, I'm sure, gone into your *American Spectator* had people not lost interest in it. I think it was the liveliest and finest monthly I ever handled. How quick it shut down when you departed. 'Cover her face; mine eyes dazzle; she died young.'[25]

In 1939 O'Casey was working on *Purple Dust* and *The Star Turns Red.* The world around the two writers was descending into complete chaos, and the Twenties seemed a long way back. The decade of breadlines and soup kitchens devolved to the decade of the gas chamber and the atom bomb. It was beyond the capability of Nathan's friends Mencken and Dreiser to cope with the Depression, Fascism, and the reality of Hitler. Nathan's bewilderment was less virulent, but he, too, had difficulty privately comprehending a world in which the theatre and drama had to take second place to the terrible realities of daily survival. Yet, Nathan insisted that "Art is a reaching out into the ugliness of the world for vagrant beauty, and imprisoning it in a tangible dream,"[26] and Nathan kept fighting as he had done before to make the dream tangible in beautiful drama produced in the living theater.

O'Casey sent *Purple Dust* to Nathan who received it in New York on March 15, 1940. Producer Eddie Dowling had a good relationship with Nathan, who sent him the plays of poetic mood and delicacy Nathan knew other producers would scorn. Nathan's creative intercession had already won Dowling praise for William Saroyan's *Time of Your Life* and for Paul Vincent Carroll's *Shadow and Substance,* and would soon do so for Tennessee Williams's *The Glass Menagerie.* So, Nathan dispatched *Purple Dust* to Dowling who immediately set to work on its production. Actress Julie Haydon was signed to play Avril and Margot Graham, Souhan. The

24 Sean O'Casey to George Jean Nathan, 8 March 1937.
25 Sean O'Casey to George Jean Nathan, September 1938.
26 George Jean Nathan, *The Critic and the Drama* (New York: Knopf, 1922).

women began rehearsals while the remaining cast and design elements were discussed between producer and critic. O'Casey believed absolutely in Nathan's astuteness and depended on the critic to protect both his aesthetic and commercial interests. Montey Wooley, who had achieved stardom in *The Man Who Came to Dinner*, was considered for the critical role of O'Killigain, but Nathan felt Spencer Tracy would be better in the role, with Laurel and Hardy as the hilariously learned and imperious Englishmen, Basil and Poges. Scripts were dispatched to the stars and verbal commitment to play the roles followed. It looked as though O'Casey and his wife, Eileen, would soon be coming to America to oversee *Purple Dust*.

On May 26, 1940, Haydon and Graham arrived at Dowling's offices excitedly prepared to celebrate the news of the acceptance of the three stars with a party. They turned on the radio to the bulletin that France was effectively lost to the Nazis and that the British had their backs to the sea at Dunkirk.

> The heart-rending retreat aided by anything that could float across the channel from England—manned by old men, women and teenagers—to bring home their battle-weary and wounded, from May 26 till June 4—called 'The Miracle of Dunkirk.'
>
> It was an abrupt end to our bright dream—for *Purple Dust*'s hilarious poke in the ribs of the British could not be given at this time in history— even the title *Purple Dust* referring to the dissolution of the British empire: O'Casey, our prophet.[27]

While Nathan finally suggested that Dowling "save *Purple Dust* for after the war"[28] and reopen *The Time of Your Life* in New York, he continued to work for the mounting of the play:

> But it was 16 years or more before George Jean Nathan was joyfully to hear of its production—during his final illness; though he must have had several dozen promises and at least two documented attempts from various prestigious producers through the years. He at last called them to task in a scorching article and book chapter accusing them all of promises made merely to have their names associated in print with the Great O'Casey.[29]

The war was doubly difficult for correspondents. Mrs. Nathan observed that, "dozens of letters and more than a few books dispatched by

27 Julie Haydon Nathan, directly quoted from her notebooks.
28 *Ibid.*
29 *Ibid.* The article and book chapter to which Mrs. Nathan refers is "Dance Me a Song," in *The Theatre Book of the Year, 1949–1950* (New York: Knopf, 1950), pp. 192–96.

George Jean to Sean are at the bottom of the Atlantic."[30] Certainly some were lost. O'Casey complained to Nathan, "I got neither the book you sent me, nor the one sent by Dick [Madden]—and I longing to read your preface."[31] Eddie Dowling tried valiantly to produce an O'Casey play in lieu of *Purple Dust*. In 1942, *The End of the Beginning* closed out-of-town and in 1948 he rejected *Cock-a-Doodle Dandy* for its perceived anti-Catholicism. The latter play also disturbed O'Casey's American agent Richard Madden and others, but it was Nathan's personal favorite—and Mrs. O'Casey's as well. In "Let 'Em Stop Grousing and Read," in the *New York Journal-American* (9 August 1948), Nathan wrote:

> Another recommended script is Sean O'Casey's new fantasy, *Cock-a-Doodle Dandy*, which, unless my critical equipment had gone to seed, is one of the finest plays of its kind to have come hopefully to the attention of the modern theatre.
>
> The theme here is the rightful joy of life and the proper dismissal from all consideration of those who would fetter it. Employing a mixture of gay symbolism and wild humour, some of it as rich in laughs as anything I've read for a long time, O'Casey filters through his natural cynicism as lively and amusing a slice of fantastic drama as one can imagine.
>
> The embodiment of his central idea in the figure of a rooster, his two boozy counterparts of the memorable Fluther and Joxer out of *The Plough and the Stars* and *Juno and the Paycock*, his fancy in such scenes as those in which the fairest and most delicate of his females suddenly sprouts devil's horns, and in which the stern males madly try to bag an innocent little fowl which they superstitiously imagine is a creature of prodigious evil—these and more, all coated with the brilliant writing for which the author is famous, combine to provide the kind of evening we too seldom are privileged to enjoy in the theatre of today.

George Jean Nathan's least favorite plays were O'Casey's "Red" or Communist dramas *Red Roses for Me* and *The Star Turns Red*, and he devoted two chapters of his *Encyclopedia of the Theatre* to the deleterious effect of Communist ideology on playwrights and their plays. In the chapter entitled "O'Casey," Nathan wrote:

> The two worst influences on present-day playwrights are, very often, Strindberg and Communism. Strindberg, for example did all kinds of things to

30 *Ibid.*

31 Sean O'Casey to George Jean Nathan, 22 September 1941. O'Casey refers to *Five Great Modern Irish Plays*, ed. with a foreword by George Jean Nathan (New York: Modern Library, 1941).

COMRADES IN ARMS: GEORGE JEAN NATHAN AND SEAN O'CASEY

Paul Vincent Carroll before he reformed, and his *Things That Are Caesar's* sufficiently attested. And Communism, one fears, has now adversely affected Sean O'Casey as a dramatic artist, as a perusal of his latest play, *The Star Turns Red*, disturbingly hints.[32]

Then, in a chapter entitled "Left Propagandists," Nathan elaborated on the problem of dramaturgical agitprop:

> The fault of the proletarian boys is that they believe the only way you can make an argument impressive is to put it into a sandbag and hit the other fellow over the head with it. As a result, the plays they write and the plays they endorse are largely indistinguishable from so many holdups. To persuade an audience fully, the weapons must be equally distributed between the play and the audience. A play can't hold a pistol against an audience's head and command it to give up.[33]

And in O'Casey's acceptance of Nathan's criticism of *The Star Turns Red* we see the completeness of the dramatist's faith in his critic friend.

> I have read your 'Encyclopedia' twice over, and a grand book on the theatre it is; outside and in, for Knopf have given it a fine cover. I have written to Knopf's thanking them for sending me your book. I have spent a very happy and stimulating time with it. How you can manage to be ever the same and always different, beats me. Excluding this one, I've read seventeen of your books; and this one is as fine as fair and as merciless and as true as witty as the best of the others. As far as the theatre goes, you are an amazing man; and amazing in a lot of other ways, too. I don't think there is anyone in the world who has the same love for theater as you have. Certainly, no one with the same knowledge; and where's the other boys who have the same courage? My volume of five Irish Plays (Juno, Plough, Gunman, End of Beginning and Pound on Demand) published by Macmillan's here [1935] I dedicated the volume "To George Jean Nathan, Drama Critic, without fear and without reproach. . . ."
>
> I've read your 'O'Casey,' and have pondered over it; and am still pondering over it. One thing I'm certain of: Communism need not injure a playwright. Almost everything I've written (except juvenile stuff) was written as a Communist. I've been a Communist for more years than I care to remember . . . And, God and you forgive me, I regard you as a Communist, too! Look at the simple life you lead; indifferent to most things really, [except] for a good play and a lovely lass.[34]

---

32 George Jean Nathan, *Encyclopedia of the Theatre* (New York: Knopf, 1940), pp. 186–88.

33 *Ibid.*, p. 225.

34 Sean O'Casey to George Jean Nathan, 4 February 1940.

COMRADES IN ARMS: GEORGE JEAN NATHAN AND SEAN O'CASEY

After his first reading of Nathan's book, O'Casey had shared Nathan's comments with the London producers of *The Star Turns Red:*

> The Unity Theatre's a Labor Group who do 'Left' plays, and they first did *Waiting for Lefty* here. How they'll make the Red Star Shine, I don't know. I read them your page on 'Left Propaganda,' and the three of us had to admit that you were right, or as right as a man can be.
>
> I, to speak honestly, hesitated to read them what you said of *The Star Turns Red,* but I did read it to them; and there was silence; and then demur. . . . I took the chance to show how, by this example, that nothing on earth would make you say you like a play you didn't like. I pointed out how deep your affection for me (one of the few things I am proud of, and justly proud of, too), and that this deep affection wouldn't weigh the fraction of a pennyweight with you, when a play was in question.[35]

O'Casey asked no quarter for his own work from such a trusted source. He did not wish to subject others to possible Nathanian thrusts, however, remarking to the critic that "I'm very chary of advising any playwright to send a play to G. J. Nathan, Esq., for so few of them are able to stand up to a fair criticism, or fight an adverse one by trying to write a better play."[36] O'Casey himself welcomed Nathan's opinion, whatever it might be. While writing *Red Roses for Me,* he reacted to Nathan's essay in *The Entertainment of a Nation* (1942): "Thank you, old son. . . . I've just read your 'Contribution of the Irish.' A hard wallop, George. And worse than that, it's terribly true. I'll have to watch my step."[37]

In 1947, O'Casey testified not only to the value of Nathan's championing of worthy new drama, but also to the paradoxically fruitful effect of Nathan's sharp criticism:

> The Irish Theatre needs a critic who will set down the comments of the chronicles of the stage with precision, knowledge, and above all, with courage. . . . A critic who will never be influenced by his paper's policy or profit; . . . who, in his criticism, will separate himself from the seduction of a friend, or from animosity toward an enemy; who will know the Theatre of the Continent as well as he knows his own, far back, and present achievement; a critic who will look upon a play as a play, indifferent to whether it hurts or heals.[38]

35 Sean O'Casey to George Jean Nathan, 27 December 1939.

36 Sean O'Casey to George Jean Nathan, 10 March 1942.

37 Sean O'Casey to George Jean Nathan, 21 February 1942.

38 Seymour Rubin, "Sean O'Casey Letters to George Jean Nathan," *Massachusetts Review* (Winter, 1964), 334.

Nathan knew that O'Casey was never merely a propagandist writer, but "a poet" of "the true music of great wonder and beauty."[39] Nathan was hard, however, on the left-wing American polemical playwrights of the Thirties, as O'Casey had discovered in 1936: "I have read your book *The Theatre of the Moment,* and it is fine reading. . . . But you are hard on 'The Little Red Writing Hoods.' All the same, I think you are perfectly just, though I'd like to be able conscientiously to say that you weren't [*sic*]."[40]

George Jean Nathan professed a deep indifference to political and economic problems. He publicly acknowledged himself a confirmed and unrepentant hedonist, with personal pleasure as his only guiding principle. Yet as O'Casey observed, Nathan lived simply, and the day-to-day program of his life, which was extremely disciplined, made a mockery of his care-for-nobody philosophy. In addition, Charles Angoff, who assisted Nathan and H. L. Mencken at *The American Mercury* in the 1920s wrote: "[Nathan] claims to be indifferent to the generally accepted moral code, yet he lives by a very strict code himself, and that code is really not so different from the generally accepted one as he thinks."[41] Much has been made of Nathan's disinterest in politics, which certainly went against the zeitgeist of the 1930s when politics equalled morality for much of the intelligentsia.

> What interests me in life [says Nathan] is the surface of life: life's music and color, its charm and ease, its humor and its loveliness. The great problems of the world—social, political, economic, and theological—do not concern me in the slightest. . . . My sole interest lies in writing. . . . Give me a quiet room, a pad of paper, eight or nine sharp lead pencils, a handful of thin, mild cigars, and enough to eat and drink—all of which, by the grace of God, are happily within my means—and I do not care a tinker's damn [*sic*] . . . whether the nations of the earth arm, disarm, or conclude to fight their wars by limiting their armies to biting each other.[42]

George Jean Nathan chose to battle for mankind's good through literature, focusing on dramatic literature as realized onstage in the live theatre. Bernard Sobel, who viewed the theatre scene from his vantage point as a theatre publicist, observed of George Jean Nathan: "Like Euclid, he retires to his tent when he finds a war raging outside and there give him-

---

39 *Ibid.*

40 Sean O'Casey to George Jean Nathan, 28 October 1936.

41 Charles Angoff, Introduction to *The World of George Jean Nathan* (New York: Knopf, 1953), p. xv.

42 George Jean Nathan, *The World in Falseface* (New York: Knopf, 1923), pp. x–xii.

COMRADES IN ARMS: GEORGE JEAN NATHAN AND SEAN O'CASEY

self over to the thing that means most to him—and much also to the world, if an art is to be sustained and preserved.[43] Nathan himself illustrates such retirement in the following six paragraphs of musing after an encounter with Sinclair Lewis's wife, the journalist Dorothy Thompson.

> The room was beautiful. The orchestra was softly playing a Strauss waltz. The girls in their flowered late summer dresses looked lovely. The champagne was excellent. I went over and sat with Dorothy Thompson. "What," she instantly and peremptorily demanded of me, "is your opinion of Molotov, Voroshilov, Kalinin, Malenkov, and Timoshenko?" "I read Sean O'Casey's new play, *Purple Dust*, this afternoon," I said. "It is rich in poetic imagination."
>
> She looked at me over her champagne glass with profound disgust. "What is a mere play, even one by O'Casey, in times like these!" she exclaimed.
>
> "But," scared half to death, I allowed, "It happens that my job is dramatic criticism, and the play interests me."
>
> "A critic!" she scoffed, as the waiter refilled her glass. "There is no place today for a mere kibitzer in life."
>
> Politely, nay with ineffable chivalry, refraining from observing that the only perceptible difference between us was that Dorothy was a critic-kibitzer in the field of war and politics whereas I was one in the field of the theatre and drama, I bowed elegantly at the middle, kissed her on each cheek, for I have long entertained a personal regard for her, and departed in the direction of the bar. There, after a brief colloquy with the bartender on the respective merits of Joe DiMaggio and Alphonse Daudet, the latter a great favorite of my bartending friend, I stood and meditated.
>
> Why, I wondered, in a world grown cruel and ugly and so famished for even a little glimpse of the old peace and fineness and beauty, why this paradoxical sudden wide distaste and even contempt for the artist and for those who would defend and champion him? Why, I pondered—and my bartending friend sympathetically pondered with me—this belief that there is no place in the world today for men and women who steadfastly hold themselves professionally, if mayhap not personally, aloof from the current confusion and who steadfastly hope and try to keep alive the inspiriting old artistic traditions?[44]

This pensive little story gives us great insight into Sean's friend George. It is true that the first five sentences reflect Nathan's hedonism; each concerns atmosphere, the senses of sight, sound, taste—and pleasure in the

---

43 Bernard Sobel, *Broadway Heartbeat* (New York: Hermitage House, 1953), p. 298.

44 George Jean Nathan, *The Entertainment of a Nation* (New York: Knopf, 1942), p. 210.

expectation of intelligent companionship. Nathan's companion, how-ever, reacts with a typically American dismissal of the importance of lit-erature and art when the world is in chaos. Her attitude is that drama is dispensable at best, irrelevant, and even morally wrong at worst. In the fourth paragraph, Miss Thompson dismisses Nathan as a "kibitzer," but George Jean Nathan was not a mere commentator, however talented, nor an uninvolved observer on the sidelines of the theatre and drama. An ac-tive mover and shaker in his sharp, subtle manner on every level of the day-to-day life of the theatre, Nathan worked constantly to obtain pro-ductions for O'Casey's plays and nourished the playwright in public and private writings regardless of the response of others, and O'Casey recog-nized this:

> The weakness of the critics is that no author can learn from them—what one condemns another praises. The one critic who had been a help and a joy to me is George Jean Nathan, the famous American Drama-Critic. The others puzzle me.[45]

To Nathan, this was important: the O'Caseys of the world were the ones who preserved the world *from* chaos. They needed defending. He defended them. This was his focus. There were plenty of fine men and women la-boring in the fields of politics, very few in the world of arts and literature. He felt there was no more important work than this.

O'Casey understood Nathan, although the semantics he used are star-tling. On the surface, it is either hopelessly naive or laughable to call George Jean Nathan a "communist," as O'Casey repeatedly did.

> To me the great proletarian dramatist of America is the bould [*sic*] O'Neill. And the great proletarian critic is—G. J. N. For, my dear George you are a red. You may say you don't give a damn about this or that, but you are a red revolutionary in the theatre, and you have always been one—at least since I began to know you, and that's twelve years ago. You want the <u>best that can be given to the art of the theatre and that's the creed of the communist.</u>[46]

For O'Casey, to call a man a "communist" was the crowning compliment. Nathan, with his very different temperament defined the identical values as "aristocratic." Nathan spoke of the aristocrat, not in a class sense—

45 Sean O'Casey to Mrs. Doris Leach, 27 February 1949, *The Letters of Sean O'Casey*, ed. David Krause (New York: Macmillan, 1980), II: 591.
46 Sean O'Casey to George Jean Nathan, 28 October 1936.

COMRADES IN ARMS: GEORGE JEAN NATHAN AND SEAN O'CASEY

although in his public persona he reflected to the world was just that—but as "man at his best."

> Drama is, in essence, a democratic art in constant brave conflict with *aristocracy of intelligence, soul and emotion*. When drama triumphs, a masterpiece like *Hamlet* comes to life. When the conflict ends in a draw, a drama, say, such as *El Gran Galeoto*. When the struggle ends in defeat, the result is a Way Down East or a *Lightnin'*. This obviously, is not to say that great drama may not be popular drama, nor popular drama great drama, for I speak of drama here not as this play or that, but as a specific art. And it is as a specific art that it finds its test and trial, not in its own intrinsically democratic soul, but in the *extrinsic aristocratic soul that is taste and connoisseurship and final judgement*. Drama that has come to be at once great and popular has ever first been given the imprimatur, not of democratic souls, but of aristocratic. Shakespeare and Moliere [*sic*] triumphed over *aristocracy of intelligence, soul and emotion* before that triumph was presently carried on into the domain of inferior intelligence, soul and emotion. In our own day, the drama of Hauptmann, Shaw and the American O'Neill has come into its popular own only after it first achieved the imprimatur of what we may term the unpopular, or undemocratic theaters. Aristocracry cleared the democratic path for Ibsen, as it cleared it, in so far as possible, for Rostand and Hugo von Hoffmansthal.[47]

Nathan called their mutual pursuit of the "best that can be given"[48] "aristocratic."[49] O'Casey called it "communist." Both are correct: few have the faculty to judge the best and many do not want it, yet all deserve and need the best. Both O'Casey and Nathan knew instinctively that

> Great drama, like great men and women, is always just a little sad. . . . Reflection, sympathy, wisdom, gallant gentleness, experience—the chords upon which great drama is played—these are wistful chords. . . .
>
> The aim of great drama? It is not to make men happy with themselves as they are, but with themselves as they might, yet alas cannot, be.[50]

Nathan never had any trouble with the mixture of tragic and comic elements for which so many criticized O'Casey. He understood that "Drama

---

47 *The Critic and the Drama*, pp. 29–30.

48 Vladimir Kozlenko, *The Quintessence of Nathanism* (New York: Vrest Orton, 1930), p. 37.

49 *Ibid.*

50 Nathan, *The Critic and the Drama*, pp. 31–32.

is a two-souled art: half divine, half clownish."[51] They enjoyed each other's writing skill and humor. O'Casey wrote, "I like you because you give me a start—at times a shock; but I like you just as much because you make me laugh, and always a laugh worth enjoyment."[52]

Sean O'Casey recognized in George Jean Nathan a kindred spirit and a complement to himself. Perhaps each man subconsciously cast himself and the other as a hero in the pursuit of the best in drama. Certainly the Gaelic Seán Ó Cathasaigh, drawing from the deep well of his Celtic ancestors, cast George Jean Nathan in the role of the powerful satirist seers of ancient Ireland who were both praisers and scourges of the warrior caste whose deeds they recorded and amplified. Nathan certainly filled an equivalent modern function where O'Casey was concerned. Both shared the "aristocratic" social values of Gaelic heroic literature: generosity, hospitality, loyalty, honor of the personal word, belief in the power of words, strength and skill. These values O'Casey of course, deemed "communist." Certainly O'Casey was a word-warrior whose deeds and works needed to be praised, sung, and recorded. Nathan sang them. Nathan well knew that, without the dramatist, the critic was nothing:

> Art is a partnership between the artist and the artist-critic. The former creates; the latter re-creates. Without criticism, art would of course still be art, and so with its windows walled in and with its lights extinguished would the Louvre still be the Louvre. Criticism is the windows and the chandeliers of art; it illuminates the enveloping darkness in which art might otherwise rest only vaguely discernible, and perhaps altogether unseen.[53]

His friend Sean O'Casey expressed their partnership thus: "The two—critic and dramatist—are two tassels hanging on the same wonderful curtain; attached to colored, silken cords pulling gorgeous curtains aside and then pulling them together again: between them they bind and loose all that is good, great, and glorious in the Theater."[54]

---

51 Nathan, *The Critic and the Drama*, p. 20.
52 Sean O'Casey to George Jean Nathan, 4 October 1949.
53 Nathan, *The Critic and the Drama*, p. 5.
54 O'Casey, *The Green Crow*, pp. 14–15.

WILLIAM CARLETON, DEMIURGE OF IRISH CARNIVAL: *FARDOROUGHA THE MISER*, 1839

DAVID KRAUSE

. . . only Carleton, born and bred a peasant, was able to give us the vast multitude of grotesque, pathetic, humourous persons, misers, pig-drivers, drunkards, school-masters, labourers, priests, madmen, and to fill them all with an abounding vitality.

. . . he was what few men have even been or can ever be, the creator of a new imaginative world, the demiurge of a new tradition.

—W. B. Yeats

THE TWENTIETH CENTURY comic world of James Joyce and the nineteenth-century comic world of William Carleton—I want to begin with an analogy between the way these two literary giants created an abounding and indestructible vision of Ireland in their fiction. According to Frank Budgen, Joyce explained one of the aims in writing his great novel *Ulysses* in the following ambitious terms: "I want to give a picture of Dublin so complete that if the city one day suddenly disappeared from the earth it could be reconstructed out of my book."[1] With proper respect for Joyce's grand scheme, it should be pointed out that the reconstructed picture of Dublin would be more faithfully accurate with the addition of some essential people and places from his *Dubliners* and *A Portrait of the Artist as a Young Man*— as well as from the indigenous and earthy Dublin of Sean O'Casey, Brendan Behan, and Flann O'Brien. And if a similar reconstruction had to be made of nineteenth-century peasant Ireland, which has indeed disappeared now, a faithful picture could be recreated from Carleton's great folk-epic comedy *Fardorougha the Miser*, as well as from his *Traits and Stories of the Irish*

---

1 Frank Budgen, *James Joyce and the Making of Ulysses* (New York: Harrison Smith and Robert Haas, 1934), pp. 67–68.

Peasantry, but it would not be necessary to add any material from the writings of Maria Edgeworth, the Banims, or Gerald Griffin.

I have decided to stress *Fardorougha* because it has too seldom been recognized and celebrated as a comic masterpiece; because, though it was apparently enjoyed by readers in Carleton's time, it has since then been ignored or misunderstood by largely indifferent critics who to this day have not perceived it to be a finely constructed and artfully rendered dark comedy; and because this novel, along with the short fiction in *Traits and Stories,* reflects the full measure of Carleton's remarkable genius. Therefore, I want to present Carleton through *Fardorougha* as a striking example of what W. B. Yeats called the Celtic Demiurge, the symbolic creator who reigned over the primal and palpable peasant world of Ireland. I want to offer this novel also as a quintessential illustration of what the Russian critic Mikhail Bakhtin called the carnival world of comic fiction, as a rare emblem of what, in their separate yet related ways, Yeats and Bakhtin saw as the vitality and variety of the rich folkloric imagination.

From many perspectives Carleton is a complex figure who has been approached with too many qualifications in an attempt to account for his minor inconsistencies and contradictions. In his own time, as well as ours, William Carleton (1794–1869) emerges as something of an enigma, for he is a towering and elusive artist who defies convenient classification. As a man and as a writer, Carleton could be both wildly creative and conservative, rebellious and insecure, strongly profane and sometimes sympathetic to religious faith, antidoctrinaire and sometimes accommodating to secular views. He lived through some of the worst years of agrarian conflict and the disastrous Famine of early nineteenth-century Ireland, and these tragic realities of necessity appear in his fiction, particularly in his tragicomic novels, where some form of violence functions as an overriding symbol of grim Irish experience, tempered only by Carleton's compassion and his comic vision of survival. Perhaps Sigmund Freud most effectively accounted for this connection between the shock of a tragic experience and a comic reaction to it as a psychological impulse that creates compensatory laughter when he wrote: "Now humor is a means of obtaining pleasure in spite of the distressing affects that interfere with it; it acts as a substitute for the generation of these affects, it puts itself in their place."[2] Carleton often

2 Sigmund Freud, *Jokes and Their Relation to the Unconscious,* trans. James Strachey (New York: Norton Library, 1963), p. 228.

evokes this substitute ironic laughter, thus mocking and taking some of the harm out of the distress, the way gallows humor becomes a compensatory method of dealing with the ultimate indignity. Such mocking or irreverent comedy may provide a way to go on living with what is too terrible, a way of laughing in order to bear the unbearable.

In his short stories and novels Carleton is a master of such comic survival techniques. Along with Maria Edgeworth's *Castle Rackrent,* Carleton's *Traits and Stories* and *Fardorougha* represent pioneering achievements in early Irish fiction, although the subtle Edgeworth novel concentrates on the big-house tradition of the decaying Protestant Ascendancy—we never see how or where the ironic or innocent servant-narrator Thady Quirk lives as one of the dispossessed lower orders—in contrast to Carleton's comprehensive portrait of distressed peasant life as seen through the sharp eyes of one of their own, an articulate hedge-school taught author. Furthermore, Edgeworth wrote about Ireland for readers in England and had her books published there, whereas Carleton was the first Irish writer whose works were published first in Ireland and for Irish readers.

The most important recent study of Carleton's early work, the late Barbara Hayley's *Carleton's "Traits and Stories" and the 19th Century Anglo-Irish Tradition* (1983), presents a careful analysis of all the revisions and additions that appear in the five editions of the continuingly popular *Traits and Stories* issued between 1830 and 1840. In her summing up Hayley is disturbed by what she sees as a pattern of careless and inconsistent revision as Carleton apparently hurried through the later editions. This leads her to the conclusion that Carleton "was not a disciplined enough writer to found and carry through a 'tradition' for himself, and certainly not for Ireland."[3] Such censure places an unfair and unreasonable burden upon Carleton's largely improvised and irregular career, as if one should expect such a nonliterary writer—a rough-hewn peasant free from all critical coteries and scholarly imperatives, free from any implications of an anxiety of influence—to be able, let alone presume, to establish a tradition of Irish fiction.

Even with the evidence of some minor refinements in Carleton's later revisions, Hayley's argument fails to convince many modern readers that there are signs of respectability in the broadly irreverent and savagely farcical peasant voices that fairly leap from the pages of *Traits and Stories* and from Carleton's best novels in which symbols of respectability and au-

3   Barbara Hayley, *Carleton's "Traits and Stories" and the 19th Century Anglo-Irish Tradition* (Gerrards Cross, Bucks: Colin Smythe, 1983), p. 394.

thority are among the chief targets of Carleton's sharp comedy. Several generations ahead of his urbane countryman Oscar Wilde, the rustic Carleton instinctively knew that respectability was the enemy of the people, and he also knew that the technique of comic exaggeration, or the guile of creative mendacity—what Wilde called the fine art of lying—was an essential literary strategy for an artist in a hypocritical world. Because Barbara Hayley limited herself to an examination of Carleton's short stories, she seemed unaware that what she called his "wild Irish voice," far from being muted, rises and echoes through his longer fiction, particularly the three big novels of his major period, *Fardorougha the Miser* (Dublin, 1839), *Valentine M'Clutchy* (Dublin, 1845), *The Black Prophet* (Belfast, London, 1847). Nor is she alone in ignoring the novels, for practically all critics—supporters as well as detractors, from his own time down to the present—have decided Carleton was incapable of controlling let alone sustaining the longer form.

Carleton began *Fardorougha* in February, 1837, and it appeared in serial form in the *Dublin University Magazine,* running irregularly for a year—he probably had some difficulty preparing new chapters since nothing appeared from June to November, 1837—and it was finally completed in February, 1838, and published in 1839 in book form. Carleton was convinced he had written a fine novel, one that was so well received by readers in Ireland and, later, in England that several new editions had to be published. For the 1848 edition, Carleton decided to write a special introduction in which he replied to his friendly detractors who had warned him not to try to write a novel, thinking that an ambitious effort was beyond his ability. After acknowledging the critical praise he had received for *Traits and Stories,* Carleton moved on to confront the warnings against the new challenge of *Fardorougha:*

> At the same time, whilst I was complimented and praised, my friends began to hint that indeed I was a clever writer; that I knew Irish life remarkably well; but that they were of opinion there was more of memory than imagination in my writing. "He is a fine fellow in his way—that is, at *a short* story or so—but he wants invention, and has not strength of wing for a long-sustained flight. He will never be able to write a novel; and it is a pity, for he is a fine fellow. . . ."
>
> "True," another friend would reply, "and if he remains as he is, all is right. Let him keep within his own range, if he is wise; but then I fear he won't have sense to do so. I wish to God some one would advise him! He

will try his hand at a novel, and fail, whereas if he keeps as it is, and sticks to short, pretty stories, he need fear nothing."[4]

Here Carleton was in the position James Joyce would have been confronted with if critics had warned him to stick to the safety of the short stories in *Dubliners*. Of course, he could not have known that Joyce would have disagreed with those friendly critics who warned Carleton that "there was more memory than imagination" in his writing. Joyce later insisted upon the reverse distinction when he stated that "imagination is memory," and proved it with his three profound novels of incomparable Irish memories, as Carleton was to prove it with *Traits and Stories*, and at least six of his powerful novels with their abounding vitality of Irish folk memories. It might be relevant to mention here that the poet Octavio Paz, in a parallel statement that could be applied to Carleton and Joyce, claimed that "Poetry is memory become image, and image become voice."[5] For Carleton, this significant statement might read: fiction is memory become imagination, and imagination become voices—the multiple and rich voices of the peasant world.

In spite of these resonant distinctions about memory and imagination, an almost unanimous chorus of critical doubters has consistently maintained that Carleton's novels were transparently unsuccessful. The disapproval came early from a largely sympathetic scholar and biographer, D. J. O'Donoghue, who edited and wrote part of the two-volume *Life of William Carleton* that was published in 1896, twenty-seven years after Carleton's death. The first volume contains Carleton's remarkable autobiography, written during the severe pain of terminal cancer and near-paralysis in 1868, the year before he died, covering only the first thirty-four years of his life. Relying upon many Carleton letters which he included, O'Donoghue completed the basic information about the remaining years in volume two. In his academic and somewhat neoclassical approach to literature, O'Donoghue qualified his praise of *Traits and Stories* with this comment on what he called Carleton's rough prose style: "He did not attempt to introduce the requisite neatness of workmanship . . . he did not stop to polish or to prune."[6] Such supposedly careless and unrefined writ-

4 William Carleton, *Fardorougha the Miser; or The Convicts of Lisnamona* With an Introduction Written for the Present Edition (London: Sims and M'Intyre, 1848), p. xv; hereafter cited parenthetically, thus: (*FM* xv).

5 *New York Times Book Review*, 8 December 1991.

6 David J. O'Donoghue, *The Life of William Carleton, An Account of His Life and Writings, From the Point at which the Autobiography Breaks Off*, 2 Vols. (London: Downey and Co., 1896), p. 352.

ing was even more damaging in the novels, according to the fastidious O'Donoghue:

> He was not a good novelist in this sense, that he did not possess the skill to construct a first-rate plot. His more ambitious works, issued as novels, are badly put together. . . . Carleton tries to depend upon the characters rather than upon the incidents in his (so called) novels proper. He resembles Dickens in relying chiefly upon his knowledge of human nature. Neither was capable of arousing and enchaining attention by their stories *as such;* it is their rich fund of humour or (as in Carleton's case especially) their pathos which keeps the reader to their pages.[7]

Apparently O'Donoghue did not realize he was paying Carleton a high compliment by comparing his novels to the supposedly ill-constructed works of Dickens. According to his rigid concept of fiction, both writers were wrong to stress characters over incidents, and to rely upon humor and pathos. It is of course possible that their intuitive knowledge of human nature and their unrestrained creative powers were more reliable and credible than O'Donoghue's narrow critical formula. No doubt the structure of the Dickens and Carleton novels was partly shaped by the fact that these appeared originally as magazine serials, which probably accounted for their open and episodic form, for their lively characters drawn in boldly colorful strokes, for their intricate plots and subplots that required cliff-hanging incidents for chapter-ending suspense, and for their balancing combination of grim tragedy, broad comedy, and intense pathos or compassion. Such striking and sprawling canvases reflected the dramatic genius of the Dickensian and Carletonian novel, which obviously represented too much exuberant and even indulgent narrative energy for the prim O'Donoghue.

The valid Dickensian parallel was not the only significant link to Carleton's unorthodox fictional form. Fortunately, the young W. B. Yeats, reacting to Carleton's reputation at the same time as O'Donoghue, came up with an important connection to the Gaelic tradition. Reviewing O'Donoghue's two-volume *Life of William Carleton* in the London *Bookman,* Yeats emphasized Carleton's peasant roots and indicated that much of his inspiration "came from the heart of Gaelic Ireland, and found there the symbols of his art. . . . He was what few men have ever been or can ever be, a creator of a new imaginative world, the demiurge of a new tradition."[8] This was, of course, an old Irish tradition newly awakened in Carleton's

7   *Ibid.,* II: 353–54.
8   W. B. Yeats, *The Bookman* (March, 1896).

WILLIAM CARLETON, DEMIURGE OF IRISH CARNIVAL

revival of the Gaelic oral speech patterns intoned by the wise old shanachie. Transposed into spoken English, Carleton's Gaelic folk idioms and rhythms follow the shape of the storyteller's humorous invocations and cleverly suspenseful digressions that become an organic part of the vivid tales. Growing up fully exposed to the legendary rituals of Irish folklore—heard from his Gaelic-speaking parents, his father's phenomenal memory of folkways and idioms, his mother's famed singing of folk ballads in Irish—Carleton inherited and reaped the bounty of their treasured racial memory. And by calling him the Celtic Demiurge, Yeats added an ancient classical touch, symbolically associating Carleton with the name Plato gave to the deity or Gnostic creator of the material world—here the earthy peasant world of the vanishing, but still vibrant, Gael newly revived in Anglo-Irish fiction by Carleton. This insight came surprisingly from the young Pre-Raphaelite and mystical Yeats who was then, and remained so all his lifetime, totally committed to an antimaterialistic view of life and art. Thus, the spiritual poet had celebrated the material peasant.

A year before he read O'Donoghue on Carleton, Yeats had already been brooding about the state of the Irish literary imagination in the first of a series of four articles on "Irish National Literature" in the *Bookman* in which Carleton is prominently featured. Literary sleuths who wish to pursue the Dickensian parallel might also consider a possible Chaucerian connection, for along the way Yeats, with his typical bell-ringing intuition, calls Carleton "the peasant Chaucer of a new tradition," a folk storytelling tradition "embodied in the customs of the poor, their wakes, their hedge-schools, their factions, their weddings, their habits of thought and feeling."[9] Then, in an attempt to suggest the magnitude of such a unique literary endeavor, Yeats envisions the enormous challenge that must have confronted a peasant artist like Carleton by offering this symbolic image of the rough and arduous shaping process of creation: "In his time only a little of Irish history, Irish folk-lore, Irish poetry had been got into the English tongue; he had to dig the marble for his statue out of the mountain side with his own hands, and the statue shows not seldom the clumsy chiselling of the quarryman."[10] Unfortunately, during the hundred years since O'Donoghue and Yeats made their contrasting comments, criticism of Carleton's novels has consistently followed O'Donoghue's negative view that they were "badly put together," missing the full significance of

9   W. B. Yeats, "Irish National Literature" *The Bookman* (July, 1895).
10 *Ibid.*

what Yeats had described as some of the expected and understandable "clumsy chiselling," and ignoring the heroic energy and self-made achievement of the powerful peasant quarryman.[11]

The best way to reply to that negative criticism is to turn directly to one of Carleton's finest novels, *Fardorougha the Miser*. To my knowledge, no one has yet presented a proper and fair critical analysis of a Carleton novel, particularly as a unified and carefully controlled comedy or tragicomedy. The book opens pointedly with a symbolic description of a lush landscape of hazel and mountain ash trees, flourishing holly and blackthorn

11 For various reasons, with several notable exceptions, most critics agree with O'Donoghue. Thomas MacDonagh, one of the martyrs of the Easter Rising, in *Literature in Ireland* (1916), decided that Carleton might have been a great writer "if he had been a patriot," an admirable but dubious asset for an artist. Stephen Gwynn in *Irish Literature and Drama* (1936), regrets that Carleton was too much of a peasant to be an artist: "He was, more's the pity, a thoroughly uneducated writer." Roger McHugh's article, "William Carleton: A Portrait of the Artist as a Propagandist," *Studies* (March, 1938), states that a didactic impulse undermines his potentially powerful novels. One of the rare exceptions, Benedict Kiely's *Poor Scholar* (1947), is a highly enlightened treatment of Carleton's life and work, and at one key point he draws an important distinction between Carleton the compassionate peasant artist and John Mitchel the pitiless revolutionary gentlemen: "He could never, like Mitchel, the gentleman who became a revolutionary, welcome murder as a weapon against murder, and disorder from below as the only answer to disorder from above. In that he was much less logical than Mitchel and the whole revolutionary Ireland and the revolutionary Europe of which Mitchel was a part. But he was much more human, in the sense in which it is human to be torn with pity for the sorrows of the poor people." Thomas Flanagan's *The Irish Novelists, 1800–1850* (1959), turns the critical tide against Carleton as a novelist with unsubstantiated generalizations that merely echo the negative views of O'Donoghue. John Wilson Foster in *Forces and Themes in Ulster Fiction* (1974) touches Carleton briefly but always with remarkable insight, especially as a comic writer. Robert Lee Wolff in *William Carleton, Irish Peasant Novelist* (1980) calls Carleton an anti-Catholic writer and says his novels lack structural control. John Cronin in *The Anglo-Irish Novel* (1980) agrees that the novels are poorly organized and adds that they are too melodramatic and sentimental. Anthony Cronin in *Heritage Now* (1982) says the novels are "not very readable" because the novel form is "an alien one" to him. A. Norman Jeffares in *Anglo-Irish Literature* (1982), echoing the negative generalizations of O'Donoghue and Flanagan, says Carleton "could not manipulate his plots." Eileen A. Sullivan in *William Carleton* (1983), in the Twayne series, offers a catalogue of information with little critical insight. In *The Pioneers of Anglo-Irish Fiction, 1800–1850* (1986), Barry Sloan stresses Carleton's gift as a fine storyteller but seldom applies his sound judgments to the novels. James M. Cahalan's *The Irish Novel, A Critical History* (1988) is a general survey, but contains some dubious psychoanalytical guesses. For example, Cahalan makes the unlikely claim that Carleton must have shared a guilt complex with the miserly Fardorougha. Kiely and Foster are the critics to be trusted here.

WILLIAM CARLETON, DEMIURGE OF IRISH CARNIVAL

bushes, highlighted with the image of a natural personification that ironically prepares the ground for the first voices: "Here grew a thick interwoven
mass of dogtree, and upon a wild hedge-row, leaning like a beautiful wife
upon a rigged husband, might be seen that most fragrant and exquisite of
creepers, the delicious honey-suckle, supported by clumps of blackthorn"
(*FM* 1). Soon, a horseman gallops up to a little whitewashed cottage to an-
nounce that a somewhat rigged husband and his not quite exquisite wife
are in urgent need of the services of the midwife who lives in the cottage,
and we hear that human nature has belatedly tried to imitate nature:

> "Is Mary Moan at home?" said the horseman.
>
> "For a maricle—ay!" replied the female; "who's *down* in the name o'-
> goodness?"
>
> "Why, thin, I'm thinkin' you'll be smilin' whin you hear it," replied
> the messenger. "The sorra one else than Honor Donovan, that's now mar-
> rid upon Fardorougha Donovan to the tune of thirteen year. Bedad, time
> for her any how—but, sure it'll be good whin it comes, we're thinkin'."
>
> "Well, betther late than never—the Lord be praised for all his gifts, any
> how! Put your horse down to the mountin' stone, and I'll be wid you in
> half a jiffy, acushla." She immediately drew in her head, and ere the mes-
> senger had well placed his horse at the aforesaid stirrup, or mounting-
> stone, which is an indispensable adjunct to the midwife's cottage, she is-
> sued out, cloaked and bonneted; for her practice was so extensive, and the
> demands upon her attendance so frequent, that she seldom slept, or went
> to bed, unless partially dressed.   (*FM* 2)

The man, who is Nogher M'Cormick, Fardorougha's loyal servant,
comes full of comic innuendoes about the very late pregnancy: "'This
quare enough business, as some o' the nabours do be sayin'—marrid upon
one another beyant thirteen year, an' ne'er a sign of a hapworth till now.
Why then bedad it *is* quare.'" (*FM* 3). But the experienced as well as sur-
prised midwife, "with an expression of mysterious and superior knowledge," warns him to leave such things to the will of God, as well as to her
own perhaps too often proven expertise, and adds the following comment
on the unusual situation:

> "Very well; seein' that, what more have we to say barrin' to hould our
> tongues. Childre sent late always come either for great good or great sarra
> to their paarents—an' God grant that this may be for good to the honest
> people—for indeed honest people they are, by all accounts. But what my-
> self wonders at is, that Honor Donovan never once opened her lips to me
> about it. However, God's will be done! The Lord send her safe over all her

throubles, poor woman! And, now that we're out o' this thief of a lane, lay on for the bare life, and never heed me. I'm as good a horseman as yourself; and, indeed, I've a good right, for I'm an ould hand at it."

"I'm thinking," she added, after a short silence, "it's odd I never was much acquainted with the Donovans. I'm tould they're a hard pack, that loves the money, honest as they are."

"Faix," replied her companion, "let Fardorougha alone for knowin' the value of a shillin'!—they're not in Europe can hould a harder grip of one."

(*FM* 3)

Throughout this urgent and amusing prelude, it is implicit, especially given Nogher's knowledge of his master's habits, and the concurring view of the neighbors, that Fardorougha and his wife, who was too ashamed to tell the midwife about her unexpected condition, kept a hard grip on their love—especially Fardorougha, who apparently was as miserly with his sex as with his money. This thirteen-year-old joke was inevitable in a village where the midwife was kept so busy at her handy mounting-stone that she seldom was able to sleep through the night without being called. Carleton himself must have had his own reason for being amused in telling this tale, for he was the last of fourteen children; and the local midwife, whom he mentions in his introduction, was actually and appropriately named Mary Moan. She is the shrewd and practical peasant throughout the opening chapter—her memorable and only appearance in the novel. There are few if any spear-carriers in Carleton's fiction, for he usually allows seemingly minor characters to come fully alive with distinctive traits and words, and they invariably make significant contributions to the story.

After the baby, Connor, is safely born, Fardorougha is immediately caught up in the unlikely but for him real "conflict between growing avarice and affection" (*FM* 7), worrying that he will now be reduced to poverty and at the same time feeling intense love for his new son to the point of tears: "'We're married near fourteen years,'" Honor says to Mary Moan, "'and, until this night, I never seem him shed a tear.'" (*FM* 11). When he disappears in distress, it is the comforting Mary who steps in and assures Honor that all will be well:

"But sure, acushla, if anything can touch a father's heart the sight of his first child will. Now keep yourself aisy, avourneen, and tell me where the whisky an' anything else may be awantin' is, till I give these crathurs of sarvints a dhrop of something to comfort thim." (*FM* 11)

After Honor's mother and sisters appear to help celebrate the occasion, they distribute "the blythe meat or groaning malt, a duty which the midwife transferred to them with much pleasure, this being a matter which, except in cases of necessity, she considered beneath the dignity of her profession" (*FM* 11).

The alert Carleton knows all these concrete and humanizing details, and the comic flow continues because Mary Moan not only has her pride but her special preferences for hot punch rather than straight liquor: "'I can't take it this-a-way,'" she protests, "'it doesn't agree wid me; you must put a grain o' shugar an' a dhrop o' bilin' wather in it. It may do very well *hard* for the servants, but I'm not used to that.'" (*FM* 15). Nogher cheerfully takes his whiskey hard, whenever he can get it, but when reminded that he must drink a triple toast to the mother, father, and child, he protests to Mary that he must have his glass replenished first:

> "Beggin' your pardon, ma'am, is it three healths you'd have me dhrink wid the one glassfull?—not myself, indeed; faix, I'd be long sorry to make so little of him—if he was a bit of a *girsha* [little girl] I'd not scruple to give him a corner o' the glass, but, bein' a young man, althers the case intirely—he must have a bumper for himself." (*FM* 13)

This statement of male principle immediately leads to an argument with a run of comic flytings as Peggy, the servant girl with whom Nogher is in love, takes exception to this insult to her sex, and she protests: "'A girsha's as well intitled to a full glass as a gorsoon, any day,'" Nogher tries to soften the dispute "good humouredly," but Peggy resists the peace offering: "'You'll have to look sharp after him, Mrs. Moan. He's pleasant enough now, but I'll be bound no man'll know betther how to hang his fiddle behind the door whin he comes home to us,'" And Mrs. Moan stands up for all women with this mysterious reply: "'Well, acushla, sure he may, if he likes, but if he does, he knows what's afore him—not saying that he ever will, I hope, for it's a woful case whin it comes to *that*, ahagur'"" (*FM* 13–14).

These two elusive remarks by Peggy and Mrs. Moan require footnotes, which Carleton provides at the bottom of the page, in order to explain what he says is an old superstitious belief that midwives "possessed the power of transferring the penalty of woman's original guilt to the husband, if he chanced to be brutal;—the wife merely giving birth to the offspring, the other bearing all the pain. In many parts of Ireland it is yet believed that they possess this power" (*FM* 14). Add to this mysterious power Peggy's suspicion that after her marriage to Nogher he will probably "hang his fiddle behind the door"—by which she means, Carleton's note says, he will "leave his good humour behind him" when he comes to her—and it becomes obvious that the women are talking in code about the original sin of sex and how to cope with it. Men should beware of the secret power of women, for the druidic midwife can transfer the guilt of the temptress Eve to the complying Adam, if the man plays a deceptive game with his fiddle—does it represent his manhood as well as his so-called good humor?—when he comes to his wife with the brutal intent of sex. According to Mrs. Moan and Peggy, men rather than women cannot be trusted, and therefore the hieratic midwife must transfer that taint of original guilt.

How is this secret power related to the serious theme of this comic novel? Had the excessively cautious Fardorougha finally left his fiddle of dubious good humor outside the door and become brutal, after waiting for thirteen long years? No direct answer to this teasing question is presented, although it is apparent that he has been brutalized by the new conflict between his strong affection for his son and his grinding avarice—"the famine-struck god of the miser" (*FM* 18), Carleton tells us, and will show us throughout the book. From the start, the comic and tragic vagaries of love, sex, and childbirth have been suggested by a carefully selected group of shrewd peasant voices, and this brilliantly controlled opening chapter closes "with the veil of a dark and fearful future unlifted before them." As we find in all traditional comedy, however, the main characters—particularly the rigid parents, and most of all, Fardorougha—must be tested by dark and potentially tragic events of their own making before they and their children can earn a happy or acceptable resolution. Thus, *Fardorougha* must begin and proceed comically, though under a veil of darkness, and it must eventually reach a comical conclusion when the veil is finally lifted and all's well that ends well.

In order to bring the conflict around rapidly to the young lovers and their star-crossed situation, Carleton wisely condenses the early action with a series of flashforward events in the following chapters. Now we see the child Connor grown up to young manhood, under the devoted care of his mother and the increasing parsimony of his father, until he meets and falls in love with the lovely Una O'Brien. At this time, having already ruined the family of young Bartle Flanagan over their inability to repay exorbitant debts on their land, Fardorougha ironically hires the secretly vindictive Bartle to work for him as a servant, which serves as a sign of Fardorougha's guilt. In this subplot, so tightly linked to the main action, Carleton develops a dominant historical theme that runs through all his novels in some form: the cruel exploitation of peasant land. Fardorougha's abuse of the Flanagans extends and darkens his culpability beyond his own family. Therefore, it is Fardorougha's well-known reputation as a miser and land exploiter that prompts Una's father, Bodagh Buie O'Brien, a well-to-do and snobbish peasant farmer, to reject the innocent Connor as a son-in-law.

The young lovers may be distraught, but the proud Fardorougha is so outraged at the snub that he insists on visiting the Bodagh Buie ("the yellow churl") in order to defend his own reputation and plead his rejected son's case. In a broadly hilarious scene that provokes his wife and son to pained amusement, the poker-faced and preening Fardorougha dresses up elaborately for his role as a "deputy wooer." In his characteristic manner of approaching what seems to be a tragic impasse with a comic point of view, Carleton, usually preferring vivid dialogue for such absurdities, offers a visual jest in the following description of the offended miser setting out on his "extraordinary mission" to the O'Briens:

> In the first place, his head was surmounted with a hat that resembled a flat skillet, wanting the handle; his coat, from which avarice and penury had caused him to shrink away, would have fitted a man twice his size, and as he had become much stooped, its preposterously long tail nearly swept the ground. To look at him behind, in fact, he appeared all body. The flaps of his waistcoat he had pinned up with his own hands, displaying thighs so thin and disproportioned to his small-clothes, that he resembled a boy in the breeches of a full-grown man, so that to look at him in front he appeared all legs. A pair of shoes, polished with burned straw and buttermilk, and surmounted by two buckles, scoured away to skeletons, completed his costume. In this garb he sets out with a crook-headed staff, in which long use, and the habit of griping fast whatever he held in his hand, had actually worn the marks of his forefinger and thumb. (*FM* 85)

In the comic episode that follows, as the well-meaning but quite ridiculous Fardorougha goes off in his absurd costume to confront the equally ridiculous O'Briens, Carleton creates a parody of a proud and miserly misfit of an outraged father. Thus, in a double view of the title character, we are presented with a comic view of a tragic miser, a pathetic and grotesque antihero reduced to a state of self-mockery. Nevertheless, here and throughout the novel, Carleton maintains a palpable degree of sympathy for the flawed and foolish Fardorougha—he who is genuinely torn between love and avarice; he who is constantly laughed at and abused; he who is always aware of his frailties. It is this underlying awareness that earns Fardorougha his measure of pity. As he stumbles about on the O'Brien farm in his ridiculous costume, one of the Bodagh's rude servants addresses him as "'my hipstriddled little codger'" (*FM* 86). When he at last confronts the O'Briens and offers his fixed term for the marriage—five times the Bodagh's dowry, but to be given to Una and Connor only after Fardorougha's death—the outraged and contemptuous Mrs. O'Brien shouts: "'The girl that we reared up as tindher as a chicking, to go throw herself away upon the son of ould Fardorougha Donovan, the misert. Confusion to the ring he'll ever put on her! I'd see her stretched first'" (*FM* 90).

This wild "deputy wooer" scene, like a one-act knockabout farce, with its outburst of comic confrontations and flytings, as Fardorougha and the O'Briens cheerfully insult each other—both sides exposed for their foolish pride and mock-respectability—follows the convention of comedy which calls for the stubborn *alazon* parents to prevent the marriage of the frustrated young lovers. Carleton often indicates, however, that the shadow of tragedy threatens to fall over such comic episodes. Like so many similar ones in Carleton's novels and short stories, this situation, while it does provoke laughter, is not a laughing matter for these self-defeating people, particularly for the grim Fardorougha. He returns home in despair and cries out repeatedly with an almost Lear-like anguish to his wife and son that the hard-hearted O'Briens "'have no bowels,'" no compassion. Though Fardorougha was equally hard-hearted and ridiculous in the comic haggling over the dowries, there is genuine pathos in his guilt-ridden lament:

> "They have no bowels, Connor—they have no bowels, thim O'Briens.... Save me! my heart's breakin'; somethin's tearin' me different ways inside; I can cry, you see; I can cry, but I'm still as hard as a stone; it's terrible this I'm sufferin'—terrible—all out of a weak old man like me. Oh, Connor, *avick*, what'll I do? Honor, *achora*, what'll become o' me? amn't I strugglin' aginst it, whatever it is. Don't yees pity me? don't ye, *avick machree*— don't ye, Honor? oh, don't yees pity me?" (*FM* 99–100)

Carleton continues to play artfully with this paradoxical dilemma, for he will go on illustrating why there can be some redemption, comic redemption in the end, for such a broken figure who is fully aware of his destructive avarice, his tragicomic hubris. Fardorougha is never as sinister as Jonson's greedy Volpone, nor as frivolous as Molière's miserly Harpagon, for, unlike these two comic villains, he is capable of honest suffering.

Meanwhile, the revenge subplot rumbles on in the background as a reminder that Fardorougha's cruel exploitation of land had provided the motive for Bartle's "black business"—the burning down of the O'Brien haggard and placing the blame on the unsuspecting Connor. Throughout the novel it is one of Carleton's recurring techniques to link together many converging ironies. Therefore, Bartle transfers his vengeance from Fardorougha to Connor, giving the impression that Connor set the fire because the perverse Bodagh refused to allow him to marry Una. At the same time, Bartle himself secretly loves Una and is planning to kidnap her. This chain of ironies continues after Bartle's betrayal of Connor when Fardorougha discovers he has been betrayed by the county treasurer, his banker, who has run away with the county funds. All along the miserly Fardorougha has unjustifiably been complaining he was too poor and now, with his money stolen, he is literally impoverished and desperate: "'I'm a ruined man, a beggar, an' will die a dog's death'" (*FM* 138). But it is his dear son Connor who is arrested and might die such a death. Because all these converging ironies add a melodramatic tone to the novel, it should be noted that such melodrama often serves as a handmaiden of comedy, as Shakespeare, Molière, and Dickens, for example, knew so well.

After Connor is condemned to the black-cap of hanging on the false evidence of Bartle, the hated informer who also turns out to be a secret Ribbonman, Fardorougha is reduced to blasphemous grief while Honor stoically resorts to prayer. At this point Carleton, for a compensatory effect, introduces a grotesque interlude of gallows humor when Bat Hanratty, a drunken Ribbonman, like the drunken Porter in *Macbeth*, roars out some comic songs and ranting: only Ribbonism or religion, he declares, could save poor Connor now. Full of high spirit, as if he were prematurely celebrating a wake, Bat pontificates that, if Connor had only "'joined the boys'" and become a Ribbonman, Bartle himself would have been stretched for breaking his secret oath and betraying "'one of the boys.'" Before he drifts into a profound snore, the blustering Bat praises Honor for having "'the thrue rallagion in her heart,'" and offers the following proof of his own potent piety:

> "I can repate the *Conwheeture* [Confiteor] in Latin myself, an', upon my sowl, I find that afther a hard day's fightin' or drinkin', it aises my mind all to pieces. Sure they say one bout of it in Latin is worth half a dozen rosaries, for, you see, the Latin bein' the mother tongue in heaven, that's what gives sich power entirely to prayers that's offered up in that langridge, an' what makes our clargy so powerful beyant all others." (*FM* 175)

Of course it is the bold Bat, the boozing Ribbonman, not Carleton, who makes a comic mockery of religion here, for throughout the novel

Carleton offers a completely sympathetic treatment of Irish Catholicism. When the young Carleton indulged in antipapist rhetoric in some of his early stories, he was reacting against what he considered to be the common practice of flagrant superstition—illustrated here by the amusingly blasphemous Bat—and not the true faith itself. All the characters in *Fardorougha* are Catholic, and those who are most admirable are the most devout, for example, the two idealized women, Honor—who, Carleton says in his introduction, he modeled after his mother—and Una, as well as the two young men, Connor and Una's brother John, who is studying for the priesthood at Maynooth and who is instrumental in helping to commute Connor's death sentence to transport to Australia. Even the sins of the wayward Fardorougha are mitigated through his suffering and rediscovered faith, though he struggles comically with his prayers: "'Will I say the five Dickens (Decades) or the whole Rosary?'" he asks Honor, who replies: "'If you can keep your mind in your prayers, I think you ought to say the whole of it; but if you wandher don't say more than five'" (*FM* 197).

The now contrite Fardorougha characteristically "wandhers," but he is on his way to salvation, for, according to comic and religious convention, the pain of incipient tragedy must be transformed into the redeeming comfort of comedy. As it turns out, a group of Fardorougha's friends, masquerading as villainous Ribbonmen, help to prove the innocence of Connor and to condemn Bartle. When Bartle enlists his Ribbon gang to help him kidnap Una so that he can secretly take her to America, the clever Ned M'Cormick and his friend Dandy Duffy infiltrate the gang and set a trap. Ned, incidentally, is the son of Nogher and Peggy, the jesting servants in the first chapter, and this is one of many instances where Carleton carefully links up thematic strands of comedy and loyalty. Ned and Dandy convince Biddy Nulty, one of Fardorougha's servants who had earlier been abused by Bartle, to dress up as Una and allow herself to be kidnapped, to be exposed as the wrong girl and thus trap a villain. A common stratagem in Shakespearean and Restoration comedy, Biddy's disguise reduces Bartle to shame and mockery in front of his gang. His treachery is revealed and he is later tried and condemned to death, while Connor is released and brought home from Australia by Fardorougha and Honor so that he can marry Una. The six-month voyage to Australia has apparently been too much of an emotional and physical ordeal for the failing Fardorougha and he is on his peaceful deathbed at the end. In the midst of the pious and happy conclusion for all, however, the shrewd Carleton opts for comedy over sentiment and allows

Fardorougha to say farewell to his son with these amusingly irreverent final words:

> "Your mother was spakin' to the priest about masses for my sowl. Now, Connor, I know that they'll say them for nothin' when they think the person's poor. I know that, for I remember myself doin' Father Fogarty out of two-an-sixpence a mass that I got to give him, by pladin' poverty; it was for my own father's sowl, an' I saved the price of a pair o' shoes by it, and had the masses sed still. That was workin' him the right way." (*FM* 294)

With this humorous lapse from virtue, in the hint of having his soul saved by cheating the priest out of a few shillings, the "wandherin'" and thieving rascal of an old miser is prepared to die true to his eccentric character, as well as in a perhaps slightly qualified state of grace. We can only laugh with compassion at this unforgettable figure with all his warts and flaws exposed, all his frustrated energies and aspirations so vividly presented in this highly entertaining and moving novel.

Because there are many memorable voices in *Fardorougha the Miser,* something should also be said about one more voice—the voice of Carleton himself which, from time to time, provides pertinent or amusing comments on the action. Some critics object to such an authorial voice, and not only in Carleton, on the assumption that it is a didactic or disconcerting intrusion that should be avoided, and that the author of a novel should be, as Joyce once suggested, "out of sight, paring his fingernails."[12] It may be unreasonable, however, to insist that there is only one way to present a work of fiction, and that the rigid rule of authorial objectivity must always be observed. As one of the exceptions to such a fixed point of view, Carleton takes the reader into his confidence occasionally. He introduces his own voice as a guide to the action, following the eighteenth-century tradition of Fielding and other novelists, where the author does not so much intrude as offer his amusing or diverting views on what we have just read or prepare us for what we are about to discover.

For a novelist like Carleton, who creates his stories in the specific context of Irish history, it is sometimes relevant for him to provide concise comments that might increase the reader's insight and pleasure. The following passages illustrate how Carleton briefly brings in his own voice to en-

---

12 James Joyce, *A Portrait of the Artist as a Young Man* (New York: Viking, 1964), p. 215.

hance the story without imposing a didactic or awkward intrusion. For example, realizing that most of his readers would not be peasants, Carleton humorously asserts his peasant credentials by slyly mocking the "higher ranks," comparing their genteel love relationships to the natural and uninhibited love-making of the lower orders:

> It is not often that the higher ranks can appreciate the moral beauty of love, as it is experienced by those humble classes to which they deny the power of feeling in its most refined and exalted character. . . . We say, however, that their love, when contrasted with that which is felt by the humble peasantry, is languid and sickly; neither so pure, nor so simple, nor so intense.
> (*FM* 53)

Carleton wants his readers to know that Irish peasants are not country bumpkins in their virtuous but intense affairs of love. Later in a more serious moment, after Connor has been betrayed by Bartle and a feeling of desperation afflicts the Donovan family, a somber chapter begins with this finely balanced introductory comment that not only sounds like the aphoristic Chorus in a Greek drama but indicates that even a peasant novelist is capable of being philosophically eloquent: "When Time approaches the miserable with calamity in his train, his pinion is swifter than that of the eagle; but when carrying them towards happiness, his pace is slower than that of the tortoise" (*FM* 144).

In other novels, like *Valentine M'Clutchy* and *The Black Prophet,* as well as in *Traits and Stories,* Carleton created many darkly tainted and comically shrewish women. In *Fardorougha the Miser,* however, he seemed determined to celebrate the heroic qualities of devout Irish women, particularly staunch Catholic mothers like Honor. When Connor is condemned to death and his father falls into hysterical despair, only the faith and strength of Honor holds the family together, as Carleton often illustrates directly and dramatically, then supports movingly here:

> Indeed it was almost impossible for any heart to exist within the influence of that piety which animated Honor Donovan, and not be warmed by the holy fire which there burned with such purity and brightness. Ireland, however, abounds in such instances of female piety and fortitude, in quiet domestic life—in hard struggles against poverty, and in those cruel visitations where the godly mother is forced to see her innocent son corrupted by the dark influence of political crime, drawn within the vortex of secret confederacy, and subsequently yielding up his life to the outraged laws of that country which he had assisted to distract.
> (*FM* 187)

Here Carleton not only celebrates the heroism of Irish peasant mothers, he goes on to stress the violent and cruel causes that corrupt and destroy the sons of grieving mothers. In a subject nation like Ireland, misruled and oppressed for too many centuries by a foreign power, religious and political loyalties have inevitably collided, and here Carleton has now exposed a conflict in the national conscience—one which Sean O'Casey dramatized almost a hundred years later in his tragicomic trilogy about the urban peasants of Dublin trapped in the crossfire of the Rising and Civil War. Juno Boyle's anguished lament in *Juno and the Paycock* for her sacrificed son echoes the tragic consequences emphasized in Carleton's remarks. Indeed, the threat of violence concerns Carleton throughout this comic novel and, at one point, he is deeply disturbed by what he sees as a paradoxical Irish propensity toward kindness and bloodshed—a confused feeling that has historical implications in an often oppressed country. When the loyal and ordinarily gentle Nogher M'Cormick tells the victimized Connor it is necessary to punish the treacherous Bartle with a bloody deed—"'to aise his windpipe a little'"—the shocked Connor rejects such terrible vengeance, and then Carleton's voice adds these ironic comments:

> Such is the anomalous nature of that peculiar Irish temperament which combines within it the extremes of generosity and crime. Here was a man who had been singularly affectionate and harmless during his whole past life, yet who was now actually plotting the murder of a person who had never rendered him an injury or given him any cause of offence, except remotely, by his treachery to Connor, whom Nogher loved. (*FM* 205)

Perhaps it would be fair to add that such contradictory behavior is not restricted to the Irish—though here it certainly bears the ironic mark of the troubled Celt—and that any kindly person confronted by an outrageous betrayal could be provoked to bloody violence. It could happen—indeed, is happening now—in any European, Asian or African country exposed to irreconcilable conflict. Nor should a reader feel that Carleton's pointed comments become an unnecessary intrusion, for they highlight a dominant theme that runs through the book, for he constantly *shows* us whatever he tells us to underscore key issues. That pervasive theme rises ominously when Bartle and his vicious gang of Ribbonmen prepare to act, and then Carleton moves in to sum up his convictions about murderous violence—"We must pause for a moment to reflect," he says—and he offers these passionate remarks:

The curse, however, of these secret confederacies, and indeed of Ribbonism in general is, that the savage principle of personal vengeance is transferred from the nocturnal assault, or the mid-day assassination directed against religious or political enemies, the private bickerings and petty jealousies that necessarily occur in a combination of ignorant and bigoted men, whose passions are guided by no principle but that of practical cruelty. . . . Persons of humane disposition declining to act in these sanguinary villainies are generally the first to be sacrificed, for, as in the case of the execrable Inquisition, individual life is nothing when it obstructs the propagation of the general principle.   (*FM* 236)

Has Carleton gone too far with this strong authorial protest during a momentary pause for serious reflection in the midst of an essentially comic novel, a comic novel about violence, to illustrate another Irish paradox? Critics who consider the author's voice a didactic intrusion will say yes, Carleton has, with the best of intentions, violated the objective tone and genre of the book. Would it be valid, however, to insist that comedy must be absolutely free from the overflow of dark or serious implications, an overflow that includes the author's compulsion to emphasize his own convictions as well as those of his characters?

Fardorougha exposes legitimate Irish fears as well as rich Irish laughter, the latter perhaps as a contemporary reaction to the former. Obviously, British injustice created the original need for such secret rebel forces as the Ribbonmen, and in his novel Carleton graphically illustrates how such underground retaliatory groups too often commit inquisitorial and indiscriminate deeds of violence that produce injustices greater than those originally imposed by the enemy. With such savagery in mind, Carleton appears to have anticipated the brutality of the gunmen on both sides of the conflict in Northern Ireland, or elsewhere, and in his even more wildly comic and tragic *Valentine M'Clutchy* he reveals the terror of the Protestant Orangemen as well as that of the Catholic Ribbonmen. With their stubborn eccentricities and fierce loyalties, Carleton's peasants reflect an accurate aspect of Irish history, and Carleton does not hesitate to present the religious and political conflicts that inspire the mixed reactions of comedy and tragedy, generosity and violence. By striking these tragicomic and paradoxical chords, sometimes in his own voice but mostly through the distinctive voices of his characters, Carleton pays his debt to history as well as to literature. In the final analysis, however, it is a dominating comic vision that illuminates his enduring art.

As an epilogue now, in an attempt to redefine Carleton's genius, I wish to suggest that one modern literary concept may properly account for his creation of all those vivid characters, their striking voices, and their unique world. Toward this end, I want to borrow the concept of *carnival* from the Russian critic Mikhail Bakhtin, who originally applied it to the works of Dostoevsky, but which requires the wild comic vision of a Carleton for its ultimate fulfillment. And I want also to add to the insight of Bakhtin, the reassuring wisdom of the young W. B. Yeats on the artistry of Carleton. Bakhtin presented his theory of carnival in *Problems of Dostoevsky's Poetics* (1929), edited and translated in 1984 by Caryl Emerson, and introduced by Wayne C. Booth. I am not primarily concerned with Bakhtin's alternately brilliant and abstruse system of theoretical criticism, for I agree with Booth's reservations about Bakhtin's method:

> My sense of Bakhtin's unique value does not, of course, leave me with a vision of perfection. To my taste the repetitiousness, disorganization, and reliance on neologisms . . . often impose unnecessary obstacles. He often seems to lapse into a hortatory mode that has little to do with the critical work in hand. Most seriously, his failure to settle into sustained study of any one of Dostoevsky's works and his persistently high level of generality often makes me impatient. . . .[13]

I must confess I share Booth's impatience with Bakhtin's failure to arrive at direct and extensive analysis of specific works. Therefore, to commend Bakhtin for his brilliance when he is a creative critic, and especially for his conceptual relevance to Carleton, I have chosen the following fragments scattered throughout his book. Taken together, they represent Bakhtin's concept of carnivalistic comic fiction:

> . . . This carnival sense of the world possesses a mighty life-creating and transforming power, an indestructible vitality. . . . What are the distinguishing characteristics of the genres of the serio-comical?
>
> For all their motley external diversity, they are united by their deep bond with *carnivalistic folklore* . . . and several of them are direct literacy variants of oral carnival-folkloric genres. . . . Characteristics of these genres are a multi-toned narration, a mixing of high and low, serious and comic.   (*PDP* 107, 108)

13 Mikhail Bakhtin, *Problems in Dostoevsky's Poetics,* ed. and trans. by Caryl Emerson, introd. by Wayne C. Booth (1929; Minneapolis: University of Minnesota Press, 1984), p. xxvi; hereafter cited parenthetically, thus: (*PDP* xxvi).

and:

> ... *Eccentricity* is a special category of the carnival sense of the world, or-
> ganically connected with the category of familiar contact—the latent sides
> of human nature to reveal and express themselves. . . . Carnival brings to-
> gether, unifies, weds, combines the sacred with the profane, the lofty with
> the low, the great with the insignificant, the wise with the stupid. (*PDP* 123)

and:

> ... Carnival is, so to speak, functional and not substantive. It absolutizes
> nothing, but rather proclaims the joyful relativity of everything. (*PDP* 125)

Wherever one looks in Carleton's fiction there is always that "indestructible vitality"; those rich "oral" and "folkloric" sources; that "multi-
toned" mixing of "the serious and the comic"; the ironic "eccentricity" of
human nature; the combining of "the sacred with the profane," "the wise
with the stupid"; the matching of Bakhtin's "verbal agons and cursing
matches" with Carleton's comic flytings; the proclaiming of "the joyful
relativity of everything" (*PDP* 125). And Carleton's fiction amply rewards
his reader with this Bakhtinian difference: "Carnivalistic legends in general are profoundly different from traditional heroicizing epic legends: carnivalistic legends debase the hero and bring him down to earth, they make
him familiar, bring him close, humanize him" (*PDP* 132–133).

All of the unique elements of "carnivalistic legend," I believe, appear in
my discussion of *Fardorougha the Miser,* as one follows the comic "debas-
ing" and "humanizing" of the tainted hero. We can find variations of all these
elements in a more savagely and more irreverent exposure in the equally
vital *Valentine M'Clutchy* (1846); even in the fatalistic *The Black Prophet*
(1847), where some of the most harrowing famine scenes are filtered through
grotesque and monstrous comedy. And there are many carnivalistic variations of comic and serious voices and gestures in novels like *The Emigrants
of Ahadarra* (1848), *The Tithe Proctor* (1849), and *The Squanders of Castle
Squander* (1852), which completes the fiction of Carleton's major phase. Always in Carleton, when he is at the top of his wild comic form, or moving
in a darker tragicomic mode, the "indestructible vitality" is maintained.

Looking at Irish carnival literature after Carleton, one would have to
single out Joyce's *Ulysses* as one of the main works in this tradition, even
though this mock-epic masterpiece has its ponderous as well as profound
comic strategies. A strong case may also be made for the essential carnival
spirit in Synge's plays with their "sacred and profane" language, "lofty and
low," "wise and stupid" characters; for the knockabout folk comedy of Lady
Gregory where the exuberant and eccentric peasants celebrate a survival

game in which "it is better to be quarreling than to be lonesome"[14]; for the "struttin' paycocks" and anarchic clowns in O'Casey's early tragicomedies and late comic fantasies; for the tragicomic tramps of Samuel Beckett who proclaim "We are inexhaustible!"[15] in the midst of their hilarious miseries; for the sacred and profane folk poetry and mock-heroic fiction of Patrick Kavanagh; and for the freewheeling tragicomic plays of Brendan Behan. No doubt there are many other Irish exemplars, but I must pause here, though not without a final deep bow in the direction of Charles Dickens, England's master of tragicomic carnival, with whom Carleton shared so many eccentric characters and voices.

Now I want to end with the wisdom of Yeats who, throughout his lifetime, pursued his vision of a mystical and heroic carnival of art and was an early and enthusiastic champion of what he called Carleton's "abounding vitality." In the introduction he wrote for his edition of *Stories From Carleton* (1889), Yeats saw Carleton's valuable role as a folk historian of ordinary and essential Irish life:

> William Carleton was a great Irish historian. The history of a nation is not in parliaments and battle-fields, but in what the people say to each other on fair-days and high days, and how they farm, and quarrel, and go on pilgrimage. These things has Carleton recorded. He is the great novelist of Ireland, by right of the most Celtic eyes that ever gazed from under the brows of storyteller.[16]

Yeats here anticipated what Bakhtin later called the oral tradition of "carnivalistic folklore." Several years later, in his article on Irish literature in *The Bookman*, after reviewing the fiction of Maria Edgeworth and of Michael and John Banim, Yeats concluded that "only Carleton, born and bred a peasant, was able to give us the vast multitude of grotesque, pathetic, humourous persons, misers, pig-drivers, drunkards, schoolmasters, labourers, priests, madmen, and to fill them all with an abounding vitality."[17] And here Yeats saw, in that vast multitude of vital Carleton voices, what amounted to a carnival world of eccentric and wise, comic and serious, debased and very humanized people whose lives, both ordinary and wild, even under some inevitable dark shadows, proclaimed "the joyful relativity of everything."

—Brown University

14 Lady Gregory, "Workhouse Ward," in *Seven Short Plays* (Dublin: Maunsel, 1909), p. 207.

15 Samuel Beckett, *Waiting for Godot* (New York: Grove, 1954), p. 40.

16 *Stories from Carleton* introd. W. B. Yeats (London: Walter Scott, n.d.[1889]), p. xvi.

17 W. B. Yeats, *The Bookman* (July 1895).

WILLIAM CARLETON, DEMIURGE OF IRISH CARNIVAL

POLICING FAMINE IRELAND

W. J. LOWE

THE IRISH CONSTABULARY had been consolidated less than a decade when Ireland's potato crop failed on a large scale in 1845. A quarter-century of new research and rewriting of Irish history has not substantially challenged the position of the Great Famine as a point of social, demographic, and economic departure for Ireland. Changes already in process were accelerated by the Famine's impact and Ireland was becoming a different country at the end of the 1840s.[1] The famine years also mark the beginning of a gradual but clear evolution of the character and role of the Irish Constabulary that, while important and of long-term significance, was obscured by the stress, tedium, and enormity of the conditions the police confronted in the day-to-day routine. In 1845, the Irish Constabulary was deployed to control a disturbed, violent countryside. Districts traditionally associated with agrarian crime, particularly in the South and West of the country, were devastated by destitution and disease during the Famine. So, even though fears of violence were at a high level in provincial landlord and merchant circles during the Famine, the police mostly found themselves witnesses to human tragedy in the communities where they were stationed. The desperation of the Famine produced violent confrontations that involved the police, but, for all the tension, drama, and seemingly interminable duty, policing the Famine was mostly an extension of customary routines.

It was during the Famine that the Irish Constabulary began a steady movement toward becoming a familiar fixture of Ireland's civic scenery. The subtle change in organizational direction was overshadowed by the magnitude and complexity of the problems that affected Irish society in the

---

1 Recent accounts of the Famine period are: M. E. Daly, *The Famine in Ireland* (Dundalk 1986); C. Ó Grada, *The Great Irish Famine* (Dublin, 1989); J. S. Donnelly, Jr., chapters 12–19 in *A New History of Ireland, V: Ireland under the Union, I, 1801–70,* ed. W. E. Vaughan (Oxford, 1989), pp. 272–371.

late 1840s. But some aspects of the Constabulary were constant and perhaps even strengthened during the Famine. Discipline and military bearing were strictly maintained, as were the barrack routines laid down by the Constabulary's *Standing Rules*.[2] The Irish Constabulary represented great stability in difficult times, and while clearly stretched thin by the scale of Ireland's needs, its performance appears to have been recognized as energetic and competent. Another indicator of the acceptance of its important role is the growth in the force's strength from 9,100 in 1845 to 12,500 men in 1850, despite heavy turnover in the ranks. The Constabulary remained staffed at the 11,000 to 12,000 level for the rest of the nineteenth century.[3] One Constabulary function that was firmly institutionalized during the Famine was the collecting of statistics. It may seem perversely mundane that Irishmen on the public payroll reduced the suffering of the Famine years to numbers, but what the government and later generations know about the Famine's impact owes a great deal to information, both statistical and narrative, recorded at the local level by the police and local magistrates. The police were responsible for compiling agricultural statistics and began reporting on the condition of the potato crop in mid-September, 1845.[4] They were also frequently on duty at evictions and in 1849 they began keeping the statistics on that sad reality.[5] Their experience with these and other administrative routines opened the door to a rapid expansion of civil responsibilities as public order in Ireland rapidly improved after the Famine.[6] It remains an historical irony that the Famine, which caused the rapid expansion in both absolute and percentage terms of the military-style

2   *Standing Rules and Regulations for the Government and Guidance of the Constabulary Force of Ireland* (Dublin, 1837).

3   Returns Relating to the Constabulary Force, 1841–1919 (Public Record Office, Kew [PRO], HO 184/54).

4   During the autumn of 1845, urgent requests were sent to Constabulary officers in local districts for information on the extent of damage to the potato crop. Similar reports were again requested in the summers of 1846 and 1847. Irish Constabulary circulars, 16 Sept. 1845, 17 Oct. 1845, 8 July 1846, 19 Aug. 1846, 31 July 1847 (PRO, 184/111, 112).

5   J. S. Donnelly, Jr., "Famine and Government Response, 1845–6," p. 277; "Production, Prices and Exports, 1846–51," pp. 286–7; "Landlords and Tenants," p. 337 in *A New History of Ireland, V: Ireland under the Union, I, 1801–70* (Oxford, 1989).

6   See W. E. Vaughan, "Ireland c. 1870" in *A New History of Ireland, V: Ireland under the Union, I, 1801–70* (Oxford, 1989), pp. 767, 769. Another important influence on the emergence of a more orderly Ireland is described in E. Larkin, "The parish mission movement in Ireland, 1850–1875," paper read at the American Historical Association, Chicago, 30 December 1991.

Constabulary, was helping to mold the conditions that would redefine its functions and, ultimately, its character.[7]

The Constabulary's role in districts seriously affected by hunger and disease derived almost entirely from its regular duties and assignments, although it was quickly acknowledged that, in a situation that changed so rapidly, duties and responsibilities would be added as needs dictated. Police barracks were used as distribution points for government agricultural information, such as the sheet entitled "Advice concerning the potato crop," and as obvious points for the collection of information on local social and economic conditions.[8] But the Constabulary's actual involvement in the provision of relief proved very limited and largely confined to the early period of the Famine. In 1846, the police sometimes found themselves supervising and administering relief programs, if other local agencies were not in place. The twenty-nine Constabulary food distribution "sub-depots" were located in the most remote portions of the West and South. The police also ran soup kitchens, one of which, in Queen's County, was actually located in the Cardtown barrack.[9] Still, the pressure and duration of duty in famine-affected districts was unprecedented and would only be approached again during the Land War of the early 1880s and the Anglo-Irish War of 1919–21. The police received little credit from those most affected by the Famine. To the Irish poor, it must have seemed that there were more police than ever before—and there were, in fact. The police looked and behaved like light infantry, and they were intimately associated with peace preservation and enforcement of laws that could only have been seen as imposing special hardships on the population.

The Irish Constabulary's first assignment was to keep the misery of famine Ireland from erupting in violence that threatened property, property owners, and good order as defined both at Dublin Castle and Westminster. By early 1846, it was clear that Ireland was not experiencing one of its too common, local subsistence crises. The Irish government received a steady stream of reports on local conditions, the best concentra-

7 See W. J. Lowe and E. L. Malcolm, "The Domestication of the Royal Irish Constabulary, 1836–1922," *Irish Economic and Social History*, (1992), 27–48.

8 Irish Constabulary circulars, 25, 31 Oct., 11 Nov. 1845 (PRO, HO 184/111).

9 Brian Griffin, "The Irish Police, 1836–1914: A Social History" (Ph.D. diss., Loyola University of Chicago, 1990), pp. 356–7; Donnelly, "Famine and Government Response," p. 279; instructions for handling relief supplies in police custody, Irish Constabulary circulars, 27 May 1846 (PRO, HO 184/111).

tions of which are found in the Outrage Papers and the chief secretary's office Registered Papers ('first division'), both preserved in the Irish National Archives. These collections are organized by county for the period of the Famine which permits a detailed view of how the Famine affected counties such as Clare, Galway, Mayo, and Tipperary.

It was already clear in January, 1846, that potatoes were scarce and the prices of provisions generally were being driven beyond the means of subsistence families, who largely relied on growing their own food rather than on purchasing it on the open market.[10] There were fears about widespread unrest and Resident Magistrate Kernan wrote from Galway Town to ask that a Royal Navy ship carrying marines be retained in Galway Bay.

> The reports which I receive daily of the continued rot of the potatoes in the pits and in the houses are truly alarming. Potatoes are now from five pence to six pence per stone, wholesale, in the Galway market, a famine price to the poor unemployed inhabitants of this locality. And I know not the moment an outbreak may take place in consequence of this state of things.

In addition, Kernan thought that a *"very large military force [sic]"* was needed to preserve order and mentioned the police only in passing because the twenty-eight resident constables were wholly inadequate to the threat that was building: "The minds of the people are excited beyond measure. They are unemployed, they are without food . . . some evil is brooding." Kernan passed on to Dublin the contents of a threatening letter received by the Galway town commissioners, which demanded the distribution of food to the people and the prevention of the export of oats and wheat, "otherwise that the people would themselves prevent the exportation, and that they were determined to rob the merchants' stores and the houses in the town."[11] At the very least, it is clear that there was excitement and foreboding in the respectable public mind and Undersecretary Richard Pennefather's minute on Kernan's plea indicates that reports of possible unrest were taken seriously. Within days cavalry, infantry, and a steamer carrying marines were arriving to reinforce Galway.[12]

10 The Constabulary in local districts was regularly asked to provide information on provision prices. Irish Constabulary circulars, 1 Dec. 1845, 28 Jan., 8 July, 4 Sept. 1846 (PRO, HO 184/111).

11 J. Kernan, R. M. to R. Pennefather, 5 Feb. 1846 (Irish National Archives [INA], Outrage Papers [OP], 1846/11/2541).

12 J. Kernan, R. M. to Lord Lieutenant, 28 Jan. 1846; Kernan to R. Pennefather, 5 Feb.

While crime related directly to destitution was a serious problem for the police during the Famine, the large-scale rioting and plundering feared by the business and professional people of Galway did not occur. Still, there were localized problems and threats that steadily increased the demands on the police. The available statistics of reported offenses during the Famine show that traditional agrarian crime declined as communities were affected by death or emigration. Families faced very immediate domestic, rather than communal, crises. There were large increases in offenses that may be attributed to hunger and privation, such as burglary, robbery, stealing of livestock, and plundering of provisions—all described by W. E. Vaughan as "a wave of crime." Crime was at its highest levels in "Black '47" when reported offenses increased by about sixty percent. There were 10,000 reports of cattle and sheep stealing, 1,200 incidents of plundering of provisions and more than 1,000 reports of stealing weapons in 1847.[13] The incidence of killing and stealing livestock was so high that the police were permitted to perform expedited investigations.[14]

Moreover, the high incidence of petty, individual crimes took on a menacing appearance. Edward Jones of Clonmel, County Tipperary, wrote that

> The country is in a state of nearly perfect anarchy. Our police force is not sufficiently strong, our magistrates are not adapted to the times. From the way in which the people conduct themselves, they appear to believe that the restraining power of the law is removed. The well disposed and industrious feel uneasy for the safety of their property. They know and hear of cattle & sheep being killed and carried away; of boats and carts being plundered and of assaults & petty robberies being daily committed on almost every road. And at the same time they are not ignorant that scarcely the least exertion is being made to check such practices.

There was great movement in Ireland during the Famine. Large numbers of destitute families left their homes by compulsion for failure to pay rent

---

1846 (OP 1846/11/1933). While military frequently accompanied the Constabulary during the Famine period, but it was made clear that troops only aided the civil police, thus avoiding the appearance of martial law. Irish Constabulary circulars, 7 Dec. 1846, 18 Nov. 1847 (PRO, HO 184/111, 112).

13 W. E. Vaughan, *Landlords and Tenants in mid-Victorian Ireland* (Oxford, 1994), p. 138. See also pp. 279, 285–6; *Return of Outrages Reported to the Royal Irish Constabulary Office from 1 January 1844 to 31 December 1880*, 25 [C. 2756], House of Commons [HC] 1881, lxxvii, 911.

14 Irish Constabulary circulars, 15 May 1847 (PRO, HO 184/112).

and in order to find subsistence and to emigrate. So, the roads of Tipperary certainly carried people who appeared threatening to the "well-disposed and industrious" and the Irish Constabulary in such districts, mostly deployed in four- and five-man stations, did not have an imposing presence. Police numbers were made to seem even less adequate by a characteristic of the public works relief effort: "The present mode of giving employment to the unemployed of collecting them in masses, by which facility is given to them to form schemes of intimidation and disturbance, is decidedly faulty...."[15] So, the more fortunate populace sensed that the scale of poverty could easily overwhelm local police parties, which caused a great increase in requests for their presence and assistance. The index to the first division of the chief secretary's registered papers in the National Archives for 1847 provides a representative selection of calls for help from the Constabulary during the Famine. There were 131 requests for protection of individual persons; 204 petitions to have police allocated to new areas; 73 calls for increases in police forces ranging from a few to 100 men; and what appear to be 157 calls for the police to assist in particular situations.[16]

The more than 275 requests for more police in 1847, either by reinforcement or new allocation and station establishment, shows that they were considered valuable in protecting life and property in areas affected by the Famine but altogether too few to provide the sense of security the respectable desired. Even the progressive increase in the size of the force during these years—by 1,265 constables in 1846 alone—fell short of local expectations. The hardship that the Famine caused for the poor was associated with "excitement" that required a controlling deterrent. Inhabitants of Louisburgh in County Mayo petitioned the Dublin government for more police at the local barrack because they

> live in a wild, remote district and have reason to apprehend danger to their lives and properties, from the dreadful excitement that at present prevails by reason of the famine which has visited the country.
>
> ... [we] can expect but little defence against the infuriated populace from four constables composing the whole force here.
>
> ... we are fearfully aware that dreadful outrages must shortly occur

15 Edward Jones to Lord Lieutenant, 3 Jan. 1847 (INA, OP 1847/27/72); see also J. Eyre to Lord Lieutenant, 27 Oct. 1846 (INA, OP 1846/11/29591).

16 The Irish Constabulary permitted resort to use of firearms only under extraordinary circumstances, but the police were advised in 1847 that the usual restrictions did not apply when assigned to special protection duty. Irish Constabulary circulars, 5 Nov. 1847 (PRO, HO 184/112).

(symptoms of which have already appeared) from the famishing state of thousands of the unemployed peasantry.

This is a good example of the pleas that reached Dublin Castle and the reception that most received there. Under the Constabulary Act of 1836 (6& 7 Wm. 4, c. 13), the cost of increasing police presence in particular areas was shared between the Dublin government and the local ratepayers. While additional protection was almost always seen as necessary, the accompanying increase in the rates was usually viewed as an outrage at least comparable to cattle houghing, threatening letters being almost preferable to notices of rate increases. Constabulary Inspector General McGregor recommended that Undersecretary Redington point out to the residents of Louisburgh that reinforcements were not possible unless formal application from the magistrates were received. This was tantamount to a refusal, since resident magistrates rarely volunteered their propertied neighbors for rate increases.[17]

Another dimension of the perceived need for police protection appears in the request of the City of Dublin Steam Packet Co. to have a detachment stationed in its warehouse at Dromineer, County Tipperary. The nearest police parties, at Tunabeg and Puckane, were "almost constantly employed alternately in protecting the mills . . . situate between Nenagh and the Shannon, and escorting . . . flour to Dromineer." The Dublin shippers' concern was a real one, but the Constabulary could add a warehouse station only if another barrack were abandoned, which would do nothing to reassure the people in the unpoliced neighborhood. County Inspector Carroll suggested to McGregor that all movement of provisions to the Shannon be coordinated on one day each week, when adequate protection would be possible without leaving any district without police.[18] The movement of food was also the concern of the Newport, County Mayo, magistrates, who requested an increase of twenty men at the seven Constabulary barracks in their area. The undersecretary's reply pointed out that, under the 1836 act, "a majority of the magistrates assembled at the sessions" had to approve such an application and the memorial received was one magistrate short. There is no indication of a response from the Newport magistrates in the chief secretary's papers.[19] Other Mayo residents, con-

17 Inhabitants of Louisburgh, to Lord Lieutenant, with cover letter to Chief Secretary from John Potter, 12 Jan. 1847; D. McGregor's minute, 20 Jan. 1847; T. Redington to J. Potter, 21 Jan. 1847 (Irish National Archives, Chief Secretary's Office Registered Papers [RP] 1847/21/46).

18 County Insp. Carroll to Insp. Gen. McGregor, 19 Jan. 1847 (OP 1847/27/332).

19 M. A. O'Donnell to Lord Lieutenant (enclosing magistrates' memorial of 5 Feb. 1847), 15 Feb. 1847; T. Redington's minute, 17 Feb. 1847 (RP 1847/21/153).

cerned about "a most determined race, neither fearing God or regarding man," at Binghamstown "inside what is called the Mullet," were also politely given the bureaucratic brush-off.[20]

In some cases, the problem of sharing the costs of police reinforcements quite aside, the Constabulary authorities simply did not agree that either additional barracks or police presence were needed.[21] In others, the fact that the Constabulary relied almost exclusively on rented accommodation for barracks could impede the stationing of a party. The Tourmakeady barrack in Mayo, which had been rented from the Church of Ireland bishop of Tuam, was abandoned owing to its poor condition. The local magistrates complained that there were "large bodies of men marching through the district at night, firing shots and terrifying the peaceable inhabitants." It was claimed that "the system of agrarian outrage known as Molly Maguirism is rapidly spreading . . . and this we must in a great degree attribute to the removal of the police station from Tourmakeady." But the police would not return until a suitable building for a barrack was found.[22] The attractive building that the Constabulary eventually occupied was abandoned and immediately burned in 1920.[23]

Even as the impact of the Famine began to subside in the late 1840s, worries about raids on provisions and general unrest persisted. The Ennis board of guardians was still sufficiently worried about attacks on boats transporting meal that in June, 1848, they successfully requested a warship in the mouth of the River Fergus. The rumors of attacks by bloodthirsty repealers on several police stations in Clare during December, 1848, were, however, simply false alarms.[24] Indeed, the abortive Irish Confederate rising of that year impinged only minimally on the Constabulary's attention. Complaints, exaggerated reports, and requests for augmented police protection and presence comprised a great deal of the Constabulary-related paperwork generated by the Famine. In the Constabulary's history,

20 T. Kirkwood to T. Redington, 19 June 1847; Redington's minute, 21 June 1847 (RP 1847/21/377). See similar response to John Eyre to Lord Lieutenant, 27 Oct. 1846 (OP 1846/11/29591).

21 Magistrates of Ballinakill and Boffin, Galway to Lord Lieutenant, [?] April 1846 (OP 1846/11/10311).

22 Memorial to Lord Lieutenant from Carra Barony [date-stamped 25 Nov. 1847]; W. Miller's minute, 29 Nov. 1847; T. Redington's reply, 13 Dec. 1847 (RP 1847/21/528).

23 Statement by J. R. W. Goulden, 23 Jan. 1956 (Trinity College, Dublin, Goulden Papers, MS 7377/7/1).

24 Ennis Board of Guardians memorial, 6 June 1848; W. Stanley to T. Redington, 22 June 1848 (OP 1848/5/545); Reports of 6, 9, 12 Dec. 1848 (OP 1848/5/1025, 1032, 1043).

however, the Famine years figure as a time of heavy expenditure of police time and energy in a variety of duties. While police sometimes had to confront the types of crime and disorder that the anxious memorials received at Dublin Castle described, most of the long hours spent by the Constabulary involved duties that varied from tediously routine to cruelly ironic.

The Irish Constabulary was not directly involved in the relief schemes brought in by the government in 1846 and 1847, but both the public works projects and the soup kitchens that replaced them required significant police attention. These projects not only employed people, they also used donkeys, whose owners received compensation. An incident in Tipperary—the exact location is not given—in January, 1847, is an example of how easily tensions could escalate. The relief project there required six donkeys and twelve animals were available. The local board of works steward, a Mr. Cosgrave, hired six of the donkeys and then the other six, "week and week about." A donkey owner named Small felt that his animal should be at work continuously, but Cosgrave refused. An armed party went to Cosgrave's house when he was not there, left a threatening message, and fired a shot through a window. As was customary, no one came forward to assist the police with their inquiries. Constabulary Sub-Inspector Crawford, assumed that the relief project workmen knew who had intimidated Cosgrave and "put a stop to the work for three days as a punishment, since which there has been no more disturbance."[25] Crawford's was a punishment guaranteed to rivet community attention in the winter of 1847.

By late 1846, there occurred robberies and attempted robberies of board of works clerks on their way to distribute wages at relief project sites, including one in Galway that left those waiting for the money at a "very great inconvenience or even to privation." Chief Secretary Sir George Grey recommended that pay clerks travel only with police escorts, but acknowledged that the "numerous demands for escorts are more than the Constabulary can furnish, as their stations usually consist of only five men, who have also to maintain a night patrol." The police, indeed, began to escort public works pay clerks, and the expense of the program was augmented

25 J. Walker to T. N. Redington, 2 Jan. 1847 (OP 1847/27/57).

by at least two policemen being shot dead in robberies.[26] There also arose dangerous disputes over the rates of wages paid on the relief works. At Lorrha, County Tipperary, wages had been increased from 8 *d.*, with subsistence, to 10 *d.* per day, but supervisors found that "the laborers so relaxed their exertions, as not to earn sixpence per day." The local engineer in charge attempted to restore the rate to 8 *d.*, a move calculated to lead to trouble. A crowd estimated at four hundred left the road works to protest the wage reduction and visited two local magistrates' houses, and at the second the man's seventy-two sheep were driven from his field "to slaughter them for their own use." The crowd and the sheep were pursued by Head Constable Rutledge and his six policemen, who reported that "The language of the body of men was that of self-destitution[*sic*], such as they would suffer to be shot, that they might as well die there as on their road home, or at their homes, that they would no longer suffer themselves to be in a state of starvation." With the aid of the local Catholic curate, the head constable spoke with men "for a considerable time, pointing out the consequences attendant, etc." The sheep were returned to the field without further trouble.[27]

In the context of widespread popular dissatisfaction with wage rates and access to relief project employment, the transition to food distribution through soup kitchens stirred fears of disturbances. At Cashel and Carrick-on-Suir fears arose that the advent of rations would cause unrest, as some people "intend assembling here tomorrow with a view of forcing their employment on the public works." The Cashel magistrates drafted in additional police and cavalry and secured the cooperation of the Catholic clergy to keep things peaceful. Trouble was averted the next day, even though there was clear dissatisfaction with the amount of relief being distributed. It was also clear to the resident magistrate that the poor much preferred even miserly employment with the Board of Works to soup kitchens because those in need wished to retain some sense of independence and control of their domestic lives.[28] At Littleton in County Tipperary "a large concourse of people" destroyed the boiler for the local relief committee's soup kitchen,

26 Irish Constabulary circulars, 17 Dec. 1846, 15 Jan. 1847 (PRO, 184/111, 112); W. Somerville to T. Redington, 8 Jan. 1847; minute, 12 Jan. 1847 (RP 1847/c/7). See also Griffin, *op. cit.*, pp. 354–5; OP 1847/27/358.

27 J. Walker to T. Redington, 9 Jan. 1847; enclosing report of W. J. Rutledge to J. Brereton, R. M., 29 Dec. 1846 (OP 1847/27/116).

28 M. Ffrench, R.M. to T. Redington, 2, 3 May 1847 (OP 1847/27/1065, 1086); [?] Murray, R. M. to Redington, 1 May 1847 (1847/27/1083).

"there being no adequate police force successfully to resist so great a multitude." Protests at the distribution of food continued in Littleton: ". . . a vast body of people assembled in Littleton, and refused to permit any person to take the meal (some even that had taken it then obliged to give it back) unless the allowances, as laid down by the Relief Commissioners, were increased."[29] Relieving officers and poor law guardians were also the objects of threats during the Famine. Head Constable Mullarkey of Kilrush was commended for securing from a witness a deposition that convicted five men for sending a threatening notice demanding increased access to relief or to "have your wills made in time."[30] Also in County Clare, an attempt was made by those outside to burn the Scariff workhouse, apparently to cover an attempt to plunder the place in the turmoil. The building was damaged in the resulting panic, but the quick arrival of the police prevented the sacking of the workhouse.[31]

The Constabulary's contact with the relief system involved less exciting and much sadder duties. The police experienced the stress of the face-to-face encounters with the famine years' depredations and victims. Constables were instructed to report immediately cases of destitution to relief officials.[32] The most common evidence of the impact of hunger and disease was the discovery of corpses in houses, outbuildings, and along roadsides. Inquests on strangers had to be organized and the police also had to arrange for numerous burials.[33] One example of the hardship that the police saw so regularly comes from Corofin, County Clare, where Sub-Constable Michael Lynch had to investigate the death by starvation of John Coleman in May, 1848. Coleman had a relief ticket for his family, but had not used it because his wife was too ill to go to the workhouse.

> The body has the appearance of long fasting, and, by all accounts, they are a destitute family. I saw a bunch of withered nettles there which I was told to be intended for breakfast.

29 J. Russell to Lords Justices of Ireland, 22 May 1847 (OP 1847/27/1235).

30 [Illegible] R.M. to T. Redington, 9 Jan. 1848 (OP 1848/5/25).

31 E. Bele, R.M. to T. Redington, 19 Aug. 1848; enclosing report of Head Constable T. Taylor, 17 Aug. 1848 (OP 1848/5/687).

32 Irish Constabulary Circulars, 11 Dec. 1847 (PRO, HO 184/112).

33 Griffin, op cit., pp. 357–8; H. Hatchett to Relief Commissioners, 27 June 1847 (RP 1847/27/1470); Sub-Insp. R. Fairsett to Relief Commissioners, 19 June 1847 (RP 1847/23/170).

The coroner's verdict was that Coleman died "for want of the common necessaries of life."[34] The desperation of life in famine Ireland was manifested in other ways that directly involved the Constabulary. A woman, Bridget O'Dea, was arrested for setting fire to a house near Scariff, which she claimed to have started in order to be transported, since she had been refused relief. Her imprisonment at Ennis indicates that her plan was on the way to some degree of success.[35] Earlier in the year, in that same neighborhood, a man was shot dead stealing potatoes by Edmond Stewart, who "was exasperated at the time, as quantities of his potatoes had been frequently stolen before." The dead man's family demanded that Stewart's bail be revoked, but the resident magistrate spoke in Stewart's favor, because he was the "son of a respectable and wealthy farmer and a young man of excellent character" who had surrendered himself to the police.[36] Class and connections did not cease to be important during the Great Famine.

The hardships of hunger and disease were compounded by another serious problem during the 1840s. Thousands of small holdings were cleared for nonpayment of rent and to make way for the further expansion of grazing, and the problems of collecting rents presented a convenient pretext to consolidate holdings. The Irish Constabulary did not actually take part in evictions, but frequently was on hand to prevent trouble. The scale of Famine-era clearances, as well as the density of population on small holdings, is starkly illustrated by a mass eviction on the property of John Gerrard, Ballinlass, County Galway, in March, 1846. Constabulary Sub-Inspector Bernard Cummins was called on to protect the sheriff's party with forty-five constables and ninety soldiers.

> Eighty houses were levelled to the ground and no resistance offered by the people, several of whom had cleared off previous to our going there. Eighty families consisting of upwards of 400 individuals were dispossessed. The townland contains about 500 acres.
>
> The tenants and laborers of Mr. Gerrard from another part of his property were obliged to attend there (very much against their will) in order to assist in levelling those houses. . . .

County Inspector W. Lewis added:

34 Sub-Insp. D. Murray to Insp. Gen., 26 May 1848, forwarding Sub-Constable M. Lynch's report, 25 May 1848 (OP 1848/5/454).

35 W. Stanley to T. Redington, 8 Aug. 1848 (OP 1848/5/1116).

36 M. Plunkett, R.M. to T. Redington, 5 Feb. 1848 (OP 1848/5/123).

The unfortunate people who were turned out are in a state of misery not to be described, scattered over this neighborhood, living in the ditches, or anywhere they can find shelter to erect a hut in. Fortunately for them, they were allowed to take the timber of their cabins with them.

The county inspector refuted a rumor that two families down with fever had been evicted.[37] The Gerrard clearance was accomplished without trouble, but two months later the tails of six heifers belonging to Gerrard's new tenants were cut off.[38]

A Dublin firm of land agents supervising a property in Galway complained that, when it attempted to divide 130 acres among seven or eight tenants, its sub-agent was met by a "mob of persons from the remaining part of the estate . . . and with threats and menaced violence declared that no persons should be put in possession of this land, but that it must be divided amongst themselves." The company was sure that this very traditional sort of agrarian resistance would not occur if the police and military were present, since "such a demonstration would overawe & prevent future interference with the rights of property."[39] A grazier from Kilkenny feared that his laborers were being intimidated and wanted additional protection for his animals, which was firmly resisted by the county inspector as being neither feasible nor necessary.[40]

Not all clearances went unresisted, as at Ballinlass. A Mr. Mannin of Dublin, who owned land in Tipperary, wrote to Dublin Castle to request assistance in clearing tenants and levelling their houses because his agent had been murdered in January, 1847. Mannin's case provided an opportunity for a clear explication of the Constabulary's role in evictions and clearances:

> . . . the police cannot be employed in pulling down houses or carrying out any other arrangements he [Mannin] may consider necessary upon his property, but if an affidavit is made before a magistrate which will satisfy him that an outrage is likely to be committed upon those employed . . . in a lawful occupation, it is competent to such a magistrate to direct a patrol

37 County Insp. W. Lewis to Insp. Gen., 26 Mar. 1846, with report of Sub-Insp. B. Cummins, 14 Mar. 1846 (OP 1846/11/6787, 7707; both with OP 1846/11/10199).

38 [Unnamed] R.M. to Undersecretary, 17 May 1846 (OP 1846/11/11981).

39 R. Guinness to R. Pennefather, 2 Apr. 1846 (OP 1846/11/8593).

40 J. Hutchinson to J. Greene, R.M., 25 Dec. 1846; McGregor's referral to County Inspector, 30 Dec. 1846; County Inspector to Insp. Gen., 2 Jan. 1847 (RP 1847/14/31).

in the neighborhood while such operations are in progress, or to take such other proper measures as may be necessary for the prevention of outrage.[41]

Legally, evictions were private matters that the Constabulary protected but did not sanction. Quite aside from the potential danger to policemen actively participating in clearances of cottiers, it is likely that there was a concern for rank-and-file morale. Being front-row witnesses to the social, economic, and human damage wrought by the famine was enough to discourage policemen, but to ask men who were the sons of tenant farmers to be an active part of evictions would have sorely tested the Constabulary's discipline. And, even if there was little sympathy for tenants being put out, there was likely to be a human hesitancy to add to the misery of the Famine.

It is not surprising that some of the most common occasions of violence during the Famine involved the transport of food and provisions to markets, warehouses, ports, or relief points.[42] The two-and-a-half years between late spring of 1846 through the harvest period of autumn of 1848, appear to have been when provisions in transit or storage were at greatest risk. In June, 1846, Head Constable Robert Rowan thwarted an attempt by two hundred persons to plunder five carts taking meal to a relief committee at Aranmore. His success was attributed to the Constabulary's characteristically strong local knowledge because local people knew that "the greater number of them were known to him and that he would prosecute them and bring them to punishment."[43] Head Constable Armstrong of Newmarket-on-Fergus station in Clare also succeeded in quickly arresting men who seized sacks of meal at gunpoint.[44] The Ballinasloe area experienced intimidation and attacks on food transports in October, 1846. Local people prevented the sale of corn one day and the police from "outstations" were concentrated to prevent a repeat of the incident. The Constabulary was assigned to escorting food after attacks near Banagher and the causes of the trouble were not lost on the local resident magistrate: ". . . if

41 Mannin to T. Redington, 10, 24 Feb. 1847, 25, 31 May 1847, 5 June 1847; Redington's minute, 20 Feb. 1847; Redington's draft for reply to Mannin, 3 June 1847; letters sent to Mannin 4, 10 June 1847 (RP 1847/27/1332).

42 For examples see Griffin, *op. cit.,* pp. 352–4. Detailed escort instructions were issued. Irish Constabulary circulars, 25 Sept., 2 Nov. 1846, 7 Sept. 1847 (PRO, HO 184/111, 112).

43 J. Kernan, R.M. to R. Pennefather, 25 June 1846 (OP 1846/11/19291).

44 B. Leyne, R.M. to T. Redington, 13 July 1848 (OP 1848/5/86).

any means could be devised to reduce the price of provisions, which are extremely high, the working classes would be very well off."[45] Another resident magistrate reported that

> ... famine & insubordination are staring us in the face, occasioned in a great measure by the cessation of the public works and the impeding of provisions in their transit from Galway to the country by lawless mobs ... there are but thirteen policemen in the town of Tuam.
>
> In a few words, we want employment for the poor; we want flour and meal for the people; we want military aid to the civil force.[46]

Tipperary experienced a series of attacks on provisions stores and transport throughout 1847 and even ships were liable to be attacked.[47] In, 1846, a vessel at Kilmaly, on the River Fergus, was plundered, but the arrival of a navy steamer in the area discouraged further trouble. The ship was withdrawn during the autumn of 1848 and another attack immediately occurred. The situation was confirmed by the Clare county inspector and the Castle undersecretary was induced to request the navy to pay more attention to patrolling the Fergus.[48]

A mill at Dunfanaghy in County Donegal, where government meal for relief distribution was being ground, was attacked three times in May, 1847, the third time successfully. The local sub-inspector reported that a Revenue Police officer, seven of his men, and one constable were guarding the meal and "made all possible resistance," being "obliged to use their bayonets ... but fired no shots." The policemen and a revenue man were severely injured before the army was able to drive off the raiders. A search the next day recovered some of the meal and four prisoners, but the sub-inspector described the difficulties experienced by the local police in meeting all the demands placed on them during the Famine: ".... four men are the number of Constabulary stationed at Cross Roads [the nearest barrack], two of which are employed at Gweedore guarding a vessel laden with Indian corn, the third was protecting the mill ... and the fourth barrack orderly

45 G. Fitzgerald, R.M. to H. Labouchere, 18, 25 Oct. 1846 (OP 1846/11/28513, 29131).

46 J. Kirwan, R.M. to Lord Lieutenant, 5 Oct. 1846 (OP 1846/11/26983); see also R. Palmer to T. Redington, 5 Oct. 1846 (OP 1846/11/26995).

47 See Irish National Archive Outrage Papers 12 Jan. 1847, 27/146; 5 Jan. 1847, 27/152; 14 Jan. 1847, 27/192; 26 Mar. 1847, 27/817; 1 May 1847, 27/1083; 8 May 1847, 27/1117; 26 Nov. 1847, 27/2289; 12 Dec. 1847, 27/2412.

48 J. Creagh, J.P. to Sir L. O'Brien, 10 Nov. 1848, enclosing memorial from inhabitants of Kilmaly; County Insp. G. Rutland to Insp. Gen., 17 Nov. 1848; T. Redington's minute, 20 Nov. 1848 (OP 1848/5/972).

[in charge of the station]." This extremely thin coverage caused the "extraordinary" circumstance in which Revenue Police, who were not peace officers or under the direct control of the Dublin government, were used for protection duty. The incident also elicited a characteristic statement of concern from the Treasury about providing appropriate protection for government property, namely corn meal for relief.[49]

Guard and escort duty so stretched police resources in the countryside that a Galway resident magistrate wrote to Dublin Castle about the "overworked police force" at Aranmore and Athenry, "arising from the escorts they are obliged to furnish for the safe transit of provisions, their nightly patrols and escorting of pay clerks through the country." A company of soldiers was requested for Athenry to assist with the escort duty, and the Galway magistrate described the elaborate system required to have the available police and troops handle different stages of provision carts' routes. Escorting alone consumed manpower and time, and the inspector general endorsed the need for reinforcements,[50] but, even as the police were reminded about the importance of routine patrolling, he worried about the effects of prolonged heavy duty.[51] When he was asked to increase off-road night patrols, he complained that

> . . . they could but very imperfectly patrol their subdistrict were they even to march the whole night. But it must be remembered that these very men have also numerous indispensable duties to perform on the following day. . . .
>
> The physical powers of even the Irish police . . . have their limits and they have been so urged beyond their limits in the disturbed counties that medical men and magistrates have justly remonstrated with me against the severity of their uninterrupted labours. . . .[52]

Clearly, there were sufficient problems and excitement in Ireland in the 1840s to keep the Irish Constabulary fully occupied with conditions directly related to the Famine. Foreshadowing the role the Constabulary would occupy in the administration of Ireland for the next seventy-five years, there was yet another duty, one that was tied fundamentally to government

49 Sub-Insp. Wright to Insp. Gen., 17, 18 May 1847; T. Redington's minute, 22 June 1847; R. Routh (Treasury) to Redington, 16 June 1847 (RP 1847/C/221).

50 J. Kernan to T. Redington, 2 Feb. 1847; McGregor's minute, 9 Feb. 1847 (RP 1847/17/1332).

51 Irish Constabulary circulars, 15 May, 18 Nov. 1847 (PRO, HO 184/112).

52 D. McGregor to Lord Lieutenant, 1 Jan. 1848 (National Library of Ireland, Larcom Papers, MS 7617).

in Ireland, that absorbed a great deal of police attention and confronted hard-pressed farmers and the police in Ireland with the relentless banality of bureaucracy.

Even in the depths of the Famine, the Irish government aggressively pursued tax collections. Costs to the public, especially in districts severely affected by the Famine, were very high and government at all levels was eager to capture as much tax revenue as possible. The establishment of the poor law system in Ireland in the late 1830s created a local tax to be collected, the poor rate, and by the early 1840s resistance among tenant farmers to the payment of poor rates required Constabulary presence when bailiffs were sent to distrain crops and livestock for nonpayment.[53] During the Famine, even substantial tenants were affected by the reduced and more expensive food supply, yet they were liable to heavier county cess and poor rates that left them sometimes unable and often disinclined to pay.[54] These ramifications in the rural economy meant that collection of money owed was difficult and poor law and county administrators resorted to distraint. From early 1847 on, as the Famine's impact intensified, tax collection became increasingly problematic. In Mayo, a cow was seized for nonpayment of county cess, but the animal was rescued by a large party of men. The baronial high constable and the local resident magistrate requested police protection. The undersecretary at Dublin Castle directed that poor rate and county cess collections should receive police protection when required.[55] Elsewhere in Mayo, the bailiff at Belmullet reported that he could not collect the cess without protection and that the local pound had been broken down and the distrained cattle driven out. Undersecretary Redington directed the local magistrate to provide whatever assistance was needed.[56] Tax collection was quickly adding to the pressure on police time and resources.

Even with a Constabulary escort, distraint attempts sometimes failed. A bailiff protected by eight policemen seized cattle and sheep in Bansha district, County Tipperary, and was then confronted by forty people blocking the road. The attempt to drive the livestock through the group re-

53 See Griffin, *op. cit.,* pp. 349–51.

54 For the pressure on both poor law unions and tenant farmers during the Famine and the problem of steeply rising poor rates, see J. S. Donnelly, Jr., "The Administration of Relief, 1847–51," in *New History of Ireland, V,* pp. 321, 326–9.

55 R. Bourke to T. Redington, 21 Jan. 1847; Redington's minute, 25 Jan. 1847, letters sent 26 Jan. 1847 (RP 1847/21/78).

56 J. Jackson to [?], 6 Feb. 1847; Redington's minute, 15 Feb. 1847 (RP 1847/21/152).

sulted in the animals being recaptured by the local people: "The police took no part on this occasion, as no breach of the peace occurred or violence offered . . . altho' Head Constable Kelly ordered his party to load, least a breach of the peace should occur and that he would have to interfere." Those involved in the rescue were arrested,[57] but resistance continued in Tipperary.[58] At Borrisokane, the rate collector was driven off twice.[59] By 1848, some collections were more successful and peaceful, but police protection was usually on hand. Anywhere from twenty to fifty police might be present and the army was often in attendance as well.[60]

The autumn of 1848 saw intense resistance to rate collections in Clare. Miles O'Bryen, the rate collector for the Gort union, went to Cranagh in mid-October, even though his police and military escorts were late. His twenty carts were damaged and harnesses cut by stone-throwing men and women. When the police arrived, the crowd was barricading the road, but the police declined to act without the authorization of Resident Magistrate F. J. Davis, who was also present. A couple of carts approached the grain intended for seizure, but they were damaged, the drivers injured, and nothing was seized. Several stonethrowers were arrested, but freed, so that the police would be not burdened with prisoners in a dangerous situation. O'Bryen completed his account by stating that "I am quite satisfied if the magistrate protected the carmen while they were bringing the cars to where the corn was, and showed a little determination, that we would have got all the rate that was due. . . ." Resident Magistrate Davis explained that O'Bryen had not given adequate notice of his intentions and he wished to avoid dividing his police and troops. Undersecretary Redington remarked that those arrested should at least have been bound over to keep the peace.[61]

News of the Cranagh confrontation spread quickly in north Clare and threats and resistance continued. The situation was complicated by the fact that two important sectors of the rural establishment were compet-

57 Sub-Insp. R. Gannon to Insp. Gen., 24 Feb. 1847 (OP 1847/27/638); see also R. Bradshaw to T. Redington, 15, 23 Nov. 1847 (OP 1847/27/2166) and Earl Glengale to W. Somerville, 27 Dec. 1847 (OP 1847/27/2511).

58 W. Reardon to T. Redington, 6 July 1847 (OP 1847/27/1498); see also 1847/27/2029.

59 E. Waller to W. Somerville, 4 Nov. 1847 (OP 1847/27/2065).

60 F. Davis to T. Redington, 30 Jan. 29 Nov., 1, 28 Dec. 1848 (OP 1848/5/86, 997, 1012, 1103).

61 F. Gibbons to W. Stanley, enclosing M. O'Bryen to Gort Guardians, 15 Oct. 1848; F. Davis to T. Redington, 21 Oct. 1848; Redington's minute, 23 Oct. 1848 (OP 1848/5/891).

ing with each other for the tenant farmers' resources. The landlords were owed the entire crop intended for taxes and they were trying to cart it off ahead of the rate collectors. Stock were rescued at Drumguane and Lissaturma. The collector of Milrook, Mr. Glynn, was advised that "the next time you come, bring your coffin, for you'll require it." Glynn concluded that "the people of that village [Milrook] are unquestionably very poor, and have scarcely any means, but whatever corn they had, which is seized by the landlord." At Arran, the bailiff was confronted by angry women, who refused to let him pass. They warned him that

> ... no matter what number of police I brought with me, they would treat them and my men in the same way as they were treated in Grennagh [sic] they day before ... It is perfectly impossible for me to bring a single beast or a grain of corn out of it without a strong force. This village certainly is very poor, as they live on the seaside and depended hitherto on the seaweed and potato. The potato is now gone and, consequently, there is no demand for the seaweed [as fertilizer].

The board of guardians was determined to collect the rate because relief expenses were very high and creditors were threatening legal action against the union.[62] A thousand inhabitants of the Kinvara area met a distraint expedition accompanied by forty-three soldiers and fifty-three police with stones and a triple line of stone barricades in the road. After some of the police and Resident Magistrate Davis were injured by stones, the magistrate read the Riot Act and ordered the police to load. The police then dispersed the crowd "with great forbearance under a constant shower of stones." Rather than attempt to cross the barricades, the collection party withdrew or, as Davis observed, "I should in self-defence have given orders to fire." Redington concluded that police should be posted ahead of collection parties to prevent blocking roads.[63] Of the Cranagh incident, "it is generally reported throughout the union that the police and military were defeated." The resistance that Cranagh inspired created a circumstance in which

> ... the stock of corn, in numerous cases the only stake for the rate, is rapidly disappearing from the lands of many of the farmers, more especially those of whom the former as well as the present rate is due, and who alone

62 H. Glynn to Gort Guardians, two reports 14 Oct. 1848; J. Slater to Gort Guardians, 14 Oct. 1848; J. Hall and J. Dunne to W. Stanley, 15 Oct. 1848 (OP 1848/5/891).

63 F. Davis to T. Redington, 23 Oct. 1848; Redington's minute, 25 Oct. 1848 (OP 1848/5/897).

are the parties we are desirous of distraining at present. In a very short period there will be nothing left on these premises available for payment, and the occupiers by their violent and lawless proceedings, will secure exemption from this rate as well as from the last.

The people so described by the Gort board of guardians were not poor relief recipients but tenant farmers who had crops to sell and rents to pay—another irony that shows the long social and economic reach of the Famine. The guardians complained that "destitution is increasing, the claims for relief are becoming daily more numerous and the creditors . . . are insisting on payment of their demands, or threatening law proceedings as the alternative." Double rescues of distraint collections were reported at Beagh and Kinvara and, despite police and military assistance at Kilmacduagh, the carts and harnesses were destroyed and the horses injured.[64] Even when overt or violent resistance was not encountered, rate collection and distraint caused very long days for the Irish Constabulary, who usually had first to concentrate from several stations and often march over long distances in the face of popular disapproval, if not open opposition.

The strain of policing Ireland during the Great Famine resulted from the combined effects of consistently long hours of duty, of the threat of violence, and of the discomfort inherent in enforcing law and order in the face of human suffering. Particularly in the West and South, the Irish Constabulary was constantly in the presence of the poor and destitute, presiding at relief programs or evictions, and escorting provisions and rate collectors. There were severe emotional and physical costs to the prolonged stress of duty during the Famine, including the impact of higher food costs on constables' families.[65] The three years 1847, 1848, and 1849 accounted for the highest death tolls of constables on active duty prior to 1919–21—respectively, 224, 150, and 221. Frequent contact with a population in which contagious disease was epidemic caused a higher death rate among the police, about twice as high as the annual average for the entire period 1841–1914—amounting to 8.75 percent of separations from the force. The incidence of gratuities to policemen who, usually for some health-related reason, left

64 J. Hall and J. Dunne to W. Stanley, 15 Oct. 1848; F. Gibbons to W. Stanley, 15 Oct. 1848 (OP 1848/5/891).

65 For five months in 1847 policemen with families were permitted to draw repayable wage advances, owing to high provision prices. Irish Constabulary circulars, 8 Feb., 29 March, 16 July 1847 (PRO, HO 184/112).

POLICING FAMINE IRELAND

the force honorably but prior to being pensionable, also rose to their highest level. Two factors probably account for this: some of the original Constabulary who were no longer effective were given an incentive to leave the force; and the stress and exposure to illness caused or aggravated policemen's health problems. In the terrible year of 1847, the highest numbers of deaths and gratuities in the force occurred. Resignations, at 526, were also at a record level, although this number would be exceeded in the waves of resignations in the 1850s and 1860s, when there was great dissatisfaction over pay and conditions. But the rate of resignation began to accelerate during the Famine.[66] Of the 120 policemen in a ten percent sample of the Constabulary personnel register[67] who resigned during 1846–51, ninety, or seventy-five percent, indicated that they intended to emigrate, which was characteristic of Ireland's response to the Famine. Inspector General McGregor worried in 1848 that "many of our respectable men have sought refuge from such excessive work by withdrawing altogether from the force ... young men of character having begun within the last twelve or eighteen months to refuse entering Constabulary service notwithstanding the general want of employment."[68] Personnel attrition during the Famine was heavy and 1847 was the Constabulary's worst year until the advent of the Anglo-Irish War. Yet, even if the magnitude and complexity of the Famine sometimes overwhelmed the human resources available to the police, there appears to have been little criticism of their performance. The complaints and petitions that poured into Dublin Castle uniformly favored *more* police. As an organization, the Irish Constabulary proved very useful and reliable in some of the hardest years in Ireland's history.

—University of Detroit-Mercy

66 The figures for separations from the Constabulary are taken from annual returns relating to the Constabulary force, 1841–1919 (PRO, HO 184/54), which are reproduced for 1841–1914 in Griffin, *op. cit.,* pp. 859–62.

67 For additional information concerning these data, see Lowe and Malcolm, "The Domestication of the Royal Irish Constabulary, 1836–1922," pp. 32–3.

68 McGregor to Lord Lieutenant, 1 Jan. 1848 (National Library of Ireland, Larcom Papers, MS 7617).

POLICING FAMINE IRELAND

DÁNTA ÚRA: NEW POEMS

SEÁN LYSAGHT

FOR JESSICA

The plastic basin hitched on your hip,
your arm falling outside, holding it
as you came down the garden,
was the tub you carried into the leasowes.

The wet damask had darkened, but would dry
to that bright, heavy fabric
you shook from the chest of drawers
and tautened, testing the winter.

As you go striding with that weight
across the water-meadows,
I glimpse your hem flailing the seed-heads,
and catching the goose-grass you'll pluck

later from your skirts at the fireside
where this new world takes hold.
The glow of a single spill
is carried in a cupped hand to the kindling.

Our home is growing with gusset,
pink fir-apple, coriander, and russets
from the shires, those love-flowers
standing in late-summer callows

that seeded first, and have spread
from beyond the sportsfield in your village,
the leasowes, where clover and vetchling
sprawled across your childhood path.

THE NAME

from TAGON

Small offal was bundled off, prayers were said for the virgin lost, and the child, cleared of the smear of his origins, was dressed and presented. The flesh became the word Tagon. He grew through the body, the body knew the name, and ran at the word, to teatimes, out of all danger.

The hair is now shorn which registered the breezes of Corca Dhuibhne. But these were the hands that reached into the nests at Mellary, to count the warm clutches. These, the legs of the light winger, AMDG, in the murk of a November afternoon.

Later, he crouched in the lavatory, then rose to the pins of spray and travelled his own extent with a flannel. At chess, or reading the crime of Raskolnikov, the members rested.

❧

THE GAZEBO AT LOUGH KEY

Beyond the tufted lichen of the alders,
with lake-water washing its base,
the folly still stands today.
built solid as a rook in chess.

The taste that framed the rampart wall
was erudite Victorian,
but is outlived this afternoon
by a restored gazebo in Roscommon.

There's no Excalibur here, no sudden
hand out of breezy waters,
no votive chalices cast, no king
grounding a love-sick daughter.

It's simply a water-studio
on the scudded, unreflecting face
choosing water as its subject
and itself as the appointed place.

In the shadow of these windows
the water-colorist could paint
on a dry sketch-pad, with a brush
immune to its own element.

And who could tell the result
as what waver of liquid force,
what dash of white spray caught
in the tincture of the source?

Still, it's measured on the instant
of the naked eye that sees
spreading waves and grazings
across the shifting surfaces.

In other words, probing the flood,
you find an otter turning at depth
on a heart of mammal blood,
and a warm, suspended breath.

TAGON'S STUDIES

from TAGON

Clearing out a hold-call lent by Melusine, Tagon found a date seed in a side pocket. It grew slowly, but sure after planting, in his vigilant care, in memory of the grove of pain, and took on its own beauty, even, in its innocence

Others were to follow into his room: an umbrella plant, papyrus, maidenhair fern. He collected and dried others from the quarries and quagmires in the vicinity.

Had he not reason, given the herbarium, to lament the ghastly victims on the shore of the Styx, where journalists and profiteers were strengthening the wrong?

But when the Princess made it to his room and broached its green spirit, he spared her this, and stuck to plant names by way of introduction.

æ

PHASES OF THE FLAP-MAN

I

The gruff farmer calls up the children,
the meek ones leaping through a meadow
of flowers whose names are unknown,

and at his bidding they disentangle from weeds
what lies fallen at the back of an outhouse,
or win things from the ash-heap:

jam-crocks, porter-bottles,
a step-ladder with missing rungs,
kettle-hooks, old cauldrons.

Then they leg-over a dormant gate
to cross into vistas of stiff corn
and crows that veer off, casually.

DÁNTA ÚRA: NEW POEMS

This is where I begin in the planted field
as whatever they drive into the ground,
scaffold and clothe, assemble, tie down.

Say the old step-ladder cloaked
in a woollen coat, my face a steering wheel
that speaks in tinkles of glass on glass.

II

They come again the following year,
the kids wading through vetch
and loosestrife. They are carrying

packaging from a building site.
A boy lobs a small, hard bottle ahead
into the unknown and runs on to it,

then follows the other boy and a girl,
truant through the gap, into the barley field.
The crow-scarer detonates.

Whatever I was has reduced to place
and direction where hedge meets hedge
and a power cable sags above a gateway.

Still presiding at about half-way,
I entice them along tight corridors of corn
to the usual zone of assembly,

and come duly, a light snowman of polystyrene
with a polythene cape and a nose-bottle,
baptised with pee as they giggle.

III

The contractors leave engines running
as they open gates to the wheatfield
and pitch scarecrows onto the headland.

I'm shifting gears towards the sea
on an old river of road
that winds past the strategies of land—

acreage, injustice, loss—
to where the farmers come
after harvest, to observe the offing.

Here's bric-a-brac for the sea-trove
as these white feet
toe their line along the shore.

Shells, stones,
beaks and skulls,
driftwood fluted or full of holes,

a little wave-worn slab of teak
with its brass lifting-ring—
a tiny door opening on an origin—

all these fill up my window sill.
I have made my own inventory
out of the immense volume of the sea

to have a list, to be sure,
a line of measured rungs
to lead where things are sung.

THE CUBE IN THE WEST

My cube was made
of cliff-faces and horizons.
The essence of sea and light
shaped in white mass,

it came shipborne
with bottled gas and pigs
and was hoisted
onto a pier of cut stone.

When the commotion cleared,
it rested.
A round sun went down.
Then the talk gathered

at a perfect window,
worrying the new—
they'd have given a right arm
to know who the designer was

who pared his nails
that evening, having sent
his project ahead.
So they spread rumours,

and spread fishing nets on the cube,
and turned a blind eye
to gulls
that soiled it with droppings.

And that might have been that,
rusting softly
beside stacks of kelp and lobster pots:
the solid idea.

The breakthrough came
when I took a die
and started tossing it
among the abandoned anchors.

That brought them round sure enough
in frayed woollens
to watch it bounce.
Ten-pound notes were wagered

on the cube's random dance,
and we played as the tide rose.
Doubles or quits,
the call had two dimensions,

like the beams of the cross
when the lots were cast
on Golgotha
at the sharing of Christ's clothes.

❧

NEMI

from TAGON

Years later, a move to the south, *in extremis*. White poppies waved on the undecorated burials of friends.

He was almost too tired to notice the figtrees in the courtyard, and hear the rasping of crickets the first evening. But he knew he had won a reprieve. A tree-frog croaked, and there was laughter from outdoor tables in the small hours.

High mountains in the east, and a dusty plain in the distance dawned on him through the small window of his attic room. He had come to be of service, so the panorama was slow to compose itself. The parsimony of vineyards. The scope of olive groves. A shimmer of sea.

None of this mattered, of course, as he hurried down the corridors with tea-trolleys, or waxed the master's shoes.

DÁNTA ÚRA: NEW POEMS

THE AIDS ORCHID

Not sweet, not blushing
for anyone now, it's just
itself in any air,
anywhere. An orchid.

Though someday it may be written
that the stricken were saved
in the spreading cities
by taking a speckled bloom.

The light in millions
from that gay mirror
they held to the self
threw back some they'd disown.

Even now they are scouring
rainforest and taiga
for a flower like a wand
yet uncut in the hazel.

Shading it into the known,
each footfall looms
in the lens of a raindrop
while the many die of desire

of the aids orchid.
Not sweet, not blushing
for anyone now, it's just
itself in any air, anywhere.

THE ECONOMIC IDEALS
OF IRISH NATIONALISM: FRUGAL
COMFORT OR LAVISH AUSTERITY?

MARY E. DALY

JOSEPH CARRIGAN, the head of the United States Economic Cooperation Administration mission to Ireland, which was the agency responsible for the Marshall Aid program, wrote in 1949 to Seán MacBride, the Irish Minister for External Affairs, to express his frustration at Ireland's apparent lack of concern about her inability to generate dollar earnings.

> As I have discussed the matter with Government officials, I find everyone most friendly and receptive to suggestions, but little action seems to follow. I have been impressed in some instances by the lightness of concern about it, in other instances by the expressed hopelessness as to Ireland's ability to do anything about it, and in still other instances by the apparent feeling that it is not Ireland's problem but that it must be solved by action entirely outside of Ireland. Some appear to feel that something is going to happen to take care of it.
>
> I have reluctantly come to the conclusion that Ireland is not facing up this problem.

Such criticism was not uncommon during the immediate postwar years. A British official commented on ". . . how self-centred and in a way isolated from reality Dublin appeared to be," and he concluded: "I was particularly anxious to get them interested in Bretton-Woods organisations but it really seemed as though the people I talked to were thinking about it for the first time." Another claimed that higher prices for Irish agricultural produce would result in

> small farmers eating more and doing less. . . . The Irish are nearer to subsistence farming mentality than we are and have yet to learn the attractions (or alleged attractions) of farming to make money for the purpose of buying things the farm cannot produce.[1]

1   University College, Dublin, Archives (UCDA), McGilligan Papers, P 35/c/6; London, Public Records Office (PRO), B.T. 11/4246 21 June 1946; B.T. 11/8821 24 May 1938.

Similar views had been expressed by a number of early nineteenth-century economists, among them Ricardo, Malthus and McCulloch, who believed "That 'a taste for other objects besides mere food' was a primary necessity for economic development in Ireland."[2] While such opinions may reflect uncritical foreign acceptance of Irish cultural stereotypes, Carrigan's views seem to be corroborated by MacBride's response:

> Ireland's approach to political and economic problems is not based on materialism; basically, Ireland is moved more by a genuine desire to serve the ideals in which she believes. These ideals are the democratic way of life, Christian social and economic principles, human liberty, the right to national self determination and family life.[3]

This is one among many litanies of cultural values enunciated by Irish nationalists. In the 1840s, the Young Irelander Thomas Davis described the Irish people as "pious, hospitable, and brave, faithful observers of family ties, cultivators of learning, music and poetry"—values jeopardized by materialist English values. In 1904, Michael Davitt described England's rule of Ireland prior to 1870 as "a systematic opposition to the five great underlying principles of civilized society as these lived and had their being and expressions in Celtic character": love of country; attachment to home and to familial land; fervent loyalty to religious faith, "unsurpassed by that of any Christian nation"; and national pride in learning. The most evocative image of this nature is Taoiseach Eamon de Valéra's famous St. Patrick's Day broadcast of 1943.

> The Ireland which we have dreamed of would be the home of a people who valued material wealth only as the basis of right living, of a people who were satisfied with frugal comfort and devoted their leisure to things of the spirit—a land whose countryside would be bright with cosy homesteads, whose fields and villages would be joyous with the sounds of industry, with the romping of sturdy children, the contests of athletic youth and the laughter of comely maidens, whose firesides would be forums for the wisdom of old age. It would, in a word, be the home of a people living the life that God desires that man should live.[4]

2   R. D. C. Black, *Economic Thought and the Irish Question* (Cambridge, 1960), p. 137.
3   National Archives, Washington, D.C., Record Group 84, Box 702 Dublin.
4   John Hutchinson, *The Dynamics of Cultural Nationalism* (London, 1987), p. 98. Michael Davitt, *The Fall of Feudalism in Ireland* (Dublin, 1904), p. xv., *Speeches and Statements by Eamon de Valéra 1917–1973*, ed. Maurice Moynihan (Dublin 1980), p. 466.

THE ECONOMIC IDEALS OF IRISH NATIONALISM

Such statements may be dismissed as the utterances of men "manipulating cultural stereotypes for political or rhetorical purposes"[5] and, perhaps for this very reason, they have been regarded as having little relevance to Irish economic history.

While numerous historical explanations have been advanced for the shortcomings of the Irish economy since independence—such as the problem of the latecomer, the postcolonial legacy, or "the rigidities reflected in the restrictive structures and mentalities fostered by the primacy of the possessor principle"—only Kerby Miller's reference to the "premodern" attitudes of Irish Catholic emigrants as an explanation for their alleged adjustment problems in the United States employs a cultural explanation. In *Ireland 1912–1985* (1989) the most lengthy treatment of twentieth-century Ireland, J. J. Lee devotes but one page of almost seven hundred to querying whether the Irish wanted economic growth, dismissing the "image of Ireland as an island sublimely submerged in a sea of spirituality" as one which carries "little conviction." Lee argues that few peoples "were so prepared to scatter their children around the world in order to preserve their own living standards," bolstering his argument with references to "the primacy of the pocket in marriage arrangements . . . the milking of bovine TB eradication schemes . . . the finessing of government grants, subsidies and loans" and other examples of Irish cupidity.[6] Yet, such comments refer to individual behavior as opposed to collective attitudes, and a contradiction between the two is by no means implausible. By concentrating on the economic ideals expressed by nationalist leaders before and after Irish independence, this discussion will give only cursory attention to popular attitudes and those of Ulster Unionists will be overlooked. While cultural attitudes may not provide the major explanation for Ireland's poor economic performance, ideals did influence policies and, indirectly, perfor-

5 David Fitzpatrick "'That Beloved Country, That No Place Else Resembles': Connotations of Irishness in Correspondence between Ireland and Australasia, 1841–1915," *Irish Historical Studies* XXVII, 108, (November, 1991), 325.

6 Kieran Kennedy, "The Context of Economic Development," in *The Development of Industrial Society in Ireland,* eds. J. H. Goldthorpe, C. T. Whelan (Oxford, 1992), pp. 5–29. Eoin O'Malley, *Industry and Economic Development: The Challenge for the Latecomer* (Dublin, 1989). Raymond Crotty, *Ireland in Crisis: A Study in Capitalist Colonial Undevelopment* (Dingle, 1986). J. J. Lee, *Ireland 1912–1985: Politics and Society* (Cambridge, 1989), pp. 517, 522. Kerby A. Miller, *Emigrants and Exiles: Ireland and the Irish Exodus to North America* (New York, 1985). For a critique of Miller, see David Fitzpatrick, "The Irish in America: Exiles or Escapers," *Reviews in American History,* 15 (1987), 272–8; Fitzpatrick, "'That Beloved Country'," 22.

THE ECONOMIC IDEALS OF IRISH NATIONALISM

mance. Analyzing late industrializing nations in *Economic Backwardness in Historic Perspective* (1986), Alexander Gerschenkron emphasized the need for both a "New Deal in emotion" and substantial government intervention as preconditions for success.[7]

The dearth of cultural explanations in recent writing on the Irish economy contrasts with the position in the early twentieth century. In *Ireland in the New Century* (1905), Sir Horace Plunkett, an unorthodox Unionist and founder of the Irish cooperative movement, claimed that when basic subsistence needs had been met, Irish peasants had "no adequate inducement to further effort." Plunkett saw this attitude as a consequence of the seventeenth-century anti-Catholic Penal Laws, abuses of land tenure, and the influence of Roman Catholicism, a religion whose tendencies struck him as "non-economic, if not actually anti-economic." He held Catholicism responsible for such failings of Irish character as "entire lack of serious thought on public questions; a listlessness and apathy in regard to economic improvement which amounts to a form of fatalism; and, in backward districts, a survival of superstition, which saps all strength of will and purpose." Writing shortly before Max Weber's *The Protestant Ethic and the Spirit of Capitalism* (1905), Plunkett poses many points in common with Weber's analysis of "traditionalistic business." Weber described behavior such as the "finessing of government grants and loans," cited by Lee to refute cultural explanations for economic retardation, as characteristic of countries "whose bourgeois-capitalistic development, measured according to Occidental standards, has remained backward." Plunkett's views were preceded by Michael McCarthy's polemical *Priests and People in Ireland* (1902), with its grasping priesthood holding the population in "mental bondage" and appropriating their savings for elaborate church-building. Filson Young's *Ireland at the Crossroads* (1907) described "an Ireland stagnant under decay and social misrule, a land of people isolated, despondent, of waning energies and without any but spiritual ambitions," whose poverty, emigration, and lunacy were attributed to the influence of Catholicism.[8]

Such issues were not unique to Ireland. The backwardness of Catholic Germany and the drain of talent to the priesthood, which inspired Weber,

7 Alexander Gerschenkron, *Economic Backwardness in Historical Perspective,* (Cambridge, Mass., 1966), pp. 25, 44.

8 Horace Plunkett, *Ireland in the New Century* (Dublin, 1905), pp. 53–57, 101, 110. The preface to the first edition is dated December, 1903. Weber's book was first published in German in 1905. Max Weber, *The Protestant Ethic and the Spirit of Capitalism,* trans. Talcott

were widely discussed around the turn of the century. Some German Catholics sought to establish Catholicism as a "principle of progress," as did Monsignor O'Riordan, rector of the Irish College in Rome. Replying to Plunkett, O'Riordan ascribed Irish poverty to past British policies and rejected allegations that Catholicism was anti-economic by referring to the success of Belgium, which had been administered by Roman Catholic governments since 1884. O'Riordan alleged that in England where "protestantism, the religion of 'self-reliance and civic virtue' has had full play, in which the 'spiritual and economic ideals have been co-ordinated', according to the mind of Sir Horace Plunkett," women and children were exploited, poverty and homelessness were common, inequality of wealth was growing, and agricultural, rural smallholdings, and the family were all in decline. In contrast, O'Riordan cited Belgium's rising population, prosperous industry, intensive rural cultivation, and widespread peasant proprietorship—a country where a Catholic government protected women and children, and one which contained less misery than a single English city. The accuracy of O'Riordan's assertions are of little concern. As MacBride was to do half-a-century later, O'Riordan distinguished between "human or social progress" and "mere material or industrial progress." He depicted pre-Reformation Europe as an era devoid of poverty, as an era when every peasant had a house and land in contrast with the adverse consequences of Protestant "individuality," "initiative" and "self-reliance" seen in modern industrial society.[9]

O'Riordan's ambivalence towards progress—and his insistence on such criteria as population growth, family welfare, and land distribution as opposed to material wealth—is echoed in many writings on the condition of Ireland. While Irish living standards rose during the second half of the nineteenth century, perhaps at a more rapid rate than in Britain,[10] economic

---

Parsons (London, 1976), pp. 57, 66–67; Michael J. McCarthy, *Priests and People in Ireland* (London, 1902), p. 560, and xiv–xv; Filson Young, *Ireland at the Cross Roads. An Essay in Explanation* (London, 1907), pp. 177–8. Davitt blamed the rising level of insanity on union with Britain. See *The Fall of Feudalism*, p. 721.

9 Weber, *Protestant Ethic,* pp. 35–6; David Blackbourn: "The Discreet Charm of the Bourgeoisie: Reappraising German History in the Nineteenth Century," in David Blackbourn and Geoff Eley, *The Peculiarities of German History* (Oxford, 1984), pp. 184–5; M. O'Riordan, *Catholicity and Progress in Ireland* (London, 1905), pp. 60, 73–121.

10 Kieran A. Kennedy, Thomas Giblin, and Deirdre McHugh, *The Economic Development of Ireland in the Twentieth Century* (London, 1988), p. 17. See also David Johnson, "The Economic Performance of Independent Ireland," *Irish Economic and Social History* (1991).

progress was at best a zero-sum outcome: larger farms and higher income were both achieved at the cost of population decline, emigration, reduced crop cultivation and falling rural employment. In fact, applying Simon Kuznets's definition of economic growth as a sustained rise in *both* population and income per capita, post-Famine Ireland did not experience economic growth until the 1960s.[11] In the early 1860s, Irish economists were divided on whether the economy was expanding or contracting. As R. D. C. Black has pointed out, the parties were arguing at cross purposes: the pessimist's case rested on declining population and crop acreage; the optimists cited rising customs and excise returns and higher bank deposits.[12] While there were economic gainers and losers within post-Famine Ireland, some of the gains and losses were borne by the same families—for example, greater prosperity for those remaining at the cost of emigration of family members— further compounding ambivalence. The fact that the Irish population peaked in the mid-nineteenth century, as did some crop acreages and yields,[13] meant that an Irish agenda for progress often entailed a backward glance.

The most frequently cited objective was population growth. The Irish population exceeded eight million at the time of the Famine of the 1840s; in the following century it declined to approximately half that figure. This loss exercised considerable power over the Irish consciousness, and virtually all nationalist leaders prior to independence dreamed of exceeding the pre-Famine population. In 1880, Charles Stewart Parnell told the United States House of Representatives that, extrapolating from statistics for the island of Guernsey, Ireland could support a population of forty-five million. Michael Davitt believed that Ireland had resources "capable of sustaining three times the present population of Belgium," or approximately twenty-two million.[14] Such optimism was bolstered by nationalist images of the Famine, and of the nineteenth-century Irish economy. Young Irelander John Mitchel's visions of six ships laden with grain leaving Ireland at the height of the Famine while a solitary relief ship arrived with food

11 Kennedy, "Context of Economic Development," *passim*.

12 Black, *Economic Thought*, pp. 47–8.

13 P. M. Austin Bourke, "The Average Yield of Food Crops in Ireland on the Eve of the Great Famine," *Journal of the Department of Agriculture*, LXVI 7, (1969), 26–39. The 1847 yield per acre of potatoes on small acreage was not exceeded until 1929. Potato acreage peaked in the 1860s, oats in the 1850s, wheat in 1847.

14 Davitt, *The Fall of Feudalism*, pp. 200, 721.

THE ECONOMIC IDEALS OF IRISH NATIONALISM

conjured up "the spectacle of millions starving in an Ireland full of plentiful crops" and suggested that the country could comfortably support a population of eight million or more.[15] Sir Robert Kane's glowing account of Irish natural resources published in 1844 led to the belief that the country could sustain the thirty-five million envisaged by Thomas Davis or the twenty million favored by 1916 Rising leader Patrick Pearse.[16] The population of pre-Famine Ireland was impoverished not because it was trapped in an archaic economic structure, but because of British maladministration, excessive rents, and undeveloped resources.

Such analysis led inevitably to a critique of British policy towards Ireland and of the prevailing ideology of economic liberalism; even such a neoclassical economist as J. E. Cairnes questioned the universal validity of laissez-faire and free trade.[17] The Famine was regarded as testimony to the folly of market forces—the export of food during the Famine years being the most glaring example. Free trade and market forces were held responsible for the collapse of nineteenth-century Irish industry, the shift from tillage to cattle farming and population decline, all of which Irish Home Ruler Tom Kettle described as "that miserable triad, famine, eviction, and emigration."[18] Free trade was frequently seen as England's weapon in the economic destruction of Ireland, which also was an argument applied to Germany by the economist Friedrich List. In phrases which echoed List, Arthur Griffith, founder of the early twentieth-century Sinn Féin move-

15 John Mitchel, *The Last Conquest of Ireland (Perhaps)*, (Dublin, 1873), p. 208. Peter Solar, "The Great Famine was No Ordinary Subsistence Crisis," in *Famine: The Irish Experience 900–1900*, ed. E. Margaret Crawford (Edinburgh 1989), pp. 112–33; P. M. Bourke, "The Irish Grain Trade, 1839–48," *Irish Historical Studies*, XX (1976), 156–69. Bourke demonstrates that grain imports greatly exceeded exports during the Famine, with the exception of the autumn of 1846. Darrell Figgis, *The Economic Case for Irish Independence* (1920), p. 7. Pre-Famine Irish food supplies were capable of feeding more than nine million people. See Peter Solar, "Agricultural Productivity and Economic Development in Ireland and Scotland in the Early Nineteenth Century," in *Ireland and Scotland, 1600–1850: Parallels and Contrasts in Economic and Social Development* ed. T. M. Devine, David Dickson (Edinburgh, 1983), pp. 70–88.

16 Robert Kane, *The Industrial Resources of Ireland* (Dublin, 1844), p. 299. Kane argued that Ireland was capable of support 17.8 million people with existing agricultural practices. Thomas Davis, "Udalism and Feudalism," in *Prose Writings of Thomas Davis*, ed. T. W. Rolleston (London, n.d.), p. 60. Ruth Dudley Edwards, *Patrick Pearse: the Triumph of Failure* (London, 1977), p. 163.

17 T. A. Boylan and T. P. Foley, "J. E. Cairnes, J. S. Mill and Ireland" in *Economists and the Irish Economy* ed. Antoin E. Murphy (Dublin, 1984), pp. 105, 111.

18 T. M. Kettle, *The Open Secret of Ireland* (Dublin, 1912), p. 90.

THE ECONOMIC IDEALS OF IRISH NATIONALISM

ment, dismissed the *Wealth of Nations* as "the best example of a subtle scheme for English world-conquest put forward under the guise of an essay on political economy flavored with that love of man which hooks in the sentimentalists of all countries." Griffith espoused List's "National Economics," which gave priority to the economic development of the nation rather than the individual, despite the fact that List regarded the union of Great Britain and Ireland as "a great and irrefragable example of the immeasurable efficacy of free trade between united nations."[19] Others sought refuge in historicism in arguing for the merits of an economic system more appropriate to Irish traditions. The English-imposed landlord system was contrasted unfavorably with the more communitarian landholding practices of Ireland's ancient brehon law. Such ideas were given legal sanction by Gladstone's 1870 Land Act which overthrew common law in favor of customary tenure. A declaration of principles read at the founding meeting of the Land League of Mayo in 1879 quoted John Stuart Mill:

> Before the conquest the Irish people knew nothing of absolute property in land, the land virtually belonging to the entire sept. The chief was little more than the managing member of the association. The feudal idea, which views all rights as emanating from a head landlord, came in with the conquest, was associated with foreign dominion, and has never to this day been recognized by the moral sentiments of the people.[20]

While Griffith's National Economics embraced capitalism, provided it was directed towards national aggrandizement,[21] most alternative scenarios condemned the promotion of individual wealth at the expense of community welfare. Irish nationalism identified capitalism with England, the historic enemy. Douglas Hyde, the founder of the Gaelic League, equated modernization with Anglicization, while Aodh de Blacam, an early twentieth-century nationalist and journalist, condemned capitalism as an alien ideology "imposed on Ireland violently from without," which failed to take hold because of the restrictions imposed by the Penal Laws. This juxtaposition of an alien capitalism with an indigenous communitarian system

19 Friedrich List, *The National System of Political Economy*, trans. Sampson S. Lloyd (London, 1904), ch xv; Arthur Griffith, *The Resurrection of Hungary: A Parallel for Ireland with Appendixes on Pitt's Policy and Sinn Fein*, 3rd ed. (Dublin, 1918), p. 122.

20 Clive Dewey, "Celtic Agrarian Legislation and the Celtic Revival: Historicist Implications of Gladstone's Irish and Scottish Land Acts 1870–1886," *Past and Present*, 64 (1974), 30–70. Davitt, *Fall of Feudalism*, pp. 160–61.

21 Griffith, "Sinn Fein Policy," pp. 146–7.

THE ECONOMIC IDEALS OF IRISH NATIONALISM

formed the basis of James Connolly's linkage of nationalism and social-ism and his commitment to restore Ireland "to the Gaelic principle of common ownership by a people of their sources of food and maintenance." For those who feared socialism, cooperation offered an acceptable, his-torically valid alternative.[22]

Capitalism was seen as not only English, but Protestant as well. Weber and Tawney's linkage of Protestantism and the rise of capitalism was fre-quently noted. In *An Essay on the Economic Effects of the Reformation* (1923), the economic historian George O'Brien stressed that "the insistence of the capitalist on the removal of all restraints by the state is strictly analo-gous to the insistence of the Protestant on the removal of all restraints by the Church. It is private judgment translated into the realm of industry." O'Brien, who regarded capitalism as a consequence of the Reformation and socialism as a response to capitalist excesses, advocated a synthesis between them, but argued that this could be achieved only by restoring the world of pre-Reformation Catholicism. De Blacam claimed that "the capitalist order as we know it could never have arisen if Catholic economics had not been departed from," suggesting that traditional Gaelic landholding prac-tices were totally in keeping with Catholic social teaching which empha-sized family rights, widespread property ownership, and the primacy of land. Outlined in the encyclical *Rerum Novarum*, Pope Leo XIII's law of wages "that the remuneration must be enough to support the wage earner in reasonable and frugal comfort"—which provided de Valéra with one of his most telling phrases—echoed the just price concept of medieval theol-ogy and was analogous to the definition of fair rent put forward in 1881 by Dr. Croke, archbishop of Cashel: "fair rent is what an honest, industrious, religious, good Irishmen could afford to pay, after suitably supporting his family."[23] Such discourse was not unique to Ireland. In late nineteenth-

---

22 J. J. Lee, *The Modernization of Irish Society, 1848–1918* (Dublin, 1973), p. 139; Aodh de Blacam, *Towards the Republic. A Study of New Ireland's Social and Political Aims* (Dublin, 1919), p. 57; James Connolly, *Labour in Irish History* (London, 1973), p. xxx; Tom Garvin, *Nationalist Revolutionaries in Ireland, 1858–1929* (Oxford, 1987), pp. 121–2.

23 Rev. M. J. Browne, "The World Economic Crisis and Catholic Teaching," *Irish Ecclesiastical Record,* 41 (1933), 345; George O'Brien, *An Essay on the Economic Effects of the Reformation* (London, 1923), pp. 91, 170, 177–80. O'Brien subsequently served as professor of political economy and national economics at University College, Dublin. By the 1930s, O'Brien had modified these views. De Blacam, *Towards the Republic,* pp. 43, 49; Lilian Parker Wallace, *Leo XIII and the Rise of Socialism* (Durham, N.C., 1966), p. 193; Mark Tierney, *Croke of Cashel: The Life of Archbishop Thomas William Croke, 1823–1902* (Dublin, 1976), p. 121.

THE ECONOMIC IDEALS OF IRISH NATIONALISM

century Germany, criticism of economic crises was "couched in language taken from older pre-capitalist traditions, like the just price or the principle of a right to subsistence" and there are obvious links with the "moral economy" notions of eighteenth-century England. In *Annals of the Labouring Poor* (1985), K. D. M. Snell has suggested that the opinions embraced by the term "moral economy" should be viewed as efforts to make legitimate practices which had once been economically appropriate but were no longer compatible with changing circumstance.[24] Irish opinions suggest an effort to restore an archaic economic order.

The nationalist vision of a more populous Ireland was an overwhelmingly rural one. An alternative economic order would reverse the Cromwellian expulsion from the rich lands of the east to the poor lands of Connacht[25] and restore the intensive cultivation of the small-holdings of pre-Famine Ireland—minus the landlord and, presumably, the poverty. The enlarged population of the idealized Ireland would live not in cities, but in the countryside. Hostility to the city was not unique to Ireland. Similar sentiments were found among nineteenth-century German intellectuals and in Victorian England.[26] The anti-urban views of such Irish literary and political figures as Davis, Yeats, and Hyde derived from German romanticism, from such English critics as Ruskin and Carlyle, or from William Morris's "merrie England." In the 1840s, the Young Irelander James Fintan Lalor urged Irish people to shun city life which he regarded as "an abomination to human feelings and human senses."[27] The Literary Revival of the late nineteenth century intensified this rural bias. Cities evoked the threat of linguistic and cultural Anglicization, despite the fact that the movement drew its major strength from urban white-collar and

24 Blackbourn, "The Discreet Charm of the Bourgeoisie," p. 207; E. P. Thompson, "The Moral Economy of the English Crowd in the Eighteenth Century," *Past and Present*, L (1971); K. D. M. Snell, *Annals of the Labouring Poor: Social Change and Agrarian England, 1660–1900* (Cambridge, 1985), p. 100.

25 Paul Bew, *Land and the National Question, 1858–82* (Dublin, 1978), pp. 82–3.

26 Blackbourn, *Discreet Charm*, p. 211. Martin Wiener, *English Culture and the Decline of the Industrial Spirit, 1850–1980* (Cambridge, 1981), pp. 46–64.

27 Davis, "Udalism and Feudalism" Hutchinson, *The Dynamics of Cultural Nationalism*, p. 97; Dominic Daly, *The Young Douglas Hyde* (Dublin, 1974), pp. 74–6; Mary E. Daly, "An Alien Institution? Attitudes towards the City in Nineteenth and Twentieth Century Irish Society", *Études irlandaises*, 10 (1985), 181–94; Mary E. Daly, "James Fintan Lalor," in *Worsted in the Game: Losers in Irish History*, ed. Ciarán Brady (Dublin, 1989), p. 113.

professional classes.[28] In many minds there was grave doubt whether Belfast could be regarded as an Irish city at all, and, if it was, few wanted it duplicated. Speaking to a committee of the first Dáil in 1920 which was examining prospects for economic development, Fr. Finlay asserted that "one Belfast is enough" and argued that it would not improve the "human lot" to transfer people from the most deprived areas of rural Ireland to the life of Belfast mill workers.[29] The acute poverty of early twentieth-century Dublin slums added to the negative image of urban life.[30]

Cultural antipathy to urbanization combined with the anti-urban views of the Catholic church. In his autobiography *Mo Scéal Féin*, Fr. Peadar Ó Laoghaire, Gaelic League activist and writer, offered what has been described as "a simple-minded, evil-city versus virtuous-village polarity." Writing early in the twentieth century, one priest claimed that "the nursery of strong and vigorous men is not in the city but in the country" and argued that "but for the constant influx of rural vigour the inhabitants of a city would die out in the third or fourth generation." Another priest proposed to settle the urban unemployed on rural small-holdings, a position also advocated by Dr. O'Kelly, bishop of Cloyne, author of a 1909 report on the Irish Poor Laws, who also claimed that an unemployment insurance scheme was unnecessary in a predominantly rural country such as Ireland, a viewpoint largely supported by the Irish nationalist party at Westminster.[31]

This identification with the allegedly traditional rural society of the western seaboard[32] appeared to conflict with aspirations to reverse Ireland's industrial decline. It was widely believed that industry had prospered in

28 Martin Waters, "Peasants and Emigrants: Considerations of the Gaelic League as a Social Movement" in *Views of the Irish Peasantry, 1800–1916* (Hamden, Conn., 1977), p. 171.

29 Sybil Gribbon, "An Irish City: Belfast 1911," *The Town in Ireland* ed. David Harkness, Mary O'Dowd, (Belfast, 1981), pp. 203–5; Dáil Éireann, *Commission of Inquiry into the Resources and Industries of Ireland,* 9 December 1919. Finlay was professor of political economy at University College, Dublin.

30 See Mary E. Daly, *Dublin: the Deposed Capital, 1860–1914: A Social and Economic Study* (Cork, 1985), pp. 308–19.

31 Garvin, *Nationalist Revolutionaries in Ireland,* p. 59; "Christianity Applied to Economic Conditions: A Lesson from the Past," *Records of the Maynooth Union, 1913–14,* pp. 20–33; "The Problem of the Poor," *Maynooth Union, 1909,* pp. 26–36; *R.C. on the Poor Laws and Relief of Distress, Report on Ireland,* 1909, Cd. 4630 XXXVIII; Ruth Barrington, *Health, Medicine and Politics in Ireland 1900–1970* (Dublin, 1987), pp. 42–3.

32 L. M. Cullen, *The Emergence of Modern Ireland, 1600–1900* (London, 1981), pp. 109, 135. Cullen argues that the survival of cultural traditions in the West of Ireland has been slight.

THE ECONOMIC IDEALS OF IRISH NATIONALISM

the late eighteenth century owing to the assistance of an Irish Parliament and had collapsed after 1800 as a result of the Act of Union.[33] Most nationalists were optimistic that government incentives, coupled with the exploitation of natural resources, would bring about an industrial revival, which they saw as an integral component of national independence. Echoing List, Griffith believed that "an agricultural nation is an individual with one arm who makes use of a foreign arm, but who cannot make use of it in all cases; an agricultural-manufacturing nation is an individual who has two arms of his own always at his disposal."[34] Such visions had to be reconciled with the preservation of the Gaelic-speaking peasant. A blueprint of decentralized rural industry was the favored option. In the 1840s, Thomas Davis urged the merits of home manufacture over factory industry,[35] and sixty years later Arthur Griffith expressed the hope that electricity and motor transport might revive decentralized industry.[36]

Griffith and his contemporary D. P. Moran have recently been presented as supporters of "re-industrialization," imbued with a "modernizing zeal . . . in conflict with the romantic rural ideals of the literary and linguistic intellectual."[37] Griffith, however, expressed deep hostility to the "industrial 'hells'" of Manchester and looked back to an idealized eighteenth-century Ireland. In one article on Irish industrial prospects, Griffith insisted that

> Every farmer should support his family on his own flour, his own meal, his own vegetables, his own pork, fowl, eggs, butter; he should support the local miller; he should have his own wool made up into blankets and clothes for his family; he should grow his own flax, and have it spun in his own house and woven by the local weaver; and when he had satisfied every want of the home, he should sell to the townsmen what he had left.

Griffith advocated a cottage hosiery industry to employ the daughters of farmers and mechanics, with knitting needles offering "a best substitute for the spinning wheel at which their grandmothers used to work in the

33 George O'Brien, "Historical Introduction," to E. J. Riordan, *Modern Irish Trade and Industry* (Dublin, 1920), p. 50.

34 Griffith, "Sinn Fein Policy," p. 145; List, *National System of Political Economy,* p. 124; Kane, *Industrial Resources,* pp. 238–9.

35 Davis, "Udalism and Feudalism," p. 63.

36 Garvin, *Nationalist Revolutionaries in Ireland,* p. 132. This opinion was repeated in the 1950s in the *Report of the Commission on Emigration and other Population Problems, 1848–54,* para. 2541.

37 Hutchinson, *The Dynamics of Cultural Nationalism,* p. 169.

good old times."[38] He also rejected materialism in tones similar to those of de Valéra and MacBride. In 1902, an unidentified correspondent to the *United Irishman* argued that infant Irish industry would be forced to pay low wages, whereas emigrants would not remain in Ireland unless material conditions equaled those abroad. Griffith responded, in language similar to that in a later speech of de Valéra, that it would be "preferable for a family to live together on three plain meals a day at home, than if by separating around the world each member could carve out for himself a fortune and live in luxury,"[39] and he continued:

> I say this from a purely human standpoint—from the belief that a larger sum of happiness is to be derived from the unfettered play of the affections than from the gratification of the passion for wealth or power. In this latter pursuit nature is hardened till it can appreciate nothing but the real and the material; but the real and the material will never satisfy the human heart—at least the human Celtic heart.

Such sentiments are worthy of MacBride or de Valéra. Griffith's ideal was to "enable our poor families, with their joint earnings, to live in moderate comfort."[40] Although D. P. Moran admitted the primacy of economic forces which had "driven Ireland into an ugly economic corner," and threatened to obliterate traditional culture, he believed that restoring the Irish language would provide a barrier against emigration and "the latest novelties from London and Paris."[41] Moreover, having rejected both Griffith and Moran, Irish economic thinking encounters some difficulty when attempting to discover an alternative modernizing figure among nineteenth- or early twentieth-century Irish nationalists. While opponents of materialism, industrialization, and urbanization may readily be found in other cultures at this time, their views were generally balanced by contrary opinions.[42] Not in Ireland.

38 *United Irishman,* 11 October 1902 and 21 May 1902. These articles written under the pseudonym "Mise" are identified as by Griffith. Seán Ó Lúing, *Art Ó Griofa* (Dublin, 1953), p. 83.

39 In 1928 de Valéra spoke of the choice open to a servant between the freedom and "frugal fare" of life in a cottage and the "luxuries" of life in a mansion. See *Speeches . . . by Eamon de Valéra,* pp. 152–3.

40 *United Irishman,* 5 July 1902.

41 D. P. Moran, *The Philosophy of Irish Ireland* (Dublin, 1905), pp. 15, 29, 111.

42 Wiener, *English Culture and the Decline of the Industrial Spirit;* Blackbourn, "The Discreet Charm of the Bourgeoisie," pp. 182–5; James Raven, "British History and the Enterprise Culture," *Past and Present,* 123 (1989), 184–5.

Irish economic blueprints invariably saw industry as the subordinate partner; consequently, major employment gains would come from intensive agriculture. This view derived from a perception of industrial success as exclusively dependent on such raw materials as coal and iron—an opinion that ignored the success of the Belfast ship-building industry.[43] The belief that Ireland's destiny was agricultural persisted and is found even in that alleged bible of modern Ireland, T. K. Whitaker's *Economic Development* (1958).[44] Some officials saw little role for industry. The 1896 *Report of the Recess Committee* compiled by Irish M. P.s asserted that "Agriculture is now, not only the main, but over the greater portion of the country, the sole Irish industry."[45] Assumptions of the dominance of agriculture left the onus for creating employment on that sector, and this entailed reversing the post-Famine shift from tillage to cattle farming.[46] Denunciations of grazing as an antisocial activity date back to the early eighteenth century. In the 1840s, James Fintan Lalor sought "not breeders of stock or feeders of fat cattle; not gentlemen who try to be farmers nor farmers who try to be gentlemen" but "a numerous, plain and home-bred yeomanry." Parnell pledged that Ireland would "undo the famine," returning land from grazing to tillage farming. Another Land League supporter, Mitchell Henry, claimed that he would "rather see a country moderately rich in men and women and happy families than in any number of cattle." This commitment to recreate tillage smallholdings permeates nationalist and agrarian politics from the Land League at the turn of the century, down to Fianna Fáil in the 1930s and Clann na Talmhan of the late 1940s. It formed a potent, if unstable, ingredient in the rise of Sinn Féin in 1917.[47]

43 National Archives, Dublin, Dept. of Finance, F. 22/11/24.

44 *Economic Development*, Pr. 5808 (1958), para. 33.

45 *Report of the Recess Committee on the Establishment of a Department of Agriculture and Industries for Ireland* (Dublin, 1896), p. 10.

46 Cormac Ó Grada, *Ireland Before and After the Famine*, (Manchester, 1988), chap. 4; Kevin O'Rourke, "Did the Great Irish Famine Matter?" *Journal of Economic History*, 51, 1 (March, 1991), 1–22.

47 Daly "Lalor," *passim;* Bew, *Land and the National Question*, pp. 82, 87; Davitt, *Fall of Feudalism, passim;* Bew, *Conflict and Conciliation in Ireland, 1890–1910: Parnellites and Radical Agrarians* (Oxford, 1987); Joseph V. O'Brien, *William O'Brien and the Course of Irish Politics 1881–1918* (Berkeley, 1976); Lee, *Modern Ireland, passim;* David Fitzpatrick, *Politics and Irish Life, 1913–21: Provincial Experience of War and Revolution* (Dublin, 1977), pp. 73, 76, 156, 158, 175.

The achievement of independence in 1922 generated pressures for a corresponding economic transformation. In 1929, Seán Lemass, a leading member of the opposition Fianna Fáil party, claimed that "if we were concerned only for the welfare of the old political unit known as the United Kingdom we would not deplore the decay of industry and loss of population here because they were more than counter-balanced by the growth of population and industry in the other island." Lemass regarded the campaign to protect Irish industry as "identical with the struggle for the preservation of our nationality."[48] The nationalist agenda sought to revive a culture which had been undermined by British conquest and to reduce economic links with Britain. Efforts were made to evolve an alternative economic model: a blend of allegedly Celtic historical traditions. Roman Catholic social teaching, and unacknowledged foreign intellectual influences. In the process, there emerged contradictory objectives—some inimical to the achievement of economic growth. Such problems were not unique to Ireland, but may be found in the histories of many developing nations.[49]

Independent Ireland experienced a conflict between economic liberalism and a more ethically determined economic strategy involving government intervention. Economic liberalism reflected the British legacy, the traditions of financial rectitude and treasury control exemplified by the Department of Finance, and the philosophy of established interest groups such as bankers, cattle graziers, and export industries.[50] Such forces dominated the economic policy of the first decade of Irish independence, 1922–32, when the Cumann na nGaedheal government operated a largely free-trade, market-driven economy, evading such issues as emigration, population decline, or the repeopling of rural Ireland.[51]

Despite such policies, the Cumann na nGaedheal party was not a monolith of economic liberalism. Undercurrents of economic discourse antedating independence survived in agriculture minister Hogan's desire for mixed farming, increased tillage, and an expanding cooperative move-

48 National Library of Ireland, Gallagher Papers, Ms 18339. Seán Lemass served as minister for industry and commerce, 1932–39; 1942–48, 1951–54; 1957–59; minister for supplies 1939–45; and as *taoiseach* 1959–66.

49 Mary Matossian, "Ideologies of Delayed Industrialization: Some Tensions and Ambiguities" *Economic Development and Cultural Change* 6 (1958), 217–29.

50 Ronan Fanning, *The Irish Department of Finance, 1922–59* (Dublin, 1980).

51 Mary E. Daly, *A Social and Economic History of Ireland since 1800* (Dublin, 1981), p. 140.

ment as an alternative to state control or private capitalism. The new government's reluctance to introduce extensive tariff protection stemmed in part from a distaste for the incursion of foreign capitalism which would follow.[52] The Cumann na nGaedheal party was divided on economic matters: J. J. Walsh, minister for posts and telegraphs staged a spectacular resignation on the issue of tariff protection.[53] The private papers of Richard Mulcahy, minister for defense and later minister for local government, reveal an obsession with emigration and population on the land rather than in the city, hostility to foreign investment, and sympathy for the *Gaeltachtaí*. Because Mulcahy viewed economic achievement as subordinate to cultural and spiritual objectives, he saw industrial self-sufficiency as essential to national identity.

> You may clothe an Irishman in west of English cloth, an Irishman may live his life in the west of England living his normal life there and you may feed an Irishman on chinese bacon or on New Zealand mutton or American meal or flour. . . . But what you cannot do is clothe an Irish civilization in English clothes or feed an Irish civilization on chinese bacon or American meal or Australian mutton. Nor have any Irish civilization in which any material part of the people is so clothed. An Irish civilization must and will only grow out of the struggle of its people to take from Irish soil their sustenance and to process from Irish resources their clothing.[54]

Such views as Mulcahy's did not predominate, however, and the alternative economic tradition became the preserve of the Fianna Fáil party, which represented the defeated forces of the Irish Civil War. Fianna Fáil proposed to develop a self-sufficient nationalist economy, driven more by Irish desiderata than by market dictates and judged by what de Valéra termed "a more rational standard," as opposed to "international standards," of well-being. This entailed settling "as many families as practicable on the land" and modest living standards as the price of political and economic independence.[55]

The contrast in attitudes between Cumann na nGaedhdeal and Fianna

---

52 Published Debates Dáil Éireann, (PDDE), 15 March 1927, P 35/b/2 and P 35/b/9.

53 Ronan Fanning, *Independent Ireland* (Dublin, 1983), pp. 101-2; J. J. Walsh, *Recollections of a Rebel* (Tralee, 1944), *passim*.

54 UCDA, Mulcahy papers, P 7b/63, P 7b/64, 1926-7.

55 *Speeches . . . by Eamon de Valéra*, p. 158; PDDE, 12-13th July 1928; E. Rumpf and A. C. Hepburn, *Nationalism and Socialism in Twentieth Century Ireland* (Liverpool, 1977), p. 100.

Fáil is evident in the reports of the Economic Committee, an all-party committee set up in 1927, which, at the insistence of Fianna Fáil first examined the merits of subsidizing wheat-growing. Rejecting a subsidy as ineffective and a distortion of existing agricultural patterns, the majority government report discussed market trends, comparative prices of agricultural produce, and the product equilibrium of Irish agriculture. The decline in tillage was attributed to the decisions of Irish farmers who were "following sound economic principles as testified by the returns of prices of agricultural produce for the period." In contrast, the minority Fianna Fáil report rejected market forces in favor of an undefined community need. It began with the statement that the primary purpose of agriculture is to produce human food and, as wheat provided the raw material for bread, the most important single article, "there is therefore, a presumption that the first function of farming in the Saorstát should be the production of wheat." The argument that growing wheat in Ireland was impractical was dismissed as "part of the general view that the policy forced upon us as individuals by the pressure of external competition is necessarily the wisest policy for us as a community." Fianna Fáil rejected this position as "unworthy of consideration, in view of the fact that Ireland is the only country in the world which for over eighty years has had a continually declining population, and is still unable to check the decline."[56] The gulf between both reports was so great that the committee abandoned further debate. Such a lack of common reference points between the liberal economic model and the more normative variety remains a constant feature of Irish economic discourse.

By the early 1930s, international depression and Britain's abandonment of free trade had increased the attraction of an economic order less subject to market fluctuations, and Fianna Fáil had taken power in 1932. De Valéra's 1932 speech to the League of Nations suggested that the "whole basis of production, distribution finance and credit requires complete overhauling" by "the deliberate shaping of economic activity to an ethical and social end" with individual countries determining how best this should be done.[57] Irish economic policy in the years 1932–38 can be seen as a conscious attempt at creating an alternative economic order—an extension of Gaelic,

56 Committee on the Relief of Unemployment. 1927. First Interim Report (R38/1).
57 *Speeches . . . by Eamon de Valéra*, p. 222.

THE ECONOMIC IDEALS OF IRISH NATIONALISM

Catholic Ireland from the cultural sphere[58] to the realm of economics. Legislation restricting foreign ownership of industry was described by Seán Lemass, the minister responsible, as bringing about "An Irish-Ireland for business."[59] An extreme version of this analysis is found in a proposed self-sufficiency program for the Irish-speaking areas of Ireland.

> In this industrial development of the Gaeltacht the main idea is the making of goods by the people of the Gaeltacht for the people of the Gaeltacht; the manufacturing of goods mainly for profit must be excluded as far as possible; the industrialisation of the Gaeltacht in the modern sense must not be permitted; industrial expansion in the individual sense does not enter into the scheme.[60]

The blueprint called for extensive land distribution and tillage subsidies, plus efforts to reduce trading ties with Britain. Industrial self-sufficiency was to be achieved by firms under Irish ownership and control, employing male rather than female workers, scattered throughout the small towns of Ireland. One aspiring industrialist was told that the farther he went from Dublin "the greater attraction would he lend to his proposal."[61] Protective legislation restricted night work, shift work, and the employment of women and juveniles, while providing for not ungenerous holidays with pay. Lemass boasted that it was the first time that such measures had been introduced by "a Government that is still a democratic Government dependent entirely upon a Parliamentary institution for its power."[62] While the program contained uniquely Irish dimensions, its somewhat utopian policies and its urge to transform Irish society in the light of Catholic social teaching closely resemble to the ideals of Catholic militants in Belgium and other parts of Europe, though it lacks the undemocratic tendencies of the continental example.[63]

In practice, Lemass's program was heavily compromised in both

58 Margaret O'Callaghan, "Language, Nationality and Cultural Identity in the Irish Free State, 1922–27: *The Irish Statesman* and the *Catholic Bulletin* Reappraised," *Irish Historical Studies*, 94 (1984), 226–45.

59 Mary E. Daly, "'An Irish-Ireland for Business'?: The Control of Manufacturers Acts 1932 and 1934," *Irish Historical Studies*, 24 (1984), 246–72.

60 National Archives, S7477, Gaeltacht, Economic Development Report 1932.

61 Department of Industry and Commerce, TID 43/63.

62 PDDE, 17 May 1935.

63 Martin Conway, "Building the Christian City: Catholics and Politics in Inter-War Francophone Belgium," *Past and Present*, 128. (1991), 134–7.

THE ECONOMIC IDEALS OF IRISH NATIONALISM

objectives and outcome. Within the Fianna Fáil cabinet strains emerged between pragmatists who took account of economic realities and those adopting more idealistic positions; between the relative priorities accorded to material and cultural goals; and between the broadly neoclassical economics, favored by Finance Minister Seán MacEntee, and the economic stances of more interventionist colleagues.[64] The partial, though largely unacknowledged triumph of economic reality emerged by the late 1930s with the program's failure to fulfill key social objectives. Despite a program of land redistribution, there were fewer smallholdings in 1939 than in 1931.[65] Growth in industrial output and employment was achieved at the cost of major compromises: thousands of female factory workers were recruited; there was a substantial influx of foreign companies; most new industry was located in the greater Dublin area; and a "new plutocracy" was created.[66] The failure of economic self-sufficiency led to the Anglo-Irish Trade Agreement in 1938, which recognized the interdependence of the two economies. Although Article 45 of the 1937 Constitution incorporated social policy directives based on papal enclyclicals, a preceding statement implied that it had no legal validity.[67]

The Report of the Commission on Banking, Currency and Credit, which body sat from 1934 to 1938, provided a reprise of the ideological contrasts found in the Economic Committee. On this occasion, the majority of the commission appointed by Fianna Fáil espoused a market-driven economic philosophy giving primacy to protecting the value of the Irish currency and criticized deviations from free-market orthodoxy which might jeopardize financial stability, including most aspects of the government's policy. The three minority reports gave priority to community interests and urged an investment program to develop resources and employment. One pointed out that "Catholic thinkers, especially in Ireland decline to accept 'economics' as the final criterion." The minority report of P. J. O'Loghlen, which based its analysis on papal encyclicals, argued the case for "the economics of the community as distinct from the individual" and urged the regeneration of rural Ireland. This forced the majority report into

64 UCDA MacEntee Papers, P 67/125, 1938.

65 J. J. Lee and M. A. G. Ó Tuathaigh, *The Age of de Valera* (Dublin, 1982), p. 178.

66 Daly, "An Irish-Ireland," *passim.*

67 Lee and Ó Tuathaigh, *Age of de Valera*, pp. 152–4; Dermot Keogh, "Church, State and Society", in *De Valéra's Constitution and Ours,* ed. Brian Farrell (Dublin 1988), pp. 110, 118.

THE ECONOMIC IDEALS OF IRISH NATIONALISM

a similar discourse. A chapter entitled "Some Social Aspects of Currency and Credit" and an appendix written by George O'Brien and Dr. MacNeely, the Catholic bishop of Raphoe, signatories to the majority report, cited papal encyclicals in defense of economic orthodoxy and noted that Portugal under Dr. Salazar, the only country which had made a "conscious and determined effort to translate the teaching of Papal encyclicals into practical action," was "free of any attempt at monetary or financial experimentation."[68] The contrasts between the majority and minority reports are best captured by the comments of Rev. Edward J. Coyne, S. J., who condemned the majority report for its belief that "increased production in itself, irrespective of the nature of that production . . . is the essential preliminary to, if not the very substance of social welfare," and he preferred one minority viewpoint that "if we want certain non-economic social values we must be ready to pay for them."[69]

The Irish population's enthusiasm for "non-economic social values" remained unproven. Trends in emigration, cattle production, and tillage, which had proved highly responsive to both national and international market forces since the Famine, remained equally so during the 1930s. The 1939 acreage of tillage was only two percent above the 1930 level, for large and small farmers persisted with cattle farming.[70] The cessation of emigration in the early 1930s was entirely attributable to international depression. When employment improved in Britain by the mid 1930s, emigration resumed. By then, economists and statisticians were predicting a continuing decline in population[71] which was confirmed by the 1936 census. Programs for land distribution, for tariff protection, for incentives to house-build-

68 Report of the Commission of Inquiry into Banking, Currency and Credit, P.2628 (1938), Minority Reports 1–3; Majority Report, chap. V and app. On Salazar as a model for Ireland, see UCDA P 67/108; on Salazar as a model for Continental supporters of Catholic Action, see Conway, "Building the Christian City," 134.

69 Edward J. Coyne, S. J. "Report of the Banking Commission," Studies (September, 1938), 401–403.

70 Cormac Ó Grada, "Supply Responsiveness in Nineteenth Century Irish Agriculture," Economic History Review, XXVIII (1975). Many Irish farmers, including small farmers, continued to depend on cattle farming during the 1930s, because of a lack of alternatives. See S9636, Small Farmers in West Cork, 1935. Daly, Social and Economic History, p. 149.

71 George O'Brien, "The Coming Crisis of Population: The Future Population of Ireland," Studies (December, 1936), 567–80. R. C. Geary, "The Future Population of Saorstát Éireann and Some Observations on Population Statistics," Statistical and Social Inquiry Society of Ireland Journal (1936-7), 15–36.

ing, and for improved transfer payments appeared to have been ineffectual in stemming the outflow.[72] By the late 1930s, de Valéra was lamenting increased migration to both Dublin and England—apparently regarding both destinations as equally undesirable.[73]

Concern over emigration increased during the "Emergency" years of World War II. Key industrial workers left Ireland, attracted by full employment and higher British wages, and British construction firms set up recruitment offices in Irish provincial towns. Reported shortages of labor for both grain and turf harvests led to the imposition of emigration controls. Increased female emigration during the immediate postwar years provoked "deep public unease" as unsullied Irish females were exposed to the moral corruption of English cities. Proposals to ban emigration by females under the age of twenty-two were considered but rejected as not in accord with long-standing traditions of freedom of movement.[74] At a time when growth rate data were not widely known and unemployment statistics were less comprehensive, population and emigration provided the most telling and complete measures of Ireland's economic achievement. Heavy emigration and rural depopulation were major factors in Fianna Fáil's loss of the 1948 general election. At a time when MacBride was emphasizing Ireland's lack of concern with materialism, mass emigration apparently testified to the contrary.

This conclusion was not immediately accepted by Irish politicians. Many appeared uncertain about the relationship between living standards and population growth. The declining birth rates experienced throughout much of Europe in the interwar years generated fears that economic development and industrialization would injure Ireland's demographic prospects. Such trends were publicized in such periodicals as *Studies*, the Jesuit journal which was one of the major sources of intellectual debate in Ireland. Richard Mulcahy pondered the issue in the mid-1920s and sought

72 Leinster, the area with the greatest increase in wheat acreage, experienced the sharpest drop in the number of agricultural laborers. Lee and Ó Tuathaigh, *Age of de Valera*, p. 135. Measures to promote tillage may have reduced the labor outflow from agriculture. J. Peter Neary and Cormac Ó Grada "Protection, Economic War and Structural Change: The 1930s in Ireland," *Irish Historical Studies*, 27, 107 (May, 1991), p. 259.

73 PDDE, 7 July 1939; *Speeches . . . by Eamon de Valéra*, pp. 401–3.

74 National Archives, Dublin, S 11582 A,B; Damien F. Hannan, *Displacement and Development: Class Kinship and Social and Change in Irish Rural Communities* (Dublin, 1979), pp. 47–56; James Meenan, *The Irish Economy since 1922* (Liverpool, 1970), p. 206.

advice from the director of the government statistical service.[75] In 1939, de Valéra explained that, while he had hoped that the availability of radio would make the rural population more content, it now appeared that, by "painting visions of town life," radio was among the principal causes of the flight from the countryside.[76] Some months later, shortly after the outbreak of World War II, Seán MacEntee, by then minister for industry and commerce, circulated a memorandum on the 1936 population census to his colleagues and appended lengthy extracts from *Laws of Life* (1941), by Dr. Halliday Sutherland, which appeared to suggest a historical correlation between high birth rates and economic hardship and declining birth rate and prosperity. The file also contains draft social welfare programs, information on dietetics, plus a pamphlet on Britain's future population by Roy Harrod. It is difficult to interpret MacEntee's thoughts on the relationship between population growth and economic prosperity, though one can sense some link with the question of children's allowances which shortly emerged as a major policy issue.[77] Emigration rather than low birthrate dominated the Irish population debate, though a 1947 memorandum from the Department of External Affairs noted that female emigration threatened the birth of the next rural generation. Emigration posed a fundamental policy dilemma: whether to abandon deeply held cultural and social ideals and aim at replicating British living standards in order to deter emigration, or to continue to uphold traditional rural society.

Journalist Aodh de Blacam, a Fianna Fáil supporter who still dreamed in 1946 of doubling the rural population, denounced the faltering commitment to national aims of language revival and increased rural population, which he believed took precedence over individual rights. De Blacam urged a ban on emigration, particularly of females; a prohibition on women working in industry; and an end to the use of commercially sponsored radio programs "for the propagation of debased and commercialised food habits."[78]

75 David V. Glass, *Population Policies and Movements in Europe* (Oxford, 1940); O'Brien, "Coming Crisis of Population"; UCDA, P 7b/63, 1927.

76 PDDE, 7 July 1939, pp. 401–3.

77 UCDA, P 67/262. It is unclear where this file was ever circulated. Lee, *Ireland,* pp. 275–83. MacEntee opposed the children's allowances. Ironically, *Laws of Life* was banned by the Irish Censorship Board, despite carrying the *imprimatur* of the Catholic archbishop of Westminster. Michael Adams, *Censorship: The Irish Experience* (Dublin, 1968), pp. 80, 84, 158.

78 UCDA, MacEntee Papers, P 67/282, Aodh de Blacam, "Rural Depopulation," Memorandum, 4 December 1946. De Blacam subsequently joined the Clann na Poblachta party.

THE ECONOMIC IDEALS OF IRISH NATIONALISM

The Vanishing Irish, a 1954 book of essays edited by an Irish-American professor at Notre Dame, saw emigration and rural population decline as reflecting some deep-seated malaise among a race predisposed to an agricultural lifestyle and large families,[79] ignoring the fact that rural migration was common to most developed countries. Similar attitudes are reflected in a 1951 speech by de Valéra, who viewed the emigrants as misguidedly deserting Ireland for living conditions of indescribable horror in English cities. Such attitudes were not the preserve of the Fianna Fáil party alone. A 1956 speech by the Taoiseach John A. Costello, of Fine Gael, dismissed the contention that emigration was caused by economic necessity as "one that cannot be sustained" in many cases, and urged prospective emigrants to

> weigh the attractions of higher monetary rewards in other lands [against] . . . comforts and happiness, real and substantial, [against] . . . the wholesome conditions of a life that is nowhere far removed from the happy peace of natural surroundings, [against] . . . certain spiritual and cultural traditions which have become our own and in which we may justly take pride [and against] . . . fellowship of family friends and neighbours.[80]

By this stage, however, even Dr. Lucey, the Roman Catholic bishop of Cork, admitted that "the rural community, no less than the urban community, attach more importance than ever before to material comforts, the pleasures of the moment and the good things of this world generally," though he believed that economic improvements would accelerate rural decline "unless we can develop a less materialistic outlook among young people."

Dr. Lucey's opinions were expressed in a minority report to the official *Report of the Commission on Emigration and Other Population Problems* (1956).[81] While offering few concrete recommendations, the report of the commission marks an important transition in attitudes. It rejected earlier utopian targets in favor of the modest aim of achieving a rising population. Emigration and late marriages were no longer seen as manifesting a national death wish but the outcome of low incomes and lack of employment. It conceded that population increase could not be achieved by "a substantial all-round reduction in existing standards of living," but only through an

---

79 *The Vanishing Irish*, ed. John O'Brien (London 1954), pp. 7, 29.

80 National Archives, Dublin, S 11582 B, G.

81 *Commission on Emigration and Other Population Problems 1948–54*, Pr. 2541, para. 211.

expansion of manufacturing and service employment, though ritual obeisance was made to the central role of agriculture and such words as "sacrifice" still occurred featured in the report's prose. This focus on living standards anticipated the 1958 government white paper *Economic Development*. Because it excluded social objectives, even increased employment, in favor of economic growth, free trade, and competitive efficiency,[82] *Economic Development* can be seen as marking the defeat of the alternative economic agenda. *Economic Development* was, however, the work on one named civil servant, T. K. Whitaker, and the product of specific crisis conditions.[83] While commitments to free trade and economic growth survived, many such traditional Irish desiderata as decentralized development, male employment, and job creation reemerged.[84] In the early 1960s, ideas of growth coexisted with earlier ideas; for example Seán Lemass, then *taoiseach*, portrayed rising living standards as synonymous with the preservation of Christian virtue and Irish traditions and culture.[85]

Such rhetoric was sustainable during the 1960s and 1970s when economic growth and industrial development brought rising rates of marriage and birth, population growth, and a reversal of emigration. However the recurrence of emigration and rural population decline in the 1980s, plus severe unemployment, all partly attributable to the earlier population explosion, has meant the questioning of such analysis. The recent attack by historian Joseph Lee on the dominant orthodoxy which measures economic performance in terms of growth and his call for the promotion of Roman Catholic economic values as well as renewed sympathy for de Valéra's ideals of "frugal comfort,"[86] suggest that the economic discourse of previous generations is not extinct.

—University College, Dublin

---

82 Ronan Fanning, "The Genesis of Economic Development," in *Planning Ireland's Future: The Legacy of T. K. Whitaker*, ed. John McCarthy (Dublin, 1990), p. 87. *Economic Development*, p. 206.

83 Garret Fitzgerald, *Planning in Ireland* (Dublin, 1968), pp. 8–21.

84 This is already evident in the *Programme for Economic Expansion* (1958), Pr. 4796; Fitzgerald, *Planning in Ireland*, p. 40.

85 Susan Baker, "Nationalist Ideology and the Industrial Policy of Fianna Fáil: The Evidence of the *Irish Press* (1955–1972)," *Irish Political Studies*, 1 (1986), 67–77.

86 *Irish Times*, 14 June 1991.

THE ECONOMIC IDEALS OF IRISH NATIONALISM

"LEAVETAKINGS AND HOMECOMINGS": DEREK MAHON'S BELFAST

TIM KENDALL

DEREK MAHON's reputation for being "culturally rootless,"[1] inculcated with all the force of critical consensus, owes its authority to no one more than to the poet himself. Noting how his contemporary Seamus Heaney digs "deeper and deeper into his home ground," Mahon by comparison pleads ignorance of his proper "place," declaring himself a poet who, coincidentally enough, "just happened to be born in Belfast."[2] However, such strenuous and often unprovoked denials betray a fundamental anxiety that the poet's home ground may have been more formative, and less easy to escape, than he would willingly admit. Heaney's telling description of Mahon as "the Stephen Dedalus of Belfast"[3] captures his friend's determination to fly by the nets of origins and obligations; but the tag—for which Heaney later apologizes— fixes Mahon in the very "home ground" of Belfast he so desperately strives to renounce.

Mahon's guilt-ridden stance, embracing both the desire for freedom and a stubborn love of the origins he would betray by refusing to serve, continually wrenches his early work. In "Glengormley," a poem dating from before the "Troubles" and titled after the Belfast district where he grew up, the poet is caught between rival forces until finally forced to acknowledge

---

1   Hugh Haughton, "'Even Now There Are Places Where a Thought Might Grow': Place and Displacement in the Poetry of Derek Mahon," in *The Chosen Ground: Essays on the Contemporary Poetry of Northern Ireland,* ed. Neil Corcoran, (Bridgend: Seren Books, 1992), p. 98. Similar recent expressions of Mahon's rootless cosmopolitanism occur in Mullaney, K. "A Politics of Silence: Derek Mahon 'At One Remove'," *Journal of Irish Literature,* XVIII, 3 (September, 1989), 45–54, and in B. Tinley "International Perspectives in the Poetry of Derek Mahon," *Irish University Review,* 21: 1 (Spring-Sumer, 1991), 106–117.

2   Interviewed by Willie Kelly, *The Cork Review,* 2, 3 (June, 1981), 10; and by Eileen Battersby, *The* [Dublin] *Sunday Tribune,* 26 August 1990, p. 26.

3   Seamus Heaney "The Pre-Natal Mountain: Vision and Irony in Recent Irish Poetry," in *The Place of Writing* (Atlanta: The Scholar's Press, 1989), p. 48.

both his origins and the concomitant impossibility of ever abandoning them. The place is described in stereotypically suburban terms, with the poem's opening line, taken from the Chorus of *Antigone*, at first seeming merely to instill disappointed bathos:

> Wonders are many and none is more wonderful than man
> Who has tamed the terrier, trimmed the hedge
> And grasped the principle of the watering-can. [4]

These "tame" pleasures are contrasted with violent, heroic struggles from myth and history, but Mahon's persona ultimately opts for a present tranquillity as rational as it is, in a romantic sense, unpoetical. This decision comes at a cost. The reference to Nerval—one of the "unreconciled" who "dangle from lamp-posts," having hanged himself from a streetlight with a length of chain—reveals that poet's discontent with mundane existence, to which Mahon adds his own voice in the conclusion: "By / Necessity, if not choice, I live here too." An admirer of Nerval, Mahon has translated *Les Chimères*. Yet, even accepting that with the death of heroes "much dies with them," Mahon nevertheless chooses the banality of peace over the poetic frisson of conflict; "Glengormley" would take issue with Yeats's comment that, for a poet, the Chinese curse "May you live in interesting times" is a blessing. Still, Mahon is tied to his place despite himself, living there "by necessity" because, even in his absence, it will always be home. The line from Sophocles, it ultimately transpires, should be taken literally; "Glengormley" is a reluctant paean to a Belfast suburb from which the poet cannot extricate himself.

The city recurs both as a metaphor and reality throughout Mahon's first volume *Night-Crossing*. "The Death of Marilyn Monroe" precludes escape as urban imagery extends to fill the whole cosmos: stars scatter ash "Down the cold back streets of the Zodiac" (*P* 7). But escape is granted to "De Quincey at Grasmere," who acquires in the Lake District all the creature comforts necessary of a "Perihelion of Paradise" yet, haunted by nightmares, yearns once more for the days of wandering "Soho after dark / With Anne" (*P* 10), looking for the "panacea" which, now, attained "home" at Grasmere, has proven illusory. A similar destiny awaits the speaker of "An Unborn Child," who interprets the mother's body as a "metropolis,"

---

4 Derek Mahon, *Poems 1962–1978* (Oxford: Oxford University Pres, 1979), p. 1; cited parenthetically, thus: (*P* 1).

"LEAVETAKINGS AND HOMECOMINGS": DEREK MAHON'S BELFAST

and eagerly anticipates the forthcoming exile, while failing to foresee the unpalatable fate which its own monologue accidentally reveals.

The opening sentence of "An Unborn Child"—"I have already come to the verge of / Departure"—rehearses imminent expulsion through its enjambment and captures the bay's impatience at its continuing confinement as it batters at "the concavity of [its] caul" and begins to "put on the manners of the world" (*P* 18). However, for all his self-assurance, the baby understands dangerously little about the world at large: the data "vested" in its bones encompass trivialities such as the goldfish on the shelf, the kitten, even the telephone's "dead filament," but this "pandemonium of encumbrances" supposedly cannot "even dwarf the dimensions of my hand." Ignorant of the potential insidiousness of "encumbrances," the baby looks forward to experiencing them sensually:

> 'I want to live!'
> This is my first protest, and shall be my last.
> As I am innocent, everything I do
> Or say is couched in the affirmative.
> I want to see, hear, touch, and taste
> These things with which I am encumbered.
> Perhaps I needn't worry. Give
> Or take a day or two, my days are numbered.

The concept of invisible restriction evades his limited intelligence. Yet, several time the monologue points to darker truths: the baby's mother sits sewing "the white shrouds / Of my apotheosis," but birth expels the child into a world where "shrouds" take on a more sinister significance than a child can solipsistically imagine. Intimations of mortality become still more intrusive as plans for the future are made: the baby's defiant boast that "'I want to live'" will be its last protest unwittingly serves as a reminder that life's end is usually unwelcome; and the poem concludes with a killing irony: "Give / Or take a day or two, my days are numbered." The longed-for escape from the "metropolis," when it finally arrives, proves a prelude to death.

While mocking the ignorance of solipsism, "An Unborn Child" tacitly insists that freedom can only exist within bounds, so that the metropolitan womb, which "fits me like a glove / While leaving latitude for a free hand," represents the optimum situation after which even such restricted liberty is denied. Because the desire for release has its origins in a fetal instinct, the poet damns all mankind as either trapped inside a claustrophobic city, or worse, nomadically exiled from an original home which is the only source of comfort and inspiration. In these circumstances, escape often becomes reduced to a daydream which placates entrapment. So, the schoolmaster of "Teaching in Belfast" imagines setting out "with a generous lady to the glittering west" where the music of the spheres can play uninterrupted by an urban din which includes "the cries of children / Screaming of bells, the rattle of milk-bottles / Footfall echoes of jails and hospitals" (*P* 31). The claustrophobia of the city, with its menacing presence of jails and hospitals, is mitigated not by escape itself, but by what the poem calls the "fantasy" of escape. By comparison, "Day Trip to Donegal," a mediocre poem which does actually seek temporary respite in the Irish West, finds, like De Quincey, that the dream of elsewhere is all, because, once attained, the promised panacea offers no cure. Deliberately sounding like a hackneyed travel brochure, Mahon notes that "As ever, the nearby hills were a deeper green / Than anywhere in the world" (*P* 17), with the pat superlative suggesting barely masked flippancy. In fact, the poem never really engages with Donegal; nothing about the area's description distinguishes it from any other piece of coastline containing a fishing village, and the journey back home to the suburbs of Belfast begins after only twelve of thirty lines. That night the protagonist feels "the slow sea" eroding his skull, and by dawn finds himself "far out at sea" and curses his "failure to take due / Forethought for this," and "this" presumably refers to the shattering of the idyllic fantasy of freedom and tranquillity in the West of Ireland, and disruption of the city's fetal comforts.

"Day Trip to Donegal" supports Mahon's disingenuous comment, describing Louis MacNeice:

> 'A tourist in his own country', it has been said, with the implication that this is somehow discreditable. But of what sensitive person is the same not true? The phrase might stand, indeed, as an epitaph for Modern Man, beside Camus's 'He made love and read the newspapers'.[5]

However, Belfast actually discomforts Mahon for the opposite reason: rather than being merely a tourist, he actually belongs there. Escape, even when possible, produces only guilty regret and the urge to return. The uncollected poem "An Irishman in London" gives early voice to Mahon's leavetaking-homecoming compulsion as his speaker boasts with undisguised élan, "Now I am truly rootless, having outstripped / The streets of home;" but

---

5   In *Time Was Away: The World of Louis MacNeice*, ed. Terence Brown and Alec Reid (Dublin: The Dolmen Press, 1974), p. 117.

having failed to locate "peace of mind," he more diffidently recognizes that "I must go forward to go back, and back / In order to go forward."[6] Similarly, "The Spring Vacation," despite its self-chastisement over a perceived infidelity to origins, unwittingly records a congenital attachment to home. An earlier version of "The Spring Vacation" was published in *Icarus,* the literary magazine of Trinity College, Dublin,[7] and the poem is dedicate to Michael Longley whom Mahon first met there. The poem's occasion is, therefore, presumably Mahon's return to Belfast between university terms and his growing disaffection from his home city; the poem's evolution seems to confirm this theme, for its current evasive title replaced the more specific "In Belfast." Yet, the poem opens "Walking among my own this windy morning" (*P* 4), an acknowledgment of belonging which contrasts, for example, with the divisive class-consciousness in MacNeice's "Belfast" of "Us who walk in the street so buoyantly and glib."[8]

One of the Mahon's earliest poems, "The Spring Vacation" broaches a theme which has since been consciously evoked by his contemporaries. Rebuking himself for indifference in the final stanza, Mahon warns himself that

> One part of my mind must learn to know its place.
> The things that happen in the kitchen houses
> And echoing back streets of this desperate city
> Should engage more than my casual interest,
> Exact more interest than my casual pity.

In "Station Island," at a moment of intense self-revulsion, Seamus Heaney despises "how quick I was to know my place," along with everything else that made him "biddable and unforthcoming."[9] In both examples, knowing one's place involves far more than just feeling at home. A community which annexes power to group values must suppress any individual liberty posing a threat to the social fabric. Heaney's apparent contradiction—"biddable and unforthcoming"—blames him for kowtowing to expectation and stifling for so long any dreams of escape and freedom. By contrast, Mahon chastises himself for detachment from home. Both poets, even

6   Derek Mahon, "An Irishman in London," *Icarus,* 42 (March, 1964) 8.

7   *Ibid.,* 31.

8   Louis MacNeice, *Collected Poems,* ed. Edward Dodds (London: Faber, 1966), p. 17. Edna Longley compares Mahon and MacNeice in "The Writer and Belfast." *The Irish Writer and the City,* ed. Maurice Harmon (Gerrards Cross: Colin Smythe, 1984), p. 83.

9   Seamus Heaney, *Station Island* (London: Faber, 1984), p. 85.

"LEAVETAKINGS AND HOMECOMINGS": DEREK MAHON'S BELFAST

while attacking them, are reinforcing the terms of their reputations—
Heaney as champion of the parochial and Mahon as urbane world-citizen.
However, in "The Spring Vacation" Mahon's treatment of home has more
in common with Heaney's than MacNeice's, as the poem's opening line
suggests. Heaney's self-loathing at being able to "sleepwalk with connivance
and mistrust" also corresponds to a similar complicity in his supposedly
rootless friend: resuming the "old conspiracy," Mahon's antennae are well
attuned to pick up the secret dialect of his tribe, and quickly yield to the
"humorous formulae, / The hidden menace in the knowing nod." Although Mahon, more often than Heaney, finds his home community con-
temptible—hence the Paisleyite rhetoric of "Ecclesiastes," or the bloody
fanaticism of "As It Should Be"—he nevertheless feels a "perverse pride"
in "being on the side / Of the fallen angels and refusing to get up." This
inverted civic pride pledges allegiance to the very home which elsewhere
in the poem Mahon accuses himself of abandoning. So, the final stanza,
boasting of freedom of spirit while apparently censuring it, is founded on
a presumption which much of "The Spring Vacation" undermines: its tone
of semi-ironic self-reproach masks the realization that the liberty vaunted
by the poet may yet prove an illusion.

Locating a latent belief in animism throughout Brian Moore's novels,
Mahon notes that in them "an object . . . is more than the sum of its atoms.
It preserves within it the racial memory of its raw material, as a wardrobe
might have heard of the Crucifixion."[10] This concept of animism, similar
to the Jungian "racial memory" often found in Heaney's early work, provides the key to several of Mahon's own poems in which the detritus of
modern civilization, exiled from its source, longs for home. In the won-
derfully economical "Nostalgias,"

> The chair squeaks in a high wind,
> Rain falls from its branches,
> The kettle yearns for the
> Mountain, the soap for the sea.
> In a tiny stone church
> On the desolate headland
> A lost tribe is singing 'Abide With Me'. (*P* 68)

10 Derek Mahon, "Magic Casements." *New Statesman*, 90, 17 October 1975, p. 479.
Quoted by Dillon Johnston, *Irish Poetry after Joyce* (Notre Dame: University of Notre
Dame Press, 1985), p. 233.

The chair, kettle, and soap yearn for their prenatal state just as the "lost tribe" of the Northern Protestant community singing "Abide With Me" remains self-righteously assured of its state of election even as it finds itself furthest from God. "Nostalgias" reiterates the crucial difference between rootlessness and uprootedness: the poem's objects long for the fetal comforts of a home from which they have been irrevocably exiled.

Mahon's most famous poem, "A Disused Shed in Co. Wexford," calls for wholesale commitment to the poet's "people." However, now the enslaved community begging its poet descendant to "speak on their behalf" is even more insultingly portrayed as indistinguishable mushrooms "in a foetor / Of vegetable sweat" (P 79) in a long-abandoned shed. The opening line—"Even now there are places where a thought might grow"—presents an enervated world in which even such limited potential gives cause for surprise. Organically rooted rather than inspirational, these thoughts grow only in long-derelict sites such as "worked out" Peruvian mines and Indian compounds where a door "bangs with diminished confidence"; the gradual winding-down into sterility is reflected by the "disused shed" located in the grounds of a "burnt-out hotel" and abandoned for half a century. The mushrooms trapped inside have remained isolated from the world at large, crowding a keyhole which is "the one star in their firmament," and hearing only rooks nearby, an irregular "shout from the blue" or "a lorry changing gear at the end of the lane." Yet, even limited contact makes them yearn for freedom: the speaker asks, "What should they do there but desire?"—some of them having been "so long / Expectant that there is left only the posture." By the time the door is opened, they have become hideously deformed, so corrupted by their confinement that there is scarcely any sign of life. Nevertheless, the free man who surveys them still recognizes his burden of responsibility:

> 'Save us, save us,' they seem to say,
> 'Let the god not abandon us
> Who have come so far in darkness and in pain.
> We too had our lives to live.
> You with your light meter and relaxed itinerary,
> Let not our naive labours have been in vain!'

The pun on "light meter" implicates the poet in the mushrooms' predicament, but the poem ends with his reaction unresolved, trapped between complicity and an outright *non serviam*—like the poem itself. He imagines the grotesque mushrooms asking him "To do something" as he stands immobile in the doorway, unable either to "close the door on them again" and walk away or to "speak on their behalf." This frozen tableau lies at the heart of Mahon's work.

The conclusion of 'A Disused Shed' typifies an exhausted torpor running throughout *Lives* and *The Snow Party*, for the contradictory responsibilities of home and flight prohibit either conciliation or a choice between alternatives. The inability to act is displayed most emphatically in "The Last of the Fire Kings," where even the imagination, a vital refuge for "Teaching in Belfast" and earlier poems, now provides no sanctuary. The Fire King has become locked in the "barbarous cycle" of waiting for a usurper to depose and kill him, take his place, and in turn wait to be deposed (*P* 64). For a moment, his assertion of free will threatens to break the chain: he pictures an escapee who "vanishes / Where the road turns," or another who jumps at night from a moving train in a land where, because he does not know "a word of the language," he can remain linguistically free. When these dreams evaporate, he toys with his last chance of escape, declaring himself "Through with history" and determining to "Die by my own hand" so as to destroy the cycle. However, the expectations of his tribe trammel in an irrevocable destiny. The refuge the Fire King perfects for himself, a "palace of porcelain" whose coldness represents the ultimate escape from the "fire-loving / People," exists only "out of time." Finally, the Fire king gives up any hope of individual volition, submitting himself to the community's demands:

> But the fire-loving
> People, rightly perhaps,
> Will not countenance this,
>
> Demanding that I inhabit,
> Like them, a world of
> Sirens, bin-lids
> And bricked-up windows—
>
> Not to release them
> From their ancient curse
> But to die their creature and be thankful. (*P* 65)

This startling reversion to the ruined site of Belfast—"Sirens, bin-lids / And bricked-up windows"—embroils Mahon's own art in the Fire King's entrapment. The contemplative life is prohibited: the tribe chains his destiny to theirs and demand that he assume the responsibilities of leader and spokesman which will eventually destroy him. Darker than Mahon's early poems, "The Last of the Fire Kings" finds no escape even in the artistic imagination.

As its title suggests, "The Snow Party" constitutes a companion piece to "The Last of the Fire Kings," embodying the "palace of porcelain" about which the Fire King fantasizes. The poem's form reiterates a sense of mutually exclusive worlds, as the poet Bashō, invited to a snow party, admires the almost epiphanic tranquillity of falling snow, while "elsewhere," hygienically cordoned off in their own stanzas, the brutalities of the Fire King's realm are enacted:

> Elsewhere they are burning
> Witches and heretics
> In the boiling squares,
>
> Thousands have died since dawn
> In the service of barbarous kings;
> But there is silence
>
> In the houses of Nagoya
> And the hills of Ise.   (*P 63*)

Although the purity of the contemplative life is sullied by the demands of "elsewhere." Bashō seems oblivious to any disruptive duty. That final stanza, returning to the snow party, creates if anything an even more serene, sanitized atmosphere than before. The poem's panoramic perspective questions the responsibility of Bashō's limited vision, the Fire King, after all, recognized a duty to stay. "The Snow Party" conveys a haiku-like economy, but also a bland world where, despite the introductions, people remain curiously faceless, where human interaction is non-existent, and where the lines describing "a tinkling of china / And tea into china" suggest, in the Mahon's masterful repetition of "china," an unappealing facade of formality. The poem does not dismiss the achieved fantasy of escape as forthrightly as "De Quincey at Grasmere" or "Day Trip to Donegal"; nevertheless, it regrets the autonomous frigidity of the aesthetic moment, which misses what the speaker of Heaney's "Exposure," freshly "Escaped from the massacre," calls "The once-in-a-lifetime portent / The comet's pulsing rose."[11]

11 Seamus Heaney, *North* (London: Faber, 1975), p. 72.

Several poems in *The Snow Party,* along with the new work at the end of *Poems 1962–1978,* mark a rejection of the "palace of porcelain" and of the snow party's realm by returning to the city from which Mahon's earlier work struggles to escape. Writing in the introduction to their *Penguin Book of Contemporary Irish Poetry,* Mahon and Peter Fallon note that throughout the anthology "home" is "the word most frequently dwelt on . . . as if uncertainty exists as to where that actually is."[12] As "The Spring Vacation" indicates, Mahon's "desperate city" exacts its fair share of "interest" because one part of his mind has learned to know its place all too well. Nor do Mahon's homecoming poems suffer any doubt about their destination, dwelling on the word "home" because it actually is the fixed point of origin around which all else revolves. So obsessed is Mahon with homecoming that even his titles become confusingly repetitious: "Going Home," for example, has been dropped from the *Selected Poems* and had its title taken by the poem originally entitled "The Return."[13] However, although he is, despite protestations to the contrary, as sure of his place as Heaney, Mahon's magnetic attraction to home—and repulsion as soon as he arrives—differs from Heaney's in one crucial respect: whereas in "Station Island" Heaney charts and relives and original escape, and so repeats the same sensations of rejuvenation and buoyancy, Mahon's urban universe is gradually winding down. Each flight becomes progressively more difficult, and each return saps more strength. So, in the original "Going Home" the "disguised" dead are shift workers who cross the Humber every day in an automatized afterlife—which is founded on their own "eschewal of metaphysics." They notice a "sunken barge" rotting on the beach "As if finally to discredit"

> A residual poetry of
> Leavetaking and homecoming,
> Of work and sentiment;
>
> For this is the last
> Homecoming, the end
> Of the rainbow—
>
> And the pubs are shut.
> There are no
> Buses till morning.   (*P* 61)

12   *The Penguin Book of Contemporary Irish Poetry,* ed. Peter Fallon and Derek Mahon (London: Penguin, 1990), p. xxii.

13   Derek Mahon, *Selected Poems* (London: Viking-Gallery, 1991), p. 96.

Through this bleak vision, Mahon argues that sentiment and insatiable desire enervate and eventually defeat their victims, condemning them to a terrible and secular afterlife.

In "Cavafy," a series of translations from the Greek poet, Mahon gives voice to the torpid despondency he feels at this homecoming compulsion. The first section, entitled 'The City,' begins with the missed possibility of having gone "to a new country, a new sea / Another, finer city," before trailing off into a resigned acknowledgment that it is now too late to escape from the vicinity of lost chances and dead ends, "Dark ruins of the life / You have wasted here."[14] The poem oozes the monotony of entrapment, with its unavoidable prospect of being shadowed by the "same old city" and growing old in the "same dim suburb," before plunging into a recognition of universal defeat:

> In this city of homecomings
> Where all voyages end
> There is now way out.
> Your failure here
> Was a failure everywhere
> In the world at large, as if talked about.

The city is a point of origin and return—a home from which, as in "Glengormley," permanent escape seems impossible. The homecoming-leavetaking compulsion becomes a Cain-like curse: failing to negotiate his freedom, the speaker is condemned to a more general, worldwide failure, unable to settle comfortably anywhere.

Neither of Mahon's two major poems of homecoming—"Afterlives" and "The Return"—provide excuses for a journey which will inevitably lead to misery and depression. "Afterlives," an effective response to its dedicatee James Simmons who was "forever accusing [Mahon] of abandoning the North,"[15] emphasizes not abandonment but an emotional self-abuse which drags Mahon compulsively back to his origins. In "Away from it All" Heaney's lobster is lifted out of its "element" to exile and imminent death, and Hercules lifts Antaeus "out of his elements."[16] Mahon claims, however, that exile is "our element," and describes in near-idyllic terms London's "soft roar," its "rain-fresh" appearance and pigeons "necking" (*P* 57). Locating in London not only his natural habitat but also the ideal

---

14 Derek Mahon, *The Snow Party* (Oxford: Oxford University Press, 1975), p. 18.
15 *The Cork Review*, 11.
16 *Station Island*, p. 16; *North*, p. 52.

city—"the bright / Reason on which we rely / For the long-term solutions"—
Mahon at first seems to reject Belfast and, in doing so, to justify Simmons's
accusation that he had abandoned his roots. However, the superficialities
of exile cannot sustain this conclusion: Mahon interrupts his rational hu-
manist vision of a better future with the brusque self-rebuke, "What mid-
dle-class cunts we are." This sudden revulsion incriminates him along with
his accuser and their class in the violence and piety of Belfast: recogniz-
ing aspects of his own identity in the "dim / Forms" which pray at noon,
Mahon bravely acknowledges the dark origins of his own life and imagination. The poems argues that supposedly enlightened beliefs serve merely
to evade responsibility, to plead ignorance of one's true place.

The bipartite structure of "Afterlives" allows the poet in the first section to pre-empt any knowledge he may gain in section two. However, in
the exiled afterlife of London, part one emphasizes kinship with Belfast.
In part two, having arrived home, the poet feels alienated: "I scarcely recognize / The places I grew up in." There is still no "doubt as to where [home]
actually is," however, for the second section begins "I am going home by
sea" and does not bother to elaborate on the obvious destination, but
merely notes in general terms the "lightship and buoy / Slipway and dry
dock" as the ship passes them on the way up the lough. The arrival home
is marked by exhaustion and bewilderment:

> And I step ashore in a fine rain
> To a city so changed
> By five years of war
> I scarcely recognize
> The places I grew up in,
> The faces that try to explain.
>
> But the hills are still the same
> Grey-blue above Belfast.
> Perhaps if I'd stayed behind
> And lived it bomb by bomb
> I might have grown up at last
> And learnt what is meant by home.

Interviewed in 1973, Mahon repeated a sentiment first expressed in "An
Irishman in London," that "Ireland is backward looking and Britain is for-
ward looking,"[17] and this underlies the phrase "stayed behind," aimed at
Simmons, with its negative connotations of lost opportunity through

17 Interviewed by Harriet Cooke, *The Irish Times*, 17 January 1973, p. 10.

"LEAVETAKINGS AND HOMECOMINGS": DEREK MAHON'S BELFAST

stubborn refusal to move. Unlike the rural Heaney, the returning city-dweller must come to terms with the realities of his home's gradual destruction. Mahon combats his resulting alienation by evoking the permanent landmark of the hills above Belfast which will outlast contemporary squabbling, and even, in "The Spring Vacation," offer the possibility of salvation. The poem's final four lines move from the surrounding landscape to the city itself, from permanence to explosion. The adult knowledge which Mahon, ironically agreeing with Simmons, suggests he may have lost through leaving is actually enacted in the chilling finality of that notorious rhyme "bomb / home."

Like "Afterlives," "The Return" presents the poet on the verge of departure from England back to Northern Ireland. Again, Mahon wishes that his home were on the other side of the Irish Sea: he flicks ash into the rose bushes "As if I owned the place," and imagines himself metamorphosed into a tree and able to "gaze out over the downs / As if I belonged here too" (P 98). In each case "as if" reveals the wishful thinking. This time England is not immune to Mahon's decaying universe: its woods are "Misted with car exhaust" and nymphs die from the pollution. However, it still compares favorably with "where I am going," because the landscape of Ireland is devoid of nymphs and woods——having, incidentally, been deforested three centuries ago to provide materials for English ships. Nor are there rose bushes. One critic who suggests that Mahon intends to deflate the grandeur of Yeats's "right rose tree"[18] identifies the correct poet but the wrong poem. Mahon's true target is actually a passage from "Meditations in Time of Civil War," where Yeats locates at "My House" "An acre of stony ground / Where the symbolic rose can break in flower." By contrast, Mahon finds "rooted in stony ground" not a rose bush but an apparently unidentifiable "stubborn growth" constantly battered by the elements.

> With nothing to recommend it
> But its harsh tenacity
> Between the blinding windows
> And the forests of the sea,
> As if its very existence
> Were a reason to continue.
> Crone, crow, scarecrow,
> Its worn fingers scrabbling

18 Robert Garratt, *Modern Irish Poetry* (Berkeley: University of California Press, 1986), p. 275.

> At a torn sky, it stands
> On the verge of everything
> Like a burnt-out angel
> Raising petitionary hands. (*P* 99)

The metaphorical fallen angel replaces the idyllic, pagan nymphs of England. Isolated, marginalized, the "stubborn growth" presents a desperate gesture of appeasement which instills in the poet the grim Beckettian determination to "continue," although it no longer seems possible, even while he longs to merge into the lush, if apparently deteriorating, landscape of England's pastoral tradition. As in "Afterlives," Mahon's initial attempt to locate home elsewhere merely results in reluctantly affirming the compulsive attraction of his origins, no matter how miserable or squalid they may seem.

Mahon's failures to sunder himself from his roots signal the same quandary later endured by Heaney in "Station Island": namely, how does the poet reconcile his disgust at the insidious corruption of his home community, with the knowledge that he is inextricably a part of it, sharing a racial consciousness and unable to grind himself down to a different core? Mahon charts this dilemma in the original version of "The Sea in Winter," his verse epistle from Northern Ireland to a friend in Greece, which begins typically with a denial of home—the poet pretends "not to be here at all" (*P* 109). When reality impinges on these escapist dreams, Mahon admits that, returning to the North, he was ". . . slow / To come to terms with my own past / Yet knowing I could never cast / Aside the things that made me what, / For better or worse, I am" (*P* 111). Repelled by his origins, Heaney in "Station Island" pragmatically salvages the enabling aspects of his community. Like the Beckettian speaker of "Matthew V. 29–30," however, who puritanically proceeds on a course of self-mutilation and global destruction while searching for a continuing "offence" (*P* 69), Mahon indicts himself along with "the things that made me what . . . I am." He slumps into "chaos and instability" and attempts to annul the internal division of rival pulls through a process of self-negation leaving him dosed up, in true Lowellian fashion, on "antabuse and mogadon," his "talents on the shelf."

Despite the suffering caused by his stubborn ties to home, Mahon searches desperately for a device of attachment capable of satisfying conflicting desires for home and exile, freedom and responsibility. Accordingly, even while "The Sea in Winter" relates his breakdown, the poem suggests a means of placating the poet's pain without renouncing his origins. Mahon sits at a window, writing, while observing the world outside: distanced from his community yet belonging to it, hovering between leavetaking and homecoming, he reproduces what the "Unborn Child" calls the "verge of departure"—that instant preceding the exile's disillusionment when the prospect of imminent release can still be enjoyed. The poet asks rhetorically why he is "always staring out / Of windows, preferably from a height," and suggests that the view of the sea, with the promise of escape, provides necessary solace. More importantly, Mahon seeks to create a higher consciousness which allows him to survey the cause of pain while avoiding guilty feelings of abandonment and betrayal:

> Yet distance is the vital bond
> Between the window and the wind,
> While equilibrium demands
> A cold eye and deliberate hands. (*P* 112)

Distance is a paradoxical bond, tying the poet to the turbulence of the external world while allowing him to remain an unruffled chronicler of his own pain. The "cold eye" is taken, of course, from Yeats's epitaph in "Under Ben Bulben"; it observes the lives and deaths in the city above which Mahon is balanced in perfect equipoise between flight and duty.

Mahon's interest in window imagery continues in two of his poems about paintings from *The Hunt by Night* (1982): he implicitly compares his responsible posture with that of artists whose frames duplicate the window from which he observes the world. Their art being spatial rather than temporal, they are granted an escapist freedom denied the poet, who envies Uccello's *Hunt by Night*—actually entitled *The Hunt in the Forest*—for its "obscurities of paint" masking the gruesome realities of the hunt and preserving the illusion of "pageantry." Similarly, Mahon attacks the idyllic wish-fulfillment of Munch's *Girls on the Bridge* which represses the sinister truth that "A mile from where you chatter / Somebody screams"[19]— *The Scream* being the most famous of Munch's nightmare paintings. By contrast, Mahon's window imagery brooks no evasion: "The Attic" provides Mahon's bathetic version of the romantic ivory tower, as he sits with his Muse-light on the city" (*P* 102) and searches for inspiration—one eye on the blank page and the other gazing out of the window. And Mahon's concrete poem "The Window" sketches the frame with the words "wood" and "window" (*P* 108), as a single, inescapable "wind" in the center hits the observer full on.

19 Derek Mahon, *The Hunt by Night* (Oxford: Oxford University Press, 1982), p. 32. See Arthur McGuinness, "Cast a Wary Eye: Derek Mahon's Classical Perspective," *The Yearbook of English Studies*, 17 (1987), 137–8.

The poem which best tackles Mahon's conciliatory posture is his "Rage for Order" which, in being translated from Wallace Stevens's Key West to the battlescape of Belfast, becomes "wretched" rather than "blessed" (*P* 44). A rioter accuses the poet of becoming distanced "far from his people," fiddling like Nero while his city burns, his protective widow isolating him from the realities of "scattered glass" while he tinkers with his "dying art." Any hope of poetry becoming a midwife to society is mocked: it is "an eddy of semantic scruples / in an unscrutable sea," and as Heaney asserts in 'Station Island', the eddy cannot reform the pool. Nevertheless, the rioter must ultimately acknowledge its relevance:

> Now watch me as I make history. Watch as I tear down
> to build up with a desperate love,
> knowing it cannot be
> long now till I have need of his
> desperate ironies.   (*P* 44)

Originally, the poet's ironies were "germinal,"[20] and although Mahon's revision detracts from their rebuilding power, the need for poetry to survive is still powerfully affirmed. The window imagery enables Mahon's most successful response to the contradictory demands of Belfast which torture him because, like irony, it evades and acknowledges simultaneously.

"The Sea in Winter" underlies the dependency of Mahon's poetic output on his new-found solution: the poet asks whether "the year two thousand" will find "Me still at window, pen in hand," and hopes that it will for the sake of his "subsidized serendipities." However, this passage was later dropped from the *Selected Poems* (1991): unable to bear even such regulated proximity to the cause of his suffering, Mahon's omission marks an abandonment of his window imagery, which in fact disappears from his poetry altogether after "The Sea in Winter." The breakdown to which that poem refers left him "resolved never to live in the North again."[21] The failure and despair which finally sap his homecoming compulsion create a serious impasse in poetry as well as life: the conflicting tensions of Belfast provide the lifeblood for much of Mahon's best work, and to abandon his home involves rejecting his crucial source of inspiration. The exile's tone of despondency running through his subsequent work reinforces the urgency of Mahon's search for an alternative stance capable of connecting the poet once again to his enabling home ground of Belfast.

20 Derek Mahon, *Lives* (Oxford: Oxford University Press, 1972), p. 22.
21 Quoted in *Irish Poetry after Joyce*, p. 225.

"MORALS FOR THOSE THAT LIKE THEM": THE SATIRE OF EDGEWORTH'S *BELINDA*, 1801

MARJORIE LIGHTFOOT

IN *NORTHANGER ABBEY* (1818), Jane Austen pays proper tribute to both Frances Burney and Maria Edgeworth. Her narrator protests against readers—and authors?—who say of novels, "'It is only Cecilia or Camilla, or Belinda'; or, in short, only some work in which the greatest powers of the mind are displayed, in which the most thorough knowledge of human nature, the happiest delineation of its varieties, the liveliest effusions of wit and humor are conveyed to the world in the best chosen language."[1] Austen objects to novelists' piously disparaging or disclaiming their own genre. *Camilla* (1796), according to Burney, is not a novel: it is a *work* showing characters and morals in action; but Edgeworth has tongue in cheek in her apologia to *Belinda* (1801) when she preserves herself from the accusation of being a frivolous female scribbler by offering *Belinda* as "a Moral Tale—the author not wishing to acknowledge a Novel."[2]

Austen was right: *Belinda* is a novel. Certainly it is a fictional prose narrative in three volumes, a courtship novel, which owes a debt to Frances Burney's *Evelina*; its plot, like hers, details the adventures of a naive yet intelligent young woman making her entry into English society. Yet, *Belinda* defies the limits of a realistic style that depicts actuality by an accumulation of detail. John Ward early complained that Edgeworth's picture of society is pervasively inaccurate and the author guilty of a travesty of the social scene.[3] By contrast, Marilyn Butler believes that Edgeworth's "talent was as a reporter of the social scene, not as a satirist or parodist," while

1 *The Novels of Jane Austen*, ed. R. W. Chapman (Oxford: Oxford University Press, 1933), 3rd edition, V: 38.

2 Maria Edgeworth, *Belinda* (London: Pandora, 1986), p. viii; hereafter cited parenthetically, thus: (*B* viii).

3 Marilyn Butler, *Maria Edgeworth: A Literary Biography* (Oxford: Clarendon Press, 1972), pp. 346–47.

her didactic message was both blunt and naive.[4] Edgeworth actually had little personal experience of English social life when she wrote *Belinda*.[5] Many characters are composites drawn from literature and from the life of her father, rather than from her own experience.[6] Edgeworth's heroine, however, is something other than the embodiment of morality in didactic fiction[7] or of the need for individualism and the education of the heart as well as the mind to secure happiness.[8] Critics have judged *Belinda* according to its success or failure in meeting the standards of literary and historical conventions that they anticipate, or else they have given preference to certain material. Avoiding presuppositions and taking a fresh look at the work as a whole provides another perspective. Observing Edgeworth's style as it affects plot, theme and characterization reveals that *Belinda*, even in its revised form, is a strikingly satirical novel.[9]

Traditionally, satire is a style of writing that mocks the follies and foibles of typical characters in life as in art; it may even encourage reform. Authors employ satire in varying degrees: it may simply embellish a work or it may be diffused through every part of it. *Belinda* is filled with satire, evident in the way Edgeworth uses irony, burlesque, parody, sarcasm, invective and innuendo. Etymologically, "satire" denotes a dish filled with mixed fruits. Examining a variety of fashionable tastes, Edgeworth offers readers a cornucopia. Her unexpected mockery of eighteenth-century assumptions about life and art may well account for the failure of many critics to do justice to *Belinda*.[10]

4   Butler, pp. 319,317.

5   Edgeworth visited Mrs. Hoare at Roehampton in 1792. See Butler, p. 107.

6   Colin B. and Jo Atkinson, "Maria Edgeworth, *Belinda*, and Women's Rights," ÉIRE-IRELAND, XIX, 4 (Winter 1984), 94, 97.

7   Twila Yates Papay, "Defining the Educative Process: Maria Edgeworth's *Belinda*," *Eighteenth-Century Women and the Arts*, eds. Frederick M. Keene and Susan E. Lorsch, Contributions in Women's Studies, 90 (New York: Greenwood Press, 1988), p. 143.

8   Elizabeth Harden, *Maria Edgeworth* (Boston: Twayne Publishers, 1984), pp. 122–23.

9   Edgeworth wrote very rapidly; she may have written better when relying on her native talents rather than accommodating her critics. Edgeworth's ultimate dislike of *Belinda*, as of *Castle Rackrent*, might not have occurred if she had had more faith in her own genius.

10   See James Newcomer, *Maria Edgeworth* (Fort Worth: Texas Christian University Press, 1967), p.137; Papay, pp.142–43; Katrin R. Burlin, "'At the Crossroads:' Sister Authors and the Sister Arts, " in *Fetter'd or Free? British Women Novelists, 1670–1815*, eds. Mary Anne Schofield and Cecilia Macheski (Athens: Ohio University Press, 1986), pp.70–71; Butler, pp. 346–47.

As a satirist, Maria Edgeworth inherited the tradition of noteworthy Anglo-Irish authors—Swift, Farquhar, Goldsmith, Sterne, Sheridan—for the Edgeworth family had established itself in Ireland during the Elizabethan Plantation.[11] But she was an innovator: *Castle Rackrent* (1800), set in Ireland, is the first regional novel; *Belinda*, though set in England, is an original contribution to the new courtship novel. The satirical perspective of both works is that of a radical and conservative Anglo-Irish woman,[12] as she questions colonialism, traditional male/female relationships, and styles of art and life while trying to preserve moral boundaries. "In her first novel, *Castle Rackrent*, Edgeworth adopts a mode that is so ironic that it becomes virtually satiric,"[13] pointing up the foibles of four generations of the Rackrent family and their Irish tenants. Ann Owens Weekes shrewdly observes that

> Not only does this subversive novel question the status of the Anglo-Irish landlord but it also looks askance at, indeed even ridicules, those who unquestioningly accept the absurd position of Irish and/or English women. Indeed Edgeworth implies that this condition is in part the logical result of its inscription and preservation in the great works of English literature.[14]

Belinda, too, is subversive, satirically addressing issues of colonialism, women's relation with men, the trustworthiness of literature as a guide to life, and conflicting views of the nature and purpose of life. Revisions in the 1802 and 1810 editions were meant to pacify family and critics.[15] She agreed to make the colonial Mr. Vincent Belinda's suitor, rather than fiancé, and to have an English farm girl wed a white Englishman rather than the black West Indian servant, Juba. But satirical insights about prejudice and self-

11 Thomas Flanagan, *The Irish Novelists 1800–1850* (New York: Columbia Univerity Press, 1959), p. 53.

12 Newcomer, pp. 3–4 131, 142, believes the Edgeworths were patriotic as both Irish and English, but Maria proudly considered herself an Irishwoman. He sees the setting of the three Irish novels, *The Absentee, Ennui,* and *Ormond,* as "insufficient reason for considering them apart from her other novels." The Irish novelist Emily Lawless did not "perceive any very marked difference between [the heroines]. Belinda—like Helen [in *Helen*], like Miss Annaly [in *Ormond*], Miss Nugent [in *The Absentee*], and the rest of her sisterhood— is at once a remarkable sprightly and a remarkable discreet young woman." See *Maria Edgeworth,* English Men of Letters Series (London: Macmillan, 1904), p. 99.

13 Frederick Reynolds Ross, "Integration of the Community: A Study of the Major Novels of Maria Edgeworth," *DAI,* 42 (1982), 5131A (University of Wisconsin-Madison).

14 Ann Owens Weekes, *Irish Women Writers: An Uncharted Tradition* (Lexington: University Press of Kentucky, 1990), p.19.

15 Butler, pp. 494–95.

deception remain in abundance. If the Irish saga novel *Castle Rackrent* strikingly discloses the damaging effects of self-deception on individuals and on society, as Thomas Flanagan affirms,[16] so too does the witty English courtship novel *Belinda*. Through characterization the author satirically demonstrates that self-deception or the failure to understand one's own identity, let alone another's—whether complex or simple, rich or poor, urban or rural, male or female, black or white, English or "alien"— arouses distrust and rivalry in families, friends, lovers, and societies. In fact, it provokes a world of trouble—and humor.

Kathryn Kirkpatrick has argued that "as a woman of the Anglo-Irish gentry, Edgeworth wrote from the conflicted position of a subordinate member of a ruling class within a colonized country," and that there are "elements of a radical critique of the colonialist enterprise" in both *Castle Rackrent* and *Belinda*.[17] In *Castle Rackrent* Edgeworth mixed her own family's stories, Anglo-Irish legends and local history with her personal experience and imagination—with no input initially from her father, her frequent collaborator and valued critic. Writing for her own pleasure, so Weekes observes, "Edgeworth drops her role of exemplum and adventures instead into ambiguous territories, registering there (whether fully conscious of the message or not) contradictory, conflicting voices . . . . "Weekes is mistaken, however, in thinking that "sadly . . . all future writing was undertaken to enlighten and reform . . . ."[18] In *Belinda*, too, the Anglo-Irish author presents contradictory, conflicting voices, satirically treated, to show a world offering multiple, conflicting values.

Belinda is characterized by a plethora of incidents and theses, of complications and contrivances that satirically mock the individual's ability to find easy answers to basic questions about life—including the best way to live. If in the novel "life does not offer a clear generic choice between

16 Flanagan, p. 69.

17 Kathryn Kirkpatrick, "A Contextual Reading of Maria Edgeworth's 'Castle Rackrent' and 'Belinda'," *DAI*, 51 (1991), 3418A (Emory University). Colonizing nations or women is a dubious practice to Irish woman authors. See Joan Tantum Kelly, "Four Irish Writers—1800–1932: Nationalism and Gender in a Changing Ireland," *DAI*, 50 (1989), 1312A (State University of New York at Stony Brook). Kelly sees Edgeworth, Edith Somerville, Violet Martin, and Lady Gregory "united in seeking class and gender identity, but divergent in their means of expression." All are "loyal to their class and their families" but "subvert the roles of their fathers and brothers, to present the roles of women differently than men perceived them, and to create a feminist literature. . . ."

18 Weekes, p. 59.

THE SATIRE OF MARIA EDGEWORTH'S *BELINDA*, 1801

modes of being,"[19] then neither does the form of the book. This is not a weakness. *Belinda* presents multiple plots, genres, and modes of being to satirize life by means of art and art by means of life. The literary maze is self-consciously created for the reader's amusement—and possible reform, if he or she can only find a way through the author's strategies to some insight.

The main plot, which centers on Edgeworth's title character, Belinda, does not simply lead the charming young heroine to the conventional wisdom of an educative domestic novel; it proves to be satiric. Belinda's conniving aunt has sent her off to London to stay with socially prominent Lady Delacour to catch a husband well-off financially and socially. As the house guest of the dissipated Delacours and then of the highly moral Percivals, Belinda learns that prudence and experience, as well as education, are necessary if one wishes to live a happy, useful life according to good principles. Belinda tries to help herself and her friends—the contentious Delacours; the disappointing colonial suitor, Mr. Vincent; and the handsome, talented, but immature and socially entangled hero Clarence Hervey—make the most of life. The irony is that prudence, experience, and education prove inadequate to secure happiness in this world, though they may foster self-knowledge. In the name of reason—as Belinda's knowledge is based on false hearsay—the heroine refuses to be rash—that is, honest about her feelings. Rather, she is ironically irrational, willing to see her beloved Clarence Hervey wed Virginia St. Pierre, whom he does not even love. Belinda accepts this marriage in the name of morality by respecting a supposed commitment, which Hervey never really intended, to a young woman, who does not actually wish to marry him. It is not Belinda who brings the farcical situation to a happy, semirational conclusion in which the right individuals are united. Nor is it the highly rational Dr. X—— or the highly moral Percivals. It is well-meaning, morally equivocal Lady Delacour, who rashly applies common sense to assist her friends and is helped absurdly by chance to resolve their problems. The author burlesques novels, plays, and fairy tales that provide artificial happy endings by means of marriage, and those that glamorize long-suffering sentimental heroines.[20]

Butler has noted that "Both Scott and Whately give due credit to Jane

19 Burlin, p. 71.

20 Lady Delacour compares *"Pamela maritata"* to *"Belinda in love,"* observing "that the prudent Belinda is more capable of feeling real permanent passion than any of the dear sentimental young ladies, whose motto is 'All for love, or the world well lost'" (*B* 427). She mocks Richardson's Pamela and Dryden's Cleopatra as heroines.

Austen for being consistently naturalistic, in her plots as well as in her characterization, whereas Maria Edgeworth, the pioneer of this kind of writing, tolerates 'absurd and lucky denouements'."[21] Edgeworth does not, however, tolerate them. She satirizes them—expressing the view of a skeptical Anglo-Irish woman.

The comedy of manners in *Belinda* is distinctive. From the Restoration period through Edgeworth's era, the comedy of manners typically ridicules the social fashions, behavior, conventions, and outlook of society—especially the artificial, sophisticated urban society. It is a realistic comedy, often satirical, pointing up aberrations of social decorum rather than more serious issues of human conduct. Verbal fencing is frequent in characteristically brilliant, sparkling dialogue. Edgeworth mocks urban society and the rural society that she prefers: the initial title of *Belinda* was *Abroad and at Home*. She violates expectations of realism, however, when she lets satire dominate form and content, and thus she deepens the import of her fiction. Typical rivalries, searches for identity, strategies, and manipulations presented in excess in *Belinda* mock not only the social and domestic milieu, but, as well, the supposed reality of the story. In their mature courtship novels, neither Frances Burney nor Jane Austen employs a comedy of manners that departs from naturalism to the same degree.

While Edgeworth intensifies her mockery of society by measuring her characters' folly against behavior found in novels, poetry, and drama of all sorts; her allusions give preeminence to plays of the Restoration period and of her own time (105, 129, 147,157, 250, 296, 433). These comedies of manners are imbued with satire, not merely embellished with it; they too mock their surface realism. In *Belinda* there are references to and parallels with Congreve's *The Double Dealer* (1694) and *The Way of the World* (1700); Farquhar's *The Beaux' Stratagem* (1707); perhaps even Royall Tyler's *The Contrast* (1787); Sheridan's *The Rivals* (1775), *The School for Scandal* (1777), and *The Critic* (1779). When Sheridan read *Belinda*, he shrewdly observed that Edgeworth should write for the stage.[22]

Edgeworth selects descriptive, mocking names for her characters, appropriate for her comedy of manners: not just Belinda Portman and Clarence Hervey, but Delacour, Freke, Lawless, Boucher, Percival, Dr.

21 Butler, p. 347.
22 Butler, p. 314.

THE SATIRE OF MARIA EDGEWORTH'S *BELINDA,* 1801

X——, etc.[23] The heroine's name conveniently reminds Lady Delacour and other characters, as well as the reader of Pope's Belinda in *The Rape of the Lock* (1712, 1714). However, Edgeworth's heroine prudently keeps her vanity in check and her locks intact; she is rewarded by being united with her manly lover, a reformed individual. In the period of the novel—late eighteenth century, but after the French Revolution—the strategies of Edgeworth and her characters provide unexpected, perhaps revolutionary, paths which lead to happier conclusions than Pope's mock-heroic poem or the French Revolution. This resolution, however, occurs arbitrarily through the author's flagrant artifice. Form and content indicate Edgeworth is doing more in *Belinda* than simply satirizing social mores.

Edgeworth's unreliable narrator, who functions as one of the formal causes of satire in her comedy of manners, offers suspect moralizing. Judgmental statements infiltrate or frame dramatic scenes, summaries of events, lengthy letters, lengthier confessions, and life histories. Well into the story, the narrator conventionally announces—didactically, even sententiously—the theme: the moral instinct needs to be enlightened or controlled "by reason and religion" (*B* 380). But the novel calls this formula into question, indirectly, through the plot. For example, religion rarely functions in *Belinda*, and when it does appear, its social role is demonstrated more than its spiritual one. Ironically, it was a chaplain who corrupted Lord Delacour with drink (*B* 289). And we are simply *told* that a chaplain like Chaucer's priest relieved Lady Delacour "from the horrors of methodism, and in their place substituted the consolations of a mild and rational piety" (*B* 292).

Reason, in contrast, is mentioned frequently by both Edgeworth's narrator and her characters; but a sustained power of logical thought proves extremely difficult to find, either in models of the urban world—the Delacours, Clarence Hervey, Sir Philip Badelly—or in moral exemplars in a rural retreat—the Percivals, or apparent noble savages like Rachel-Virginia from the New Forest and Mr. Vincent from the Indies. Even the exceptionally rational Dr. X—— is not wholly reliable.[24] Nor do the working classes show superiority as rational creatures. Belinda herself believes in using

---

23 Clarence Hervey is not like Pope's Baron Hervey, satirized as "Sporus" in "Epistle to Dr. Arbuthnot," any more than Miss Portman is like Pope's Belinda. In 1800, Freke's name refers to "a caper, a capricious humor or whim" (Atkinson, 100). A "dasher," Freke is a "bizarre version of the masculine-woman stereotype and the Dreadful Warning figure in the didactic plot" (Atkinson, 115).

24 Dr. X—— fails to use reason when Lady Delacour pretends that her expressed fear

reason to judge habits and principles, in order to determine conduct (*B* 210). The Percivals help her to establish "in her own understanding the exact boundaries between right and wrong upon many subjects" (*B* 211–12). Yet, when Belinda would like to forget Hervey, who has not proposed, and rationally considers Mr. Vincent as a suitor, as the Percivals advise, she discovers only by good luck that Vincent is her anathema—a gambler. The unreliable narrator overtly affirms that one *ought* to live a moral, rational life; but Edgeworth implicitly demonstrates her satirical view that it is easier said then done. First, one must determine what is moral and what is rational, and then discover whether human nature will support such standards.

Edgeworth's theme, like her plot, is satiric. In *Belinda*, life is tragicomic: the story shows that no path that one chooses can guarantee earthly happiness, though much can be said for choosing the heart's instincts and mind's logic as guides, and then acting according to sound practical judgment and common sense. Edgeworth makes a satiric attack on those who foolishly follow sentiment, superstition, or fashionable social conventions. Those who seek self-knowledge, like Belinda and Hervey, have a greater possibility of achieving at least psychological insight. A sense of humor, a touch of guile, and an enormous measure of good luck are needed if earthly happiness and a life of moral consequence may be hoped for. Edgeworth shows no expectation that moral worth will win worldly happiness beyond the possibility of psychological peace. *Belinda* is essentially a comedy of manners in which "virtue" and "vice" do get what they deserve—quite incredibly, thanks to the poetic justice of the arbitrary author satirizing life and art.

Life can be satirized by means of art. Edgeworth plays off against all forms of art the wholly suspect "reality" of *Belinda*, as individuals absurdly impose upon life the meaning that they hope or expect to find. Irrationally, Edgeworth's characters use various genres as artistic metaphors for life in order to glamorize their existence and define their own roles—whether in a moral tale, novel, sentimental romance, Gothic thriller, picaresque tale, mock heroic poem, Shakespearean drama, comedy of man-

---

of dying that night has merely been a hoax to postpone an operation. Belinda realizes that Lady Delacour's laughter is a ploy to prevent him from sitting up with her. A surgeon thinks that cowardice has influenced the patient. "After having expressed their opinions, without making any impression upon one another, they retired to rest," observes the complacent narrator, whereas the author satirizes their rational discussion as fruitless (*B* 278).

ners in the form of a novel or play or some other genre. "Virtues" and "vices" are identified variously, relative to the viewpoint of each observer, in terms of the genre the person currently embraces. Yet, the unreliable narrator does not call into question the existence of essential virtue and vice. Common sense, reason, and sensibility—observation, education and experience—are the means by which the unreliable narrator and heroine confidently identify virtue and vice, making a leap of faith: "virtue" ought to be rewarded, not "vice." The comic happy ending of *Belinda*, which provides poetic justice only through ridiculous contrivances, confirms and highlights with artificiality the author's philosophical doubts and her satirical inquiry into the nature of being.

Consider the ways in which various characters try to turn life into art. Lady Delacour most often sees her acquaintances as figures in an absurd comedy of manners, whether a novel or a play, which she is determined to direct. Lady Delacour jests that, despite society's disapproval of novels, Belinda identifies with Burney's Camilla, fearful of being misled by a devious woman like Lady Delacour (*B* 60). Life is essentially a moral tale to Belinda, but she and Lady Delacour ironically learn from each other, and save each other from unhappiness.

Likewise, Hervey sees life in multiple genres: as a picaresque tale—when he roguishly pursues adventures at home and in France; or as a comedy of manners—when he attends Lady Delacour and Belinda; or as a sentimental tale—when he calls Rachel Hartley Virginia St. Pierre. Hervey's three "goddesses" (*B* 119) complicate his life and the author's plot, which climaxes when he irrationally decides to marry Virginia, as if living out a moral tale.

Logical Dr. X—— with fine satirical wit mocks mankind's irrational taste for sentimental or Gothic literature.[25] Like the hero of a didactic tale, he speaks from the heart, but uses reason to urge Hervey to live a more meaningful life by employing his talents and acquirements to "be permanently useful to his fellow creatures" (*B* 101-2). Therein lies the obvious moral of

25 See *A Memoir of Maria Edgeworth with a Selection from Her Letters* by the Late Mrs. [F.A.B.] Edgeworth, ed. by her children (London: Printed by Joseph Masters and Son, 1867), III: 273. Edgeworth's original sketch called for a Doctor Sane, based on author Dr. John Moore, "a benevolent man who knows human nature and what is called the world, perfectly: who has polite manners and talents for conversation in a high degree." Perhaps Dr. X—— in the novel reflects also Dr. Erasmus Darwin, whose principle of moral activism was reinforced in Mr. Edgeworth between 1766 and 1771, when he associated with scientists and industrialists known as the Lunar group. See Butler, pp. 31-34.

Edgeworth's tale. The doctor is a minor character, however, and the only person who may live up to this ideal, outside of family life and a small circle of friends, where Belinda, Hervey, and Lady Delacour function with mixed results. Perhaps Edgeworth is suggesting that one begin transforming the world first by cultivating the fruits of one's own garden, as did the Edgeworths, whether in England, Ireland, or elsewhere.

The name Percival suggests that Mr. Percival may turn the story into a didactic novel based on the legend of the chaste Sir Parsifal, who quests for the Holy Grail and tries to make the waste land fertile by healing the impotent Fisher King. Mr. Percival assists Hervey to mature somewhat, but he fails with his colonial ward, a Jamaican, Mr. Vincent. Mr. Percival's moral, rational behavior very nearly lands Belinda in a marriage with the unsuitable Mr. Vincent, rather than Hervey, her first love.[26] Mr. Percival rejected his first love, the domineering Lady Delacour, for her vanity; with Lady Anne he has created a model household based on their equality, not on a colonial relationship.[27] Ironically, many women in this society offensively try to "colonize" men, just as men conventionally try to "colonize" women, with negative results.

26 Are Mr. Percival's good intentions and equivocal results with the English and colonial youth a reflection of Mr. Edgeworth's experiments to improve education and his efforts to reconcile the English and the Irish? Mr. Percival's character, like Hervey's, is based on that of Edgeworth's beloved father, Richard Lovell. Mr. Edgeworth was the originator of the positive educational views promoted in *Belinda* by the Percivals—but was also a practitioner earlier of the folly of educating his eldest son according to the principles of Rousseau's *Émile*. See Butler, pp. 37–38. Though Mr. Edgeworth favored the union of Ireland with England as advantageous to the Irish, he voted against it in 1800 because he saw money rather than conviction determining the outcome. See Butler, pp. 181–84.

27 Conservative Mr. Percival asks the feminist revolutionary Mrs. Freke, "Should we find things much improved by tearing away what has been called the decent drapery of life?," thus echoing the Anglo-Irish Edmund Burke in *Reflections on the Revolution in France* (1790). See Atkinson, pp. 113–14. But equality in marriage is seen in the chapter "Domestic Happieness" as a rational principle. Equality of the sexes is actually supported by the author and her chief characters, Lady Delacour and Belinda (*B* 106) and Hervey (*B* 344), as well as by the model Percivals. Practical regard is given, however, to the particular strengths and actual weaknesses exhibited by individual men and women; there is ambivalence about gender roles. Harden notes that "if [Edgeworth] did not campaign publicly for women's rights, she quietly challenged women all along in her fiction to accept their rights to self-realization" (121–22). Weekes points out that Irish women authors since Edgeworth have characteristically concerned themselves with "the value and the cost of human relationships" (23).

THE SATIRE OF MARIA EDGEWORTH'S *BELINDA*, 1801

Though Lady Anne embodies wisdom and goodness suitable to a happy marriage in a domestic novel, Lady Delacour cannot help liking her the better for being wrong and admitting to Belinda that she was "so rash in her advice" to marry Mr. Vincent (*B* 407): "It saves her, in my imagination, from the odium of being a perfect character" (*B* 408). More obviously, simple Virginia St. Pierre, having no experience of society, is misled by a romantic governess to make life copy romantic fiction (*B* 372). Endlessly "grateful" to Hervey, she feels she ought to marry him, even if she is really in love with another—a man of whom she dreams, a man seen in a picture.

Not only can life be satirized by means of art; art can be satirized by means of life. Edgeworth's fiction is no sentimental novel, nor a Gothic novel, nor a didactic novel, any more than is life. *Belinda* does use elements of all three genres, however, in its comedy of manners in order to satirize literary kinds. Edgeworth provides literary criticism indirectly through allusions, for example, to Sterne's *Sentimental Journey*, to Radcliffe's picturesque writing, to Fordyce's *Sermons for Young Women* (*B* 248), and through burlesques of various other genres and styles. The author travesties the sentimental novel in the subplot involving the child of nature, Virginia. Satirical Lady Delacour sarcastically affirms that, at best, Virginia "is only half mad" (*B* 430). Romantically, Hervey has renamed Rachel Hartley Virginia St. Pierre (*B* 171) in honor of the French author of the sentimental *Paul et Virginie* (1788). His lack of success in educating her to become a perfect wife for him indicates—through parody—that Rousseau's *Émile* is an inadequate guide to life.[28] Rashness and reason fall under the author's scrutiny in art as in life. The sentimental subplot with Virginia slides into the central comedy of manners with Lady Delacour and the moral Belinda. The heroine's admitted effort to light the torch of Cupid on the altar of Reason (*B* 255), as in a moral tale, is forestalled when life proves her literary model to be as doubtful an object of worship as Mr. Vincent. There are also slippery, because feigned, Gothic elements: a ghost, voodoo, and behind a locked door, a secret lover. Belinda has discovered that a frantic feminist, Mrs. Freke, has played a phosphorescent ghost to scare gullible Lady Delacour, and she similarly scared the black colonial servant, Juba, with "voodoo." And "the mysterious boudoir" in which either Lady Delacour or Belinda may be hiding a lover, to the dismay or either Lord

28 Richard Edgeworth's friend, Thomas Day, tried in the manner of Russeau to educate a naive young woman to become his wife—with bad results. See Butler, pp. 39, 243.

Delacour or Clarence Hervey, actually proves to be a cabinet suited to the "retirement of disease, and not of pleasure" (*B* 117).

The real horror of the story is that Lady Delacour secretly thinks she is dying of breast cancer and determines to live out her life in dissipation, masking her pain with brilliant wit, opium and a painted face.[29] Disappointed in Lord Delacour, her inferior in understanding, she flirts with talented Clarence Hervey, who reminds her of Mr. Percival. However, she hides in her boudoir not an illicit lover, but laudanum. It relieves the pain of an injury she incurred when her gun backfired while she was engaged in a foolish but fashionable duel. Out of vanity and fear, she refuses to see a physician, until Belinda, her only true friend, pressures her either to submit to examination, or be left to face death alone. The injury is not really serious; Lady Delacour will recover. The author never allows possibilities for tragedy in life or art to overpower the witty, satirical style that governs this novel which calls for a happy ending. Comedy of manners, too, is mocked as a mere picture of existence; it is untrustworthy as a guide to life,

Characterization in *Belinda* involves many stereotyped characters appropriate for a comedy of manners in which reality is stylized, artificial, and in which types are satirized for their follies. Dr. X—— and Lord Delacour are simply conceived, two-dimensional individuals. The former is the wise doctor, whose reasoning may nevertheless be wrong. The latter is the boorish, belligerent husband, whose good nature and talent may be fostered by considerate attention, though he remains quite determined not to be seen as governed by his wife (*B* 29, 316). Most of the characters are simple stereotypes whose few traits are exaggerated to emphasize that they are unrealistic figures: for example, the noble savages, Virginia and Mr. Vincent; the hasty, hot tempered moralist, Lady Margaret Delacour; the would-be rake, Sir Philip Badelly; the irrational feminist, Mrs. Freke—whose capers, innuendo, and invective are outrageous in the "Rights of Woman" chapter; the dishonorable "other woman," Mrs. Luttridge, who is Lady Delacour's social and domestic rival; the moral Percivals; the exceedingly good little girl, Helena Delacour. Manly Clarence Hervey proves

---

29 Lady Delacour is said to be modeled on Sir James Deleval, a dissipated young man whom Richard Edgeworth knew in London during his youth. See Atkinson, p. 97. Lady Delacour's speech to Belinda about her mortal illness and her regret over a life of folly seems to be based on Deleval's confession to Richard Edgeworth. See Butler, pp.28–29. Though Maria Edgeworth initially intended Lady Delacour to die from cancer, as if punished for her vices, the author created a much more sophisticated role for her character as an embodiment of one who comes to recognize her own follies and foibles.

a bit more complex. He exhibits some capacity to mature, as he comes to esteem Belinda above Virginia, preferring Belinda's virtues, which he thinks spring from reason, to Virginia's, which arise from sentiment (*B* 344). The sophisticated Lady Delcaour and the naive but intelligent Belinda are familiar types, but are given more intricate three-dimensional characterization which enriches the satire.

At the center of the dynamic narrative, thematic and psychological interest in the novel is Lady Delacour, an exemplar of satire: what will she say or do next that mocks English society? Lady Delacour is incomparable; as Belinda's sometime hostess and friend, she "trample[s] on impossibilities" to achieve her own ends (*B* 431). Telling her life story to Belinda, she proudly affirms her rash character:

> I never read or listened to a moral at the end of a story in my life:—manners for me and morals for those that like them. My dear, you will be woefully disappointed if in my story you expect any thing like a novel. (*B* 28)

Lady Delacour's life is not only *like* a novel, it is *part* of a novel, with more love than hate in the balance.

Few women in English literature can compare with this manipulating, articulate coquette, villain, and goddess of machination. Lady Delacour's sophisticated folly creates considerable misery, domestic and public, especially for herself. But her essential good nature and inimitable wit demand the reader's capitulation, and she does precipitate the happy ending. Lady Delacour steals the show: she calls into question conventional moral behavior in life and in art through satire, demonstrating as much in her own behavior as in that of others the follies and foibles of mankind. The prominence of Lady Delacour—a chief exponent of a satirical, existential view of life—may account for the critics' embarrassment over *Belinda*, which does not conform to their expectations of a realistic courtship novel designed to convey a conventional moral based on domestic ideology embodied in the heroine.[30]

Belinda Portman, the nominal heroine of Edgeworth's novel, surprisingly turns out to be another complex character. When Edgeworth was asked

---

30 See Beth Kowaleski-Wallace, "Home Economics: Domestic Ideology in Maria Edgeworth's *Belinda*," *The Eighteenth Century: Theory and Interpretation* 29 (Fall, 1988), 260; Papay, p. 143; Hawthorne, p. 148; and Jane Spencer, "Maria Edgeworth's *Belinda* (1801)," *The Rise of the Woman Novelist: From Aphra Behn to Jane Austen* (London: Basil Blackwell, 1986), p. 161.

by Mrs. Barbauld to revise the novel for the fifty-volume "British Novelists" series, the author responded, "I was really so provoked with the cold tameness of that stick or stone Belinda that I could have torn the pages to pieces—and really have not the heart or the patience to *correct* her."[31] Admittedly, good-hearted Belinda is stiff as a heroine when behaving conventionally, which attests to the author's striking satirical outlook, for such idealization does not make Belinda effective in securing her own domestic happiness. Ironically, Belinda becomes an interesting, complex character because she finds it impossible to remain conventional when dealing with Lady Delacour. The young woman learns from her worldly friend something about using guile to achieve her own ends, and yet she maintains integrity. She manipulates Lady Delacour to bring her friend domestic happiness in spite of herself.

Belinda's good deeds include emotionally blackmailing Lady Delacour into consulting a physician; reconciling her to her husband by inadvertently arousing her jealousy; restoring the Delacour's daughter to the domestic circle as a mystery guest; and unmasking the "ghost" of Colonel Lawless as Mrs. Freke.[32] When Belinda shows Hervey that Lady Delacour is worthy to be reformed, they become accomplices in fostering good will between the Delacours by manipulating their views of each other. Thus, Edgeworth's comedy of manners accommodates a moral tale without her satire losing its preeminence.

Lady Delacour reciprocates Belinda's good deeds in headstrong fashion, bringing Belinda and Hervey together by sweeping away their supposedly rational reasons (*B* 327, 379) why their love can never be fulfilled (*B* 409—11). At the climax of events, active appeals to the heart and to common sense are the methods by which Lady Delacour, still using devious means, manages to arrange ends to her personal satisfaction and that of her friends, winning both our applause and our laughter. She pays tribute to all those who have inadvertently brought about a happy ending, saying, "we might have been all making one another unhappy at this moment, if it had not been for Mr Vincent's great dog Juba—Miss Annabella Luttridge's billet-doux—Sir Philip Baddely's insolence—my Lord Delacour's belief in a quack balsam—and Captain Sunderland's humanity'" (*B* 429). A dog named Juba—like the colonial servant, two self-serving exploiters, a hus-

31 Quoted by Butler, p. 494.

32 Lady Delacour is haunted by her guilt: Lord Delacour wrongfully killed Lawless in a duel to preserve his honor—though technically his wife never lost hers to the rake.

THE SATIRE OF MARIA EDGEWORTH'S *BELINDA,* 1801

band gullible as herself, an a stranger are the formula out of which Lady Delacour has created an ending as good as gold. This is quite extraordinary if Edgeworth is serious about presenting *Belinda* as a moral tale. Jovially, Lady Delacour admits, "Things have turned out contrary to all my expectations, and yet better" (*B* 431). With poetic justice fortuitously granted, everyone can feast on the fruit of the satire.

Edgeworth concludes her tale self-consciously, with Lady Delacour identifying life with a novel and asking her friends, ". . . shall I finish the novel for you?" While they agree, they each have their own ideas to contribute to the dénouement. She is reminded by Belinda "that there is nothing in which novelists are so apt to err as in hurrying things toward the conclusion: in not allowing *time* enough for that change of feeling, which change of situation cannot instantly produce" (*B* 432). A variety of endings are suggested, but the technique actually used to close the novel is that of a scene concluding a play: the typical tableau ending of a traditional comedy of manners. Lady Delacour positions everyone conventionally and, speaking as a "reformed rake" (*B* 158), addresses the audience, to conclude the story with a moral: "Our *tale* contains a *moral*; and, no doubt, / You all have wit enough to find it out" (*B* 433–34). This ending, which states no moral, teases the audience for its hypocritical insistence on didacticism to justify literature that is actually read, as *Belinda* is, for its universal delight and subversive insight.

—*Arizona State University*

DUBLIN LETTERS:
JOHN EGLINTON AND *THE DIAL,* 1921–1929

MARY E. BRYSON

AMONG THE essays in John Eglinton's *Irish Literary Portraits* (1935)[1] are "Yeats and His Story" and "A. E. and His Story," which both first saw print as Eglinton's contributions to *The Dial* magazine.[2] Critical reception of the *Portraits* collection suggests the significance of the nearly thirty *Dial* pieces Eglinton wrote as its Irish correspondent throughout the 1920s. The interest of the *Dial* pieces is not limited, however, to Eglinton's literary criticism as such. Beginning with the premise that a tradition in Ireland had passed with the "passing of Kathleen ni Hoolihan,"[3] Eglinton was often as much social historian as literary critic. For example, he analyzed the new voices in Irish literature—F. R. Higgins, Liam O'Flaherty, Eimar O'Duffy— as signaling an historic change in the Irish cultural scene, with a correlative change in the Irish psyche. The biographical-critical "portraits" of established Revival writers also reflect this interest in the cultural context, as in this depiction of John Synge, in the "typical attitude of Anglo-Irish literature," as Synge listened "through a chink in the floor . . . to the talk in the public room below . . . ." It was

> . . . essentially the observation of one cultivated people (the Anglo-Irish) of a race supposed for a long time to be naturally subject. the spirit of an agreeable hostess who delights her guests with scraps of the conversation below stairs (raising a laugh in which none joins in so heartily as the strangers from the other side of the Channel) persists even in Lady Gregory's

1   John Eglinton, *Irish Literary Portraits,* (London: Macmillan and Co, 1935).

2   This was the fourth incarnation of the magazine begun by Ralph Waldo Emerson and Margaret Fuller in 1840. *The Dial* of the 1920s was a monthly established by Scofield Thayer and James Sibley Watson, who bought the fortnightly *The Dial,* for which Ernest Boyd had been Irish correspondent, in 1920. It ran until 1929.

3   "Dublin Letter," Nov. 1921, 593. Except where confusion might occur, articles from *The Dial* will be cited parenthetically, thus: (Nov. 1921, 593).

Kiltartan note-books, and in most of the plays which have made the fortune of the Abbey Theatre.   (May 1926, 361)

Eglinton's perspective, while it originated in this same Anglo-Irish background, did so with a difference. He was acutely aware of the attitude, and wary of its bias.

Eglinton began his first "Dublin Letter" to *The Dial* with a glum warning to "American and English collectors of Anglo-Irish literature" that "the bulk of this literature is uncanonical": "Irish nationality as interpreted by the writers of the 'Literary Renascence' is an ideal entity; the real Irish nation, though it may differ as much from the romantic Ireland of story and song as did Queen Elizabeth personally from the Glorianna of her courtiers and poets, is Catholic Ireland . . ." (Mar. 1921, 332). That a body of literature to be "canonical" should take on the burden of interpreting the "nationality" of its origin may have seemed rather reactionary to Eglinton's peers at *The Dial,* probably the most avant-garde American magazine of its time. As such, it was a sounding board for radically new theories of literary criticism inclined to dismiss matters of origin—biographic or ethnic[4]—a theory to emerge as the New Criticism. *The Dial'*s staff included a number of such critics who came to be associated with that movement as T. S. Eliot, I. A. Richards, Kenneth Burke. Eliot wrote the "London Letter," Ezra Pound, the "Paris Letters."

Into this company came the rather traditional, Wordsworthian Romantic John Eglinton (William K. Magee), an Irish critic-essayist and a member of the coterie of Revival writers, although often at odds with them. Ironically, he, himself, had opposed Revival leaders on this very issue of "nationality" when he argued in 1902 for the purging of Irish literature of this "impurity," that is, the "getting rid of the notion that a writer is to think first . . . of interpreting the nationality of his country and not simply of the burden he has to deliver." In short, he called for the "De-Davisation of Irish Literature."[5] Even earlier he had engaged Yeats and A. E. (George Russell) in a newspaper debate about the related question of the function of a national literature. For Yeats, this function was to "express

4 See "Comment," Jan. 1923, 107, for a statement of the *Dial'*s policy toward "such matters of origin, including approaches through history, biography, ethnology" as "quite aside from the high road of criticism."

5 *The United Irishman,* May 31 1902, 3. The phrase achieved some scattered unattributed fame. Sean O'Faolain simply identifies Eglinton as "our first historian" when he refers to it. See *The Irish* (Devin-Adair Co., 1949), p. 159.

the soul of a nation,"[6] and for A. E., it was "to reveal Ireland in a clear and beautiful light" (81). Eglinton argued that they had got it backwards: national ideals are a product, not a source, of literature; a nation receives its ideals from the poet, not the other way around; thus, "Poets and thinkers have owed far less to their countries than their countries have owed to them" (13).

But Eglinton was out of joint with the time, when few Irish critics were free from the convention of using "nationality" to evaluate a work, a custom which produced such absurdities as Thomas MacDonagh's elevation of Alice Milligan as the "Best Living Irish Poet" because she was "most Irish,"[7] while critics rejected James Stephens's *Insurrections* for the absence of the "Celtic Convention."[8] As such identities as "Anglo-Irish" and "Gaelic Irish" became more politically charged, Eglinton often found himself defending the legitimacy of the Anglo-Irish writers. Rather early on he enlarged, for the record, the national canon to include Swift and other Anglo-Irish figures of the eighteenth century, by redefining the term "Irish Literature" as "the utterance of humanity in Ireland."[9] Ernest Boyd, in his history of the Revival had excluded these "Anglicized" writers, as well as such contemporary counterparts as George Bernard Shaw, as not "informed by the spirit of the race" (*ILR* 10). Even more exclusively, Daniel Corkery called the literature of Boyd's history "alien-minded," and "incapable of further growth."[10]

In the *Dial* period, Eglinton began to concern himself with the nationality issue more frequently. One probable reason for this turn is quite simple: he was here addressing a non-Irish audience and, thus, was himself more self-consciously Irish. Then too, Eglinton's tenure with the *Dial*, beginning in 1921, coincided with a new cycle of the problem of Irish identity, as Ireland passed from the Anglo-Irish War with the agonies of the Treaty, through the Civil War, thence to an ambiguous dominion status as Free State. Moreover, as Eglinton saw it, Irish literature presented

6 First published in the *Daily Express* in 1898. The series was republished as *Literary Ideals in Ireland* (London: T. Fisher Unwin, 1899), p. 131; hereafter cited parenthetically, thus: (*LII* 131).

7 *Irish Review,* September-October 1914, 287.

8 Ernest Boyd, *Ireland's Literary Renaissance* (New York: John Lane Co., 1922) 266–67; hereafter cited parenthetically, thus: (*ILR* 266–67).

9 "Life and Letters," *The Irish Statesman,* July 5, 1919, 42.

10 Daniel Corkery, *Synge and the Anglo-Irish Tradition* (Cork: Cork University Press, 1931), pp. 1–28.

some peculiar conditions for the critic, particularly the fact that the Irish public required "that Irish authors should be true and disinterested interpreters of Irish nationality" (Aug. 1923, 179). Ironically, a few months after writing this statement, Eglinton left Ireland to take up permanent residence abroad, joining a number of literary Wild Geese.

Eglinton's 1921 dismissal of the Anglo-Irish Revivalists as alien to the national psyche was not so final as it may have appeared. He went on for nearly ten years in his *Dial* articles to analyze these writers in the national context, as he did the newer writers, most of them out of the newly ascendant Roman Catholic, "Gaelic" majority. The biographical monographs on George Moore, Yeats, and A. E. were given lead status in *The Dial*. Eglinton called them "stories" and prefaced "George Moore and His Story" with a small defense of the form, perhaps for the benefit of his more "pure" colleagues at *The Dial* who had dismissed "matters of origin." Eglinton never abandoned the Romantic doctrine of literature as self-expression, or as he had earlier expressed it, "Personality in Literature."[11] In *The Dial* article, he mildly suggested that "there are many ways of being interested in literature"; he believed that the "vitality of a work of literary art is in proportion to the interest it excites in the author."

> People who say: "Why trouble about whether Bacon or Shakespeare wrote the plays, so long as we have them" are people whose real interest is not in the arts, and I have more sympathy with the Shakespearean scholar who replied to some observation of this kind, "Well, if I thought it was Bacon who wrote the plays, I would go and blow my brains out!" (Aug., 1926, 91).

In these and other articles, Eglinton also explored an important corollary of the nationality approach, "to see literature as a device for the examination of the Irish mind and character," as one historian put it.[12]

Thus, for Eglinton, just as "Yeats was born to be the poet of Romantic Ireland," James Joyce in his "malign irony" and Moore in his "good-humored indecency" indicated a "profound . . . and as yet a hardly suspected movement of change in the Irish mind."[13] Or was it a change? Perhaps it was a return to the character of Gaelic Ireland. In 1905, Eglinton had seen a similar liberated skepticism in Merriman's "Midnight Court,"[14] and he

11 *Daily Express,* Sept. 17, 1898, 3.

12 E. Ruth Taylor, *The Modern Irish Writers: Cross Currents in Criticism* (Lawrence, Kansas: University of Kansas Press, 1954), p. 39.

13 "George Moore and Holy Ireland," Apr. 1929, 342.

14 "The Best Irish Poem," *Dana,* Feb. 1905, 18.

had noted in the Medieval Oisin-Patrick dialogues[15] something akin to the "confidence in the elemental passions, and scorn of all the timidities of our hesitantly-Christian civilization," he found in the 1927 work of Eimar O'Duffy and in the "buoyant irreverence of the Shavian drama." O'Duffy had "emerged from his studies in Gaelic lore and literature with a spirit emancipated by mockery and mischief. . . . The gaiety and gusto of *King Goshawk and the Birds* quite carry you off your feet" (May 1927, 410). Change or not, it was a new day for Irish literature, and perhaps for the Irish psyche. James Stephens was the "St. John"—the intermediary for the new literature, whose "messiah" might "take the form of a jester, causing a ripple of laughter to pass over the countenance of the Ireland of the Sorrows" (Mar. 1921, 335).

This is not to say that Eglinton used the ethnic approach as a normative standard, nor was it his only concern; in fact, he often considered it in connection with the aesthetic issues more consistent with those of the *Dial* critics—matters of language, for example, as articulated by the Imagists, who elevated the concrete in literary language over the abstract. A related concern, the problem of "thought" in literature had some years earlier absorbed his contemporary Revivalists, Eglinton reported. He recalled that Moore's aesthetic of "pure poetry"—poetry in which no "reflection entered"—had its origins at one of Moore's "evenings" at Ely Place with A. E., who had come up with an almost instantaneous anthology of such poetry.[16]

Unwilling to consider "thought" an impurity, Eglinton developed his own interpretation of the principle, something he called "impassioned intellection," a balance between the emotions and intelligence. It is assertion, not thought, that is the impure ingredient, according to Eglinton. He objected to Yeats's later tendencies to such assertion, which "interrupt the mood in which his art should enwrap us." He suggested that "here we possibly discover the cause of a kind of disjointedness in Mr. Yeats' later work."[17] But Eglinton feared that notions of the "pure" in fiction had influenced Moore to go too far in the other direction in his later novels. *Héloise and Abélard* was one "long series of visualizations" (June 1921, 483), and in *Ulick and Soracha*, the narrative became "rarified to the interest of the visual." Still, for Eglinton, Moore's language did much to redeem such flaws (Nov. 1926, 432).

15 "St. Patrick on the Stage," *The Shanachie*, 5, (1907).
16 "Mr. George Moore as Shanachie," review of *Ulick and Soracha*, Nov. 1926, 432.
17 "Mr. Yeats's Tower," Jan. 1929, 64.

In general, technique in language became much more critical to Eglinton in his *Dial* articles. His review of Yeats's 1921 collection focused on the "curiously felicitous yet often whimsically selected phrase," but he also worried about Yeats's everlasting tinkering—the alterations, "themselves with no air of finality in every new edition." And he asked half-playfully, "Is the moral perhaps that a poet should not entertain too many ideas?" (June 1921, 683).[18] He commended the "objectivity" of Padraic's Colum's language and contrasted it with the abstraction-laden poetry of the early Revival "Protestant poets, with Mr. Yeats at their head," who filled Irish literature with "an ambiguous twilight, peopled with phantom divinities and shadowy beings . . . ."[19] The later poetry of A. E. was similarly fuzzy. A. E. avoided the "inevitable word," substituting "facile epithets like 'mystic,' 'dreamy'. . . . 'starry,'" which produced the effect of "hurried rhetoric rather than intimate recollection." Parenthetically, Eglinton confessed that it was his own inability to conceive of beauty as an "abstraction" which lay behind his "failure to enter into the poetic idealism of the Celtic Renaissance . . . ."The "much admired line . . . 'Eternal beauty wandering on her way'" was to Eglinton "a conception without meaning." For Eglinton, beauty "lives and has its being in the present moment, and to make of beauty an abstraction is to make it an object of belief rather than apprehension."[20]

Colum, however, had "the eye for externals, which do not with him lose their outline in a crepuscular reverie" (Feb. 1928, 124). The "Colum world, clear and distinct [was] interpreted by an eye far more conversant with the things that make up the Irish folk than is that of Mr. Yeats."[21] The explanation, Eglinton speculated, might be found in Colum's fixed Roman faith, "which had left his vision clear for the things of life and nature" (Feb. 1928, 124–25). Thus, while engaging the critical tools of the *Dial* critics—the focus of technique in language—Eglinton was at the same time exploring a new criterion for measuring nationality in literature, accord-

18 Probably *Michael Robartes and the Dancer.* Eglinton did not specify the title of this collection, only that it was a "new volume from Cuala Press." A footnote added that "ten of these poems appeared in the *Dial* for Nov., 1920." In what is described as its "happiest coup," the *Dial* acquired exclusive magazine rights to Yeats's poetry in America at a time when Yeats had only a small national following. See *A Dial Miscellany,* ed. William Wasserstrom (Syracuse: Syracuse University Press, 1963) P. 371.

19 "New Poems of Padraic Colum," Feb. 1928, 124.

20 "A. E. and His Story," Apr. 1927, 275.

21 "The Irish Poetic Tradition," Mar. 1923, 294.

ing to certain national traits: in this case, Colum's Catholicism and his roots in rural, Gaelic Ireland.

Eglinton went to the bardic literature of Ireland to identify a related ethnic characteristic: the "preoccupation" with language. He selected James Joyce as the "key figure" for the new literature partly on the basis of his "almost pedantic preoccupation" with words. Citing the "tundish" passage from *A Portrait of the Artist as a Young Man,* Eglinton warned that, "the foreign critic, unacquainted with Joyce's race and upbringing," was at a disadvantage in understanding Joyce's attitude to language" (May 1929, 420). Irish word-obsession, however, could carry a writer too far, as with the poet Austin Clarke, who in "Pilgrimage" was a modern counterpart of the bards. Eglinton reflected on the abuses of the bardic colleges and their subsequent decline:

> The Irish bard thought no end of himself if he could find fifty adjectives for the word "sea." Language, in fact, was everything to him, and the consequence was that ancient Irish literature, of which the unpublished manuscripts load the shelves of the Royal Irish Academy, is curiously deficient in poetic personalities. (Nov. 1927, 426–27).

"These haughty poets . . . grounded like Senior Wranglers in metrical subtleties and verbal tropes" might have influenced F. R. Higgins. Eglinton thought "Polonius might have approved" of some of the metrical flights of Higgins with his "stalk-crashing marshes," and "moon-drenching orchards" (425).

In any case, the national literary tradition began to take on new dimensions, indicating, perhaps, a corresponding change in the Irish character. This decade saw the emergence of a new genre—"the short, violent tale of peasant life"—with Aodh de Blacam and Daniel Corkery as representative writers (Mar. 1921, 333). Seumas O'Kelly's "The Weaver's Grave" was the masterpiece; it was to "the Irish short story what Synge's *Playboy* was to Irish drama" (Feb. 1923, 357). Eglinton compared the new fiction writers to the Russians, but found the Irish lacking in "that grave contemplation of humble life [practiced by] the Russians," and wondered whether there was "some inherent lack of gravity in the Irish temperament."[22] An exception was Liam O'Flaherty, "a Carleton [who had] read the Russians" (May 1927, 408), and O'Flaherty's work was a striking development in another way: he was "writing as if the Celtic Renascence had never been."

22 "Yeats and His Story," May 1926, 357.

O'Flaherty, "hailing from the last stronghold of an ancient culture . . . the miracle for which Ireland has waited, a pure Gael with literary genius" . . . had turned away from the Celtic sources and instead "hies him to the slums and brothels of Dublin in quest of elemental passions." What did it mean? Eglinton did not see that "abjuring his birthright" had diminished O'Flaherty's power, and asked:

> What secret of human affinities is disclosed in the zest and understanding with which this young islander, his coat still drenched with Atlantic spray, looks round him in this fetid world? Must we conclude that the slum-dweller is an intensified form of the peasant? (409–10)

It was Joyce, however, who produced "a violent interruption" of the Irish Literary Revival with *Ulysses*—Ireland's "most important contribution to literature for some time," (Oct. 1922, 437). It was a "bonfire, glorious while it lasts, of all the pious illusions of provincial and Catholic Ireland," appropriate to a Dublin where "conflagration is the order of the day" (Aug. 1923, 180). "The day," a season of bombings and assassination, colors the tone of some of Eglinton's letters of the early 1920s. Eglinton was far from politically sympathetic to the revolutionaries, and he was, moreover, a pacifist. He prefaced his major discussion of *Ulysses* with a report of a "monstrous explosion" shaking Dubliners, who, rushing out . . . saw going under black volumes of smoke . . . the shreds [of the] ancient archives of Dublin" (Oct. 1922, 435). This report set the scene for a discussion of the reception of *Ulysses* in a city which had no "corporate sentiment likely to take offense at *Ulysses'* cruel realism." Dublin, "no nurse of moral enthusiasms," produces "the scholar and the mocker," typified in Joyce (435–37). Joyce, then, seemed to have taken up the mantle of satirist, a role Eglinton himself had urged on the Revivalist poets in 1903,[23] but for Eglinton Joyce failed as a "philosophic humorist," because he did not "universalize the objects of his mockery." Joyce was too "minutely personal . . . prejudiced by something short of good humor," suggesting the "mere local satirist: thus A. E. passes by, and Mr. Joyce sets us all cachinnating. It is extremely well done, and we cannot help joining in, but it is not—shall I say, very high class" (Oct. 1922, 436).

As further evidence of *Ulysses'* lack of universality, Eglinton reported that, although non-Catholics called it "epoch-making," a "highly intelli-

---

23 "On the Relation of Poets to their Country," *United Irishman*, Feb. 21, 1903, 3. Eglinton contrasted the powers of the Celtic satirists with those of the moderns, and declared that the poet's true relation to his country is one of "admonition and reproof."

gent Catholic, born and bred in Dublin could really savor it perfectly" (435). Eglinton excepted from this charge all that related "to Bloom in this epic work": in the "philosophic Bloom," Joyce had "added a new character to that company of real-imaginary personalities whom we know better than we know ourselves" (436). Also admirable were the "unfailing vitality and purity of his phrase . . . ; his superb powers of mimicry and literary impersonation . . . the half-kindly and painstaking exactness which mitigates his cruelty" (437).

Eglinton's 1922 *Dial* article was a relatively early review of *Ulysses,* which did not get the widespread early coverage Joyce expected.[24] It has some historic interest in its report of the reception of *Ulysses* in Dublin, where such phrases as "it puts Ireland at the head of European literature," circulated "chiefly among the newly emancipated youth of the National University, who disparage the Protestant-minded Shaw . . . and turn to the pure diabolism of Mr. Joyce as to the living powers of a new art." For all this, Eglinton found *Ulysses* a flawed masterpiece in the unrelieved mockery of its tone, which produced a "monotony" of mood—the monotony of "the cinema or the hippodrome" (436). The references to Joyce's cruelty might remind us, if it is necessary, that these comments came from a writer who is also one of the characters in the novel. And however, "half-kindly" Eglinton is presented, his words and ideas are part of the joke of *Ulysses.* Eglinton referred to this situation when he admitted that Joyce's method is puzzling even when he "relates incidents in which I have myself taken a humble part" (June 1922, 622).

By 1929, in his last "Irish letter," Eglinton's perspective had developed to the point that he saw Joyce as perhaps that literary "messiah" he had called for in 1921—"a champion spirit in the new national situation." He selected Joyce as "key-figure" not just for his "preoccupation with language" but also for his influence on literary style in the English language:

> In him for the first time, the mind of Catholic Ireland triumphs over the Anglicism of the English language and expatiates freely in the element of universal language: an important achievement, for what has driven Catholic Ireland back upon the Irish language is the ascendancy in the English language of English literature which . . . is 'saturated with Protestantism,' that is, of the English spirit. . . . In Joyce, literature has reached for the first

24 Two months after publication, Joyce was complaining, "still no review in the English Press." *Letters of James Joyce,* ed. Stuart Gilbert (New York: The Viking Press, 1957), p. 183. Eglinton was one of the few Irish critics to review the novel so early. (Taylor, 65).

time in Ireland a complete emancipation from Anglo-Saxon ideals."

(May, 1929, 419–20).

Joyce also signaled the "ascendancy of the National University over the expiring tradition of Trinity College in Irish culture." As Yeats had been the leading figure for Eglinton's generation, so Joyce had won that place for the youth of the new university, who can "feel they have produced a writer whose influence reaches out . . . to the whole English speaking world." Perhaps Eglinton was approaching this assessment when in 1922 he called *Ulysses* a "violent interruption" of the Revival and looked to the new edition of Boyd's history, in which he would "study its significance" (Oct 1922, 437).

For Ernest Boyd, *Ulysses* was far from an interruption—it was another step in Ireland's "literary and intellectual evolution" (*ILR* 404). In a tone almost combative, he refuted efforts to cut Joyce off "from the stream of which he is a tributary" (404). Like Eglinton, Boyd viewed Joyce as quintessentially Irish, but referred only obliquely to the Catholic dimension when he described Joyce as showing "the imprint of his race and traditions," and *Ulysses* as "a most original dissection of the Irish mind in certain of its phases hitherto ignored." Nor did he see Bloom as a universal; both Bloom and Stephen were "two types of Dubliners" (410). Joyce, then, like the other figures in Boyd's history, was part of the Anglo-Irish canon. It should be noted, however, that Boyd and Eglinton used the term "Anglo-Irish" somewhat differently. Boyd used it to describe Irish literature written in English but "informed by the spirit of the race" (10). For Eglinton, "Anglo-Irish" defined a cultural-religious class. For the most part, they were talking about the same group of writers, but the difference to Eglinton was an important one. They had also some basic disagreements about the staying power of the Anglo-Irish literary tradition. For Boyd, it had produced a "nucleus of a national literature." The Eglinton of 1921, as noted, was more pessimistic but had considerably softened his view by mid-decade.

Aside from this difference in basic assumptions, Eglinton had few quarrels with Boyd's revised history when he reviewed it for *The Dial*.[25] He called it a "complete story." But he found the "story" framework had tempted Boyd to "make heroes out of his characters." Much as Eglinton admired Yeats and A. E., "their figures [dilated] upon the mind after reading Mr. Boyd." And this was "true even of the subordinate characters"—and Eglinton

25 "Anglo-Irish Literature," Apr. 1923, 395.

regarded himself as one of these—who, "even in proportion to our importance in that moment . . .get more than our share of attention." He confessed, "with regard to some pages devoted to my own humble efforts, that I have risen from their perusal with the conviction that after all I am rather a fine fellow." Furthermore, a literary historian should not "hate any of his characters." Boyd had obviously disliked some of the writers, and his manner was uncomfortable toward others. Eglinton did not specify which, but regretted some of the omissions, Shaw and Stephen Gwynne among them (April 1923, 396).

An important difference between Eglinton and Boyd lay in their critical standards. Boyd defended his judgment as "relative" in the world of Anglo-Irish literature (April 1923, 10–17); Eglinton took his standard from comparative literature, evaluating Irish writers in relation to their international counterparts, the Russians, Americans, Spanish, as well as the English. Though he wrote no history of the Revival, Eglinton often wrote as much as an historian as critic in his contributions to *The Dial,* which frequently moved into his own retrospects of that movement, sometimes in seeming digressions. But Eglinton does this more fully in those literary portraits he first published in *The Dial* as biographical-critical studies of the Revival's leading figures and in reviews of their contemporary work.

As a critic-historian in these studies and reviews, Eglinton gave his *Dial* readers fresh glimpses into that world of the Revival and its people, many of whom he knew personally from the beginning. He met Yeats when both were students at the High School in the 1880s. It is interesting to note that, although Yeats's biographers describe him as shy and unhappy at public school in England, this is far from the picture Eglinton gives us of Yeats at the High School, where he was much admired and where "we all felt it a kind of distinction to be seen walking with him." Yeats the schoolboy of Eglinton's memory cribbed his Greek with a cavalier nonchalance, was strong in Euclid and Algebra, and kindly allowed the younger Eglinton to "cog" from him in math exams (Mar. 1922, 299).

After Yeats had left the High School "with small Latin and less Greek" (Mar. 1922, 299), he continued to be an influence there. Indeed, Yeats changed the lives of some when he introduced them to theosophy with the loan of Sinnett's *Esoteric Buddhism* to one of the boys. With some gentle self-parody, Eglinton described the excitement at the school when the book captured the intelligence of half-a-dozen youths "who now had our own views of what the universities could teach us." The stir it created among them—"I read it and I believed!"—was the beginning of the Dublin theosophical movement.[26]

For Eglinton, the involvement with theosophy did much to explain Yeats the man and the poet. It was theosophy which empowered him to "divine the spirit" of Celtic mythology. Eglinton judged Yeats superior to Coleridge partly because "with Yeats, the poet and philosopher were one" (May 1926, 363). If the Abbey Theatre failed Yeats in his dream of a "mystical, ideal drama," it was partly the fault of an audience largely made up of more or less agnostic Anglo-Irish. Eglinton doubted that "even an Athenian audience went to the theatre in the spirit which Yeats demanded of our poor modern mentality with its shreds of belief hanging about it . . . " (362). But when his friends in Dublin heard of Yeats's London success with the Noh drama, they saw it not as a new direction, but as coming full circle: ". . . it was from the East that Yeats snatched the clue to the interpretation of Celtic mythology . . . and it was in the East—in the Noh plays of the Japanese—that he was one day to find the solution of those dramatic problems . . . he had long wrestled somewhat thanklessly in the Abbey Theatre" (358). Yeats was "himself again" (362).

Did the mature Eglinton share the "spirit of belief," which empowered Yeats the poet, even in old age, the spirit which underlay the whole of A.E.'s life? Not so. Although historians frequently identify Eglinton as a "Dublin Theosophist," Eglinton denied that he had ever become one.[27] He confessed he had inherited the "malady of the nineteenth century—doubt" (April, 1927, 271). His characteristic skepticism is recorded in *Hail and Farewell*, as Moore contrasts him with A.E.: "he and you [A.E.] are opposite poles . . . You stand for belief, John Eglinton for unbelief. On one side of me sits the Great Everything, and the other side the Great Nothing." In the same passage, Eglinton calls A.E.'s "interesting heresy" "*AE*-theism," and A.E. says of Eglinton's "contrairy [*sic*] nature," that he was only happy "when contrairy or contradicting. . . ."[28] He became "Contrairy John" in Moore's story. Skeptic though he was, Eglinton was closely associated with the theosophical movement; his brother was a chela with A.E. in the theosophy commune, and theosophical journals published his first essays. The affinity was strongest in Eglinton's attitude toward nature. He prefaced

---

26 "A. E. and His Story," Apr. 1927, 273.

27 *A Memoir of A. E.* (London: MacMillan and Co., 1937), p. 21.

28 George Moore, *Hail and Farewell*, Vol. II, "Salve" (New York: D. Appleton and Co., 1912), pp. 114–16.

"A.E. and His Story" with a rather lengthy summary of the alternative views toward nature from Brahmanism and Buddhism, as contrasted with the Westerns ideals of the "scientific conquest of nature," in order to bring the reader "fully in the thoughts of A.E." (April 1927, 272–73).

The friendship with A.E.—a relationship Eglinton later described as one of master with straying disciple[29]—also began in early youth at a theosophy meeting. A.E.'s youthful intensity, which he never lost, is caught in an account of how he used to haul the sometimes unwilling Eglinton out of his late, homeward-bound train to regale him with recitations of the poet's newest verses and visions, while Eglinton listened a little uneasily. When A.E. translated his theosophical beliefs into a kind of Celtic pantheon, peopled with the "forlorn figures" of Celtic deities, Eglinton was again at a loss. But the popularity of A.E.'s first poetry demonstrated to Eglinton "how widely diffused was the interest in Theosophy" (April 1927, 275). He was not a whole-hearted admirer of the poetry, but granted that as a "poet of ideas," A.E. was unique. As social critic, editor and reformer, A.E. "saw every book and met every distinguished visitor to Ireland." His wide influence included some of the 1916 revolutionaries and may have contributed to their mystic sense of destiny. Eglinton recalled that, in his hearing, P. H. Pearse, a devout Catholic, "avowed his belief in the semi-divine inspiration in the Epic of Cuchullin" (April 1927, 227). And it was Eglinton's view that Russell's ideals had prevailed over those of Arthur Griffith in the new state. "A.E. and His Story" is aptly titled: it is, indeed, quite a story. In 1927, the critic marveled that the somewhat exotic young visionary he had known in his youth should develop to so distinguish himself in the "world of action, art and literature."

> Had I heard that he had suddenly taken wing into the Orient and assumed the yellow robe of a Bikkhu in a Burmese forest, it would have seemed a more appropriate translation from Pim's warehouse than that which the destinies had prepared for him. (272–73)

Eglinton's several *Dial* articles on George Moore are themselves part of a much larger body of writing on this subject. Eglinton reviewed all of Moore's novels of the 1920s for *The Dial*, and Moore figured prominently in Eglinton's reminiscences of the Revival. They met during Moore's Dublin period, and the Eglinton of *Hail and Farewell* is one of the kinder and most accurate portraits in that gallery. Their friendship was one of the

---

29 *A Memoir of A. E.*, p. 30.

few to survive the publication of *Hail and Farewell*. For Eglinton, Moore constituted an excellent specimen for demonstrating the "personality in literature" doctrine. As he put it in "George Moore and Holy Ireland,"

> . . . with the style you must be prepared to accept the man, with his genial vaingloriousness, his incredulous conservatism, the absence from his mind of any hierarchy of ideas, his hatred of all abstractions. . . . The importance with him of all that can be seen, heard, felt, smelled, or tasted over all that can be divined, believed in, prayed for.   (Apr. 1929, 339)

As a critic, Moore had some attitudes about writing that baffled and amused Eglinton—for example, Moore's "humility and assurance, which enabled him to believe that if only he could master grammar, he could attempt anything."[30] As for Moore's notion of literature as a "craft," Eglinton owned that he had often "looked askance" at such judgments as Moore's praise of "Paradise Lost for being well written or Romeo and Juliet for its 'construction'" (Aug. 1926, 93).

Moore's return to Revival Ireland was the turning point for his writing, according to Eglinton, for there "dwelt his best muse, the muse of Recollection" (97). He came into plenary possession of himself in *Hail and Farewell*, where "style and personality are one" (99–100). But his success in *The Lake* and *The Untilled Field* was not so much the effect of Moore's having "learned to write," as Moore had claimed, as it was from the sense of community he found there: " . . . he felt he had colleagues; and these works rightly belong. . . . [to] the Irish Literary Renaissance, for in writing them Moore felt for a brief period that he was writing for friends who had a common aspiration and also a common enemy" (97). Even so, critics have wondered why Eglinton never wrote a full-blown memoir of Moore, as he had done for A. E., and as Moore, himself, desired. Whatever the reasons, one thing is clear: Eglinton was not always an admirer of Moore's work. Moore once autographed a copy of one of his novels, "To John Eglinton, who likes me better than he likes my books" (99). In his letters, Moore's responses were rarely so resigned; he was once infuriated when he felt that Eglinton had given more space to Yeats's "poem about his daughter" than to *Héloise and Abélard*, and, after a rift of some months, he wrote, rather sadly, "You are without aesthetics . . . and I with little else."[31]

In Eglinton's Moore articles, especially, we have some rather interest-

30 "George Moore and His Story," Aug. 1926, 99–100.
31 John Eglinton (ed.) *Letters of George Moore*, "with an Introduction by John Eglinton to whom they were written" (Bournemouth: Sydenham, 1942), pp. 60–61.

ing perspectives on this phase of the Revival: how that "daemonic man'
Yeats fetched Moore to be the "Voltaire of Ireland," and how Moore's
"quizzical attention was more and more diverted from the enemy to these
new friends," until he saw that "it was they rather than the powers he had
come to make war upon could provide him with a new literary subject"
(98–99). And often, as in the impressions of other Revival leaders, Eglinton
got at something essential about his subject, whatever the validity of his
theories about "the style and the man."

> Life at any rate remains perennially wonderful to George Moore. His orig-
> inal endowment from nature was a gift of startled curiosity about every-
> thing that life was to unfold before his gaze, and he must have disconcerted
> his nurse with the same amazed and speculative pair of eyes which in early
> manhood he directed upon Manet while the latter painted his portrait.
>
> (98)

As retrospects of the Revival, Eglinton's *Dial* articles have much to
recommend them. And while we have a number of such retrospects, they
are often from the point of view of the second generation, like those of
Colum, Stephens, or Lennox Robinson. Eglinton offers, to set beside the
accounts by Yeats, Lady Gregory, and Moore, another glimpse by one of
that same generation, with neither the hero-worship and reticence of Lady
Gregory nor the malice of Moore. The more general "Dublin Letters" also
supplement the record of the critical climate and literary production of the
immediate post-Revival period: a discussion of Yeats as senator of the Free
State, an event Eglinton could not resist comparing with a similar situation in *The King's Threshold* (Feb. 1923, 191); the state of such periodicals as
A. E.'s *Irish Statesman,* to which Eglinton contributed; the progress of the
Abbey Theatre, and other literary-cultural matters.

As for Eglinton's Anglo-Irish, "unionist" bias, we might note that it
sometimes flared up in irritated reaction to some of the exaltations of the
new state like that of Arthur Clery, who proclaimed: "The Age of Pearse
will, after time, have a glory like that of Pericles" (Nov. 1921, 333). The bias
might also account for the occasional lapse into a tone almost bitter, at times
petulant. He was inclined to object to novels that used political revolutions
as subject, particularly when written with the "biblical unction," he saw
in Aodh de Blacam's *Holy Romans* (Mar. 1921, 333). When he reviewed the
1928 Tailteann Games, he suggested disqualifying "your Irish correspondent" for reasons of "temperament hardly less than by force of circumstances." He described the celebration as "pathetic" in the ironic incon-

sistencies of a state distributing awards for literature with one hand, while with the other it was drafting censorship laws. (Nov. 1928, 423).

In this mood, Eglinton fell into some inconsistencies of his own. He ridiculed the awarding of a prize to Shaw for *St. Joan,* an achievement "no more Irish than the winning of Waterloo" (423), apparently forgetting that he had criticized Boyd's history for excluding Shaw. In a similar case, he objected to A.E.'s promotion of the eighteenth-century writers to the national canon (Dec. 1925, 496), when a few years earlier, Eglinton had made the same move. Was this a change in Eglinton's point of view of what was "Irish" in Swift and Shaw? Or was he demonstrating the "contrairiness" of the John Eglinton of *Hail and Farewell?* According to Moore, on at least one occasion, "Contrairy John was confused and roundabout and at the end of many an argument found himself defending the very principles that he had started out to controvert" (347). But on the other hand, the narrator (if not Moore himself) of that fiction does not strike one as very astute in perceiving the subtleties which are a hallmark of Eglinton's expression.

An ironic charm pervades much of Eglinton's writings, including those historical-philosophic digressions, with which he intertwined his essays. He once defended such digressions, claiming that "the best of writing about literary personalities . . . [is that] you can bring in so many things before literature!"[32] But many of these flights need no justification beyond the pleasure of this supple and insightful prose, as in this small musing on the "love of animals" which emerged from a discussion of Colum's *Creatures:*

> The love of animals has not been enjoined by ethical teachers, springing as it does from affinities within us, original like sin; yet if I should hear of a man that he was pre-eminently concerned with the weal of his neighbors, I would not have the same expectations . . . were I told . . . that he was fond of tigers. Such a man could not fail to be endowed by nature with some real and lucid disinterestedness of soul. . . . The two sympathies which enter into our feeling for animals, admiration and pity—admiration for [their] ruthless efficiency . . . within their limitations, and pity for their imprisonment within these limitations—are also perhaps the specifically human instincts, and in the exercise of them we are least likely to forget that we are animals ourselves; animals who have lost contact with nature, saving in so far as we can recapture lost affinities through the exercise of a

32 "Life and Letters," *The Irish Statesman,* Sept. 13, 1919, 290.

comprehensive, all-atoning human faculty which we name imagination. ("New Poems," 125–26)

Certainly no accusation of religious bias can be directed at Eglinton's treatment of Colum, who was admirable "both as a poet and as a human being" (126). In "Irish Poetic Tradition," Eglinton compared Colum to Robert Burns and suggested that Ireland had just missed having in Colum such a national poet, who "might have put new heart into the Irish countryside." What interfered with this development? Eglinton wondered whether it was "his exile, now apparently voluntary" (Mar. 1923, 295). Soon to be an exile himself, the critic looked wistfully after the exile poet and complained of the "air of wistfulness" brought into Colum's poems by his move to America.

—*Montana State University*

COVER

We close the twenty-ninth volume of ÉIRE-IRELAND with the last of four photographs depicting artifacts of popular, material culture housed in the collections of the Ulster Folk and Transport Museum at Cultra Manor. Our readers may remember that our first cover depicted a vivid and touching sampler from Ballyhay, County Down; the second a silver snuff box incised with Orange symbols, from Dromore; and the third a chaste and autumnal bar-and-stripe quilt from Teeshin, County Derry. Appropriately wintery in coloration, our last cover depicts an unfinished cuff of braid lace crafted in the 1900s. Crafted as either a pastime or a cottage industry, this type of lacework involved first twisting a braid or tape into a decorative or utilitarian shape, then stitching it to a ground fabric, and then working decorative embroidery between the basted tapes following lines marked on the ground fabric—working, however, over rather than through the ground. A finished piece of lacework was released from the ground by unpicking the basting holding the tapes. The ground and its design often were stored for reuse. In this instance, the lace cuff, being unfinished, remains attached to the blue material of the ground. As before, the photograph is by Kenneth Anderson and appears by kind permission of Dr. R. A. Gailey, director of the Ulster Folk and Transport Museum.

DUBLIN LETTERS: JOHN EGLINTON AND *THE DIAL,* 1921–1929

"A PARTICULAR FLAIR, A HOUND'S NOSE, A KEEN SCENT": SEAN O'FAOLAIN'S EDITORSHIP OF *THE BELL*

HEATHER BRYANT JORDAN

SEAN O'FAOLAIN chose the occasion of the first birthday of his monthly magazine *The Bell* to reflect upon its progress toward "distinguish[ing] between life and non-life."[1] In the autumn of 1941, it was his view that continued success could only be assured through vigilant application of a "hound's nose" to all matters Irish.[2] Such spiritedly self-conscious exhortations mark O'Faolain's editorials which opened almost every issue of his determinedly eclectic journalistic enterprise. In April, 1946, when O'Faolain passed the torch to his managing editor Peadar O'Donnell, a great deal was lost, although the diminishment did not make itself immediately apparent. It became clear that it had been O'Faolain who made cohere the contradictory and energetic paradoxes *The Bell* embodied; when he turned his attention elsewhere, the pressing vitality continued to dissipate until it flickered out in the fragmentary last issue of December, 1954. His editorship became synonymous with an era of imaginative and practical possibility in a time of war and isolation.

It comes as no surprise that the magazine O'Faolain founded expressed his own far-reaching attitudes and interests. Every issue plays out the conflicting convictions he held in tension. What is perhaps more remarkable is the way he fearlessly and eagerly sought to expose and explore these clashes. He craved intellectually honest debate, a goal that sounds all too elusive today. His editorials and the myriad monthly choices he made show him mediating passionately among the debates informing his time: between old and new, regional and international, rural and urban, Catholic and sectarian, isolated and unified, sophisticated and plain, myth and

1   *Bell* 2(6): 12.
2   *Bell* 2(6): 12.

reality, romantic and sentimental, native and European, Gaelic and English, literature and politics, artifice and laissez-faire, church and state, intellectual and practical, northern and southern, colonial and independent, established and fledgling, subjective and objective.

His selection of a name for the magazine, taken from *Kolokel*, a Russian newspaper supplement edited by Alexsandr Herzen and published in Geneva and London from 1857 through 1867, illustrates O'Faolain's many-layered quest. Such a choice underscores Hubert Butler's observation that O'Faolain was "not merely making a magazine but shaping a literature, or calling it into being."[3] Saying he was taken by "bell" as a "spare and hard and simple word," he also claimed to want a word with no associations.[4] By following in the liberal tradition of Herzen's earlier publication under an oppressive regime—one which had inspired the imaginations of Tolstoy, Dostoevsky, and Turgenev—he was placing himself within a context, within a parameter of associations already made. At the same time that he longed to strike out on his own, to create a new and unsullied medium for expression, O'Faolain was recalling an already established nontraditional tradition.

Such paradoxes color every aspect of O'Faolain's tenure at *The Bell*. Hoping the magazine could simultaneously see within and without Ireland, O'Faolain yearned "to see clearly" into the heart of a "young nation" but also to direct "a telescope on the busy coast of Europe."[5] He also found himself caught between his articulated desire to provide the life spirit of the publication while fervently and repeatedly declaring his mandate to his readership "This is your magazine."[6] Even as he wished to allow "nature" "to give the magazine its own time created character," he fought to impose his own unmistakable imprint.[7] This was a sleight of hand extraordinaire. In his juggling act, O'Faolain further struggled with the defining schism of his career: the life of the mind and the life of action. By heeding his perennial desire to forge a link between idealism and realism, he set up his criteria for discourse "decent, friendly, possibly hot-tempered, but always polite and constructive."[8] Whatever the internal

3   Hubert Butler, "*The Bell*: An Anglo-Irish View," *Irish University Review* 6(1): 71.
4   *Bell* 1(1): 5.
5   *Bell* 1(2): 6; *Bell* 10(5): 434.
6   *Bell* 1(1): 5.
7   *Bell* 1(1): 5.
8   *Bell* 1(2): 5.

dichotomies, they spoke to an eager audience; *The Bell* sold out on the first day it appeared in Dublin.[9] According to its proud editor, only the *Nation* had met such an enthusiastic reception.[10] Eventually, the magazine would make its way into the inner reaches of the country; in later years O'Faolain remembered the way *The Bell* was sold in small towns "under the counter with a furtiveness associated with pornography."[11]

Eventually enjoying a circulation of three thousand, or half that of *The Partisan Review, The Bell* quickly began to assume a recognizable identity. The circulation reached significantly beyond Ireland; a thousand of its readers lived abroad. In his mission, O'Faolain relied on a talented editorial board: Peadar O'Donnell, Anthony Cronin, Maurice Walsh, Rosin Walsh, and, as poetry editor, first Frank O'Connor and then Geoffrey Taylor. Regular feature writers like Larry Morrow, alias "The Bellman," and Michael Farrell, or "Gulliver," began to appear in each issue. Together they drew on an astonishingly wide range of contributors from the well-known Elizabeth Bowen, Erskine Childers, John Hewitt, Patrick Kavanagh, Freda Laughton, Louis MacNeice, Vivian Mercier, and Honor Tracy, to amateurs and professionals in a variety of fields. The words of lawyers, doctors, nurses, and even a former prisoner, identified as such, graced the pages. The Christmas, 1942, number included the following: a poem by Maurice James Craig, fiction by Bryan MacMahon, articles on crime in Dublin, Trollope in Ireland, "People and Pawnshops," and the inimitable "A Day in the Life of a Dublin Mechanic."[12]

In a magazine known for publishing and furthering the work of some of the most important creative writers of the period, it is always refreshing to note the emphasis on the practical and the everyday. Indeed, *The Bell's* merging of the two realms challenges our familiar division between the two. Never did O'Faolain show patience with lofty intellectualism. In keeping with his own definition of the intellect as "the source of the moral sense that keeps the imagination in touch with whatever is sane in common life," O'Faolain wanted to know of what and of whom northern and southern Ireland were composed.[13] He set inquiries into what people ate, drank, where they lived, how much money they made, what they got sick

9   *Bell* 1(2): 5.
10 *Bell* 1(2): 5.
11 Julia O'Faolain, "Sean at Eighty," *London Magazine* 20(3): 22.
12 *Bell* 5(3):
13 Sean O'Faolain, *Vive Moi!* (Boston: Little Brown, 1964) 246.

with, how they raised their children; in essence, how they lived their lives. Consequently, the publication offered commentary on such concerns as fashion with a wide range of attitudes. In answering a query on women's hats for an article by Eileen O'Faolain on the topic, Elizabeth Bowen shared her hopes for "simplicity" in the new designs, complaining that "too many Irish ladies ruin their style by trimmings."[14] An article on Irish whiskey, by Maurice Walsh, declared it "the best . . . in the world."[15] And an anonymous report of a country doctor claimed he would rather work with the Irish because they are "more human, if more demanding."[16] Reviews of spring flower shows, Dublin pubs, museums, and other treasures of culture solidified the impression that O'Faolain sought to convey life in Ireland. Yet, by such focus on matters Irish, on the concrete and near at hand, the erstwhile editor left himself open to frequent charges of what he despised most—provincialism.

Intensely aware of his critics, O'Faolain constantly took the magazine's pulse in an effort to gauge how well he was succeeding at the task he had set for himself.[17] A self-consciousness at odds with his immersion in the objective and external world suffused the editor's apparent purpose. In an extended series commissioned by O'Faolain on the press, "The Fourth Estate," Vivian Mercier gave his own opinion of both *The Bell* and the man who presided over it: "Sean O'Faolain *is the Bell*. . . . He is not just a figurehead—he is the magazine . . . and if I am not careful, he will write most of this article too."[18] Mercier found that the editor's active involvement cut both ways; he was on the one hand the "most stimulating editor one could hope to find" and on the other hand he was overly "in love with the written word—provided he himself had written it."[19] This "hard task master" had achieved a great deal in *The Bell*, but Mercier argued his overinvestment led to "too much free criticism and advice" combined with an "editorial condescension" that he viewed as a serious mistake.[20] Mercier's most compelling comment addressed O'Faolain's and thus, *The Bell*'s confusion over its roles. The critic pointed to the implicit and enduring tension between the descriptive tag on the magazine's note-

14 *Bell* 1(4): 73.
15 *Bell* 2(5): 24.
16 *Bell* 3(1): 6.
17 *Bell* 1(1): 5.
18 *Bell* 10(2): 157.
19 *Bell* 10(2): 157.
20 *Bell* 10(2): 157.

paper proclaiming it a "Magazine for Creative Fiction" and the subtitle on every cover, "A Survey of Irish Life."[21]

Throughout his years at *The Bell*, O'Faolain labored to bring the imaginative creative life together with the frequently less than fascinating details of everyday existence in Ireland. The result of his work gives a sense of just how many expectations the journal tried to answer as it combined, in Mercier's comparison, the characteristics of *Horizon, New Statesman and Nation, John Alantin's Weekly,* and *World Review.*[22] For American reference points he chose an amalgam of *Partisan Review, The New Republic, The Saturday Review of Literature,* and *Harper's Magazine* with *Life* or maybe *Picture Post* as well.[23] To this composite one could add *Yankee Magazine, Good Housekeeping,* and the *New York Review of Books.* O'Faolain's desire to gain a wide audience, to open the minds of what he perceived to be his constituency led to an unusual pastiche of features. Despite Mercier's fairly pointed criticisms, he concluded that O'Faolain must have been doing something right: "The fact that *The Bell* has been able to win and keep a public for itself" was a hopeful sign.[24] In a climate highly toxic to the survival of such ventures—*Ireland To-Day,* for example, had recently collapsed—O'Faolain's journal was paying its way and could, Mercier speculated, sell more copies than the paper quota allowed.[25]

O'Faolain himself summarized the responses to a questionnaire he had run in the spring of 1945. After ranking the readers' preference for features—editorials on the world first and book reviews last—he shared some of the commentary, selectively pruned. In the "Verdict on *The Bell*," O'Faolain described the kindness of the reactions, saying that ultimately the outpouring had been "something of a Roman holiday" for the editor.[26] Yet, he too recorded the now familiar point of contention: had the journal "lived up to its birthday promise of being a magazine of creative fiction?"[27] Defensively, the editor replied with characteristic surety that "the general *Bell* public do not want a literary magazine."[28] Not to be accused of unwarranted partisanship, he did select some negative press as well: re-

21 *Bell* 10(2): 158.
22 *Bell* 10(2): 158.
23 *Bell* 10(2): 158.
24 *Bell* 10(2): 164.
25 *Bell* 10(2): 164.
26 *Bell* 10(5): 437.
27 *Bell* 10(5): 434.
28 *Bell* 10(5): 434.

porting that one reader called the enterprise a "pretentious attempt to instill Paris atmosphere into agricultural Éire."[29] The gentler responses were easier to take: he took justifiable pride in the comment on his balanced nature: "Your editor is one of those unique Irish writers who use their heads as well as their stomachs."[30] He was also pleased with a reader's down-to-earth commendation of *The Bell* as "the healthiest periodical in the country."[31] For the gutsy leader, such talismans confirmed that he was adhering to his desire to remain grounded in the real world, the realm of the mind and the body.

By the spring of 1945, just a year before O'Faolain stepped down, the magazine had assumed a predictable, if eclectic shape. One could count on poems and short stories by established writers side by side with work by younger ones, always heartily encouraged. In fact, much space was devoted to advice to new writers, with O'Connor noting nostalgically that "the Editor wishes to keep in each number of *The Bell* a few pages for people trying their hand at literature, as he and I once tried it in Cork."[32] In a feature on "New Writers" O'Faolain kept his promise. He selected one story for extended criticism, with the aim of helping the "author and other younger writers."[33] O'Connor also commented, as requested, on a "mediocre poem" cautioning, "don't write verse unless you have to. . . . Don't write out of your head."[34] Both established writers saw this column as an opportunity to nourish the next generation, to keep literature alive through innovation and continuity. Together they remembered the vitality and cooperation of their early days and sought to create a forum where such literary experimentation could take place within a continuing dialogue. They sympathized with those eager souls who were struggling to break into a closed and depressed literary world.

At base, O'Faolain's perennial fascination with the writer as a person was palpable in every issue. Consider his selection of biographies of both major and minor figures, as well as sometimes idiosyncratic autobiographical reflections like "The Swaggering Caravan," Micheál Mac Liammóir's spirited recollections of life in the country theater. In Mercier's

29 *Bell* 10(5): 436.
30 *Bell* 10(5): 436.
31 *Bell* 10(5): 436.
32 *Bell* 1(1): 92.
33 *Bell* 1(5): 61.
34 *Bell* 1(5): 61.

view, such features reflected the writer's attempt to "exploit their personalities."[35] Conversely, serial articles such as "Penal Servitude," penned by "a man who has paid the price of his folly and now bravely looks backward and forward," attempted to record important, if less appealing, "facts" of Irish individualism.[36] Side by side with interpretations of the vicissitudes of human frailty existed art and architecture and book reviews, usually, in Mercier's opinion, "the most capriciously treated of all."[37] Michael Farrell's reviews of amateur theater all over Ireland closed each issue with vigorous and lively commentary. The journal was more than the sum of its parts; each section depended heavily on the person responsible for it.

In addition to the more familiar components of a monthly magazine, other items peculiar to *The Bell* gave the publication its distinctive character. "Public Opinion," or the letters section, "Interviews" with the "Bellman" (Larry Morrow), "Mise Éire," and "The Open Window" all had an enchanting, if alternately infuriating, tone. "Mise Éire," modeled on the *New Statesman's* "This England," asked for press cuttings on "Good critical snippets on Irish life . . . rather than howlers, bulls, misprints, or inane idiocies."[38] A book token was promised for the prizewinning entry, once awarded to the selection, "We need some straight information regarding lovemaking in Ireland."[39] Another star contender hailed from a "sign in Hospital in west": "During this intense cold and owing to the scarcity of coal, no unnecessary operations will be performed."[40] Begun in January, 1943, "The Open Window," modeled on *Dana's* "Literary Causier," encouraged exchanges with its readers.[41] Also known as "A Monthly Perambulation by Gulliver," it was declared a place where "personal opinions will have full scope and the editor abdicates (growling impudently)."[42] For articles of unusual interest on matters Irish at home and abroad, Gulliver (Michael Farrell) offered book tokens, welcoming "prejudices of

35 *Bell* 10(2): 161.
36 *Bell* 9(1): 41.
37 *Bell* 10(2): 161.
38 Peter Denman "Ireland's Little Magazines," in *Three Hundred Years of Irish Periodicals,* ed. Barbara Hayley, Edna McKay (Mullingar, Co. Westmeath: Lilliput Press, 1987), 133; *Bell* 2(3): 47.
39 *Bell* 1(4): 32.
40 *Bell* 2(2): 58.
41 Denman, 133.
42 *Bell* 5(4).

all sorts."[43] Indeed, Gulliver set competitions of varying degrees of relevance and difficulty. He once staged a contest for the best statement on the place in Europe that meant the most to the writer. "The Open Window" came in third for reader's preference after the editorials, so it must have spoken well to its audience. For Mercier, it was *The Bell*'s "most successful attempt to run an 'amateur corner'."[44] Although at times it resembled an insider's box, it certainly distinguished the journal from its competitors.

Looking back on *The Bell*, we can see repeated examples of O'Faolain's concerted attempt to play off the established tradition of small magazines while at the same time creating his own forum. Particularly evident in his self-conscious mission was his sense of competition, simultaneously spoken and unspoken, with his most obvious rival, the English journal *Horizon*. He had set himself a rough task. Begun in the same year, Cyril Connolly's London-based magazine ran until 1950. This other journal born of wartime fears about the starvation of culture became a continuing and oftentimes vexing benchmark for O'Faolain. When he raised the price of the *Bell* from one shilling to one shilling six pence in December, 1941, he justified the move on a comparative basis: *Horizon* had to raise its price "long before we did."[45] When he advised his readers to sell, rather than lend, their copies of his magazine, he prized this method over Connolly's "Begging Bowl." This practice encouraged readers to send extra money to authors of articles they favored; to O'Faolain, this seemed a scandalous practice for a journal "centered in a wealthy country, at the heart of an Empire, . . . and like nine English periodicals out of ten, heavily subsidized."[46]

The Irish editor kept *Horizon* in his readers' minds for more reasons than financial ones. Advertisements for the English journal frequently appeared and sometimes acrimonious exchanges occurred. When *Horizon* branded *The Bell* provincial, O'Faolain bristled in his editorial on the topic in May, 1941.[47] And when *Horizon* published an Irish issue in January, 1942, to which both O'Faolain and O'Connor contributed, O'Faolain wanted to answer with an English one, until logistical difficulties interfered, transforming the response into an "International Issue." In March, 1946, the dialogue continued with Donat O'Donnell (Conor Cruise O'Brien)

43 *Bell* 5(4).
44 *Bell* 10(2): 161.
45 *Bell* 5(1): 1–2.
46 *Bell* 5(1): 2.
47 *Bell* 2(2): 5.

offering a critique of *Horizon*, emphasizing that the journal "never pretended that its heart was in politics."[48] Noting the "internationalism" on which *Horizon* "prides itself," he too wrote of how it "condemns the provincialism of such magazines as *The Bell*."[49] Even after O'Faolain had left the helm of *The Bell*, the sense of internal competition he had instilled in it remained. The presence of *Horizon* had allowed O'Faolain to define himself against what he was not. To found a magazine and to keep it running in wartime required not only ingenuity but also a sense of purpose and audience. O'Faolain kept himself busy cultivating both.

Not content to let the project be, O'Faolain was eager to pronounce on what he was doing while he was doing it. Conscious of cultivating his own tradition in Ireland without recourse to many immediate practical resources, he filled the pages of *The Bell* with references to past editorials, advertisements for future issues, thanks to advertisers, notes on books by contributors, and advertisements for boxed sets of the magazine. He favored boxes over binding as a "more elegant method," open at the back, with title and volume number, and finished in "attractive red cloth."[50] In 1944, he gladly announced the publication of *The Bell* anthology of poetry, *Irish Poems of To-Day*, sponsored by an "anonymous donor," who also made possible yearly prizes for the best short story and poem published in the magazine. He established other mementos by running offers of subscription notice cards printed by the Cuala Press, as well as sometimes off-beat invitations to readers, such as the recreation of a particular week in the Earl of Tyrone's diary. O'Faolain selected the week his subject had eloped, hoping for some outrageous responses. Not to be deterred when he received no entries, he set another competition for an elegy on the Death of a Censor. For this verse, to be based on Gray's churchyard poem, he received some less than satisfactory entries. These sometimes peculiar, but always imaginative, requests show the editor actively establishing and preserving his perceived piece of culture in a time of trouble.

Unlike *Horizon*, *The Bell* had to keep World War II in perpetual shadow, precisely because of the rules of censorship O'Faolain so despised. But external events exerted a tremendous pressure on the editor, a pressure he found exhilarating if, at times, daunting; in recalling these years, O'Faolain remembered feeling "fully integrated because I was on the attack. I had ac-

---

48 *Bell* 11(6): 1033.
49 *Bell* 11(6): 1035.
50 *Bell* 2(2): 38.

cepted my responsibility as a citizen and thought of myself as speaking for a great and silent majority."[51] For several years, he could meld all his Yeatsian elements together and by magic and hard work make them all cohere in *The Bell.* Nowhere was this more apparent than in his sometimes lengthy, yet always intense, editorials at the beginning of each issue. To read these is to get a sense of the course of O'Faolain's journey through the "Great Emergency." Not surprisingly, however, the debates he argued, the fights he fought against advocates of censorship, the overbearing Gaelic League, the shrill intellectuals, the petty demagogues, the mourners of the past, the Anglophiles, the foolish sentimentalizers, and the peddlers of the mindless symbols, began to wear thin. As long as the war was on, O'Faolain could unite his efforts in a compressed focus; the Emergency allowed him to see clearly as he labored to mitigate against provincialism through editorials such as the series entitled "One World."

But when the boundaries imposed by isolation and censorship expanded, O'Faolain became restless to return to his own work. By his account, "Tired of the fight" he "wanted to be a private person again."[52] Such dedicated editorial missions had certainly taken away from his other work. After being held taut in wartime, his own ambivalent and many-layered energies began to emerge as disruptive rather than cohesive forces. With fatigue came a certain regretful bitterness and vituperation; in his final editorial blast O'Faolain described growing "weary of abusing our bourgeoisie, little Irelanders, chauvinists, puritans, stuffed-shirts, pietists, Tartuffes, Anglophobes, Celtophobes, et alii hujus generis."[53] He had come a long way from his enthusiastic "memo for Businessman" in July, 1941, when he wrote: "we were warned that our printing order for 5,000 copies was just a 'poet's dream' and the new order is 500 pages above 1st, with 60 pages of advertising over six numbers."[54] After O'Faolain, *The Bell* was not to attain such success.

Although the magazine continued to appear, under O'Donnell's leadership it slowly lost in editorial distinctness and fire. He wrote fewer of his own editorials, increasingly asking guest writers to contribute, as O'Faolain had only rarely done. This abdication makes us all the more aware of the former editor's presence throughout the magazine. In these later years,

51 Julia O'Faolain, 20.
52 Julia O'Faolain, 22.
53 *Bell* 12(1): 1.
54 *Bell* 2(4): 54.

SEAN O'FAOLAIN'S EDITORSHIP OF *THE BELL*

proprietary feelings would occasionally surface and the former editor would return, as in a heated 1947 debate with Peadar O'Donnell on the Palestinian issue, or to argue with the bishop of Galway's charge of "rancour" toward *The Bell*.[55] But gradually O'Donnell's interest in rural conditions, economic, and social problems began to nudge the journal in a different direction as editorials such as "The Donkey Cart" and "Grand Children of the Insurrection" suggest. With a less present editor, the energy of *The Bell* began to diffuse as its vibrancy diminished, concurrently decreasing in humor and in self-consciousness. Many familiar features appeared only intermittently, or disappeared altogether. By December, 1947, O'Donnell was appealing for renewed readership, crying financial distress. The following spring, *The Bell* suspended publication for the first time in its history. When it resumed in November, 1950, it was even more irregular, trying a stint at seasonal publication in the summer of 1953. It became a monthly again in the winter of 1954, costing 2 shillings. The last issue of December, 1954 was, in the editor's own words, "frankly a miscellany."[56] Even for him, this was an understatement. It began with a reprinting of Sartre's address on the atomic bomb, "A Weapon Against History," was followed by articles on cancer, Henry Matisse, and two childrens' stories by Yeh Sheng-Tao. Without O'Faolain's vision and editorial posture the *Bell* had lost its center and had fallen victim to its own policy of inclusiveness. What Maurice Harmon has identified as the "force and vigor of his creative imagination" had made such eclecticism—and cultivation of audience—possible.[57] Under O'Donnell, after the war, both personality and circumstance had altered and *The Bell* had lost its focus and purpose.

Years later, O'Faolain wrote in his autobiography that "Every writer is a man with one deaf ear and one blind eye, who is possessed by a demon and unteachable by anybody but himself."[58] It was precisely this demonic quality which made *The Bell* what it became: lively, eccentric, all-encompassing, sometimes passionate, sometimes bizarre, unceasing in its drive to explore every particle of life in Ireland. O'Faolain's daughter described what he had accomplished in *The Bell* as a clearing away "of the ground of

55 *Bell* 17(6).

56 *Bell* 12(11): 5.

57 Maurice Harmon, *Sean O'Faolain: A Critical Introduction* (Dublin: Wolfhound Press, 1984), 18.

58 O'Faolain, *Vive Moi!* 242.

myths so that people could start to think."[59] This enterprise was not without its costs; she pointed to the struggle at the center of his editorship between "Sean the citizen" and the "writer who preferred personal relationships, privacy, and art."[60] For six years he had been a magician, able to forge a union among wildly disparate people and ideas under the pressure of the demands and opportunities provided by war. He had brought a lively and provocative debate to a troubled and uncertain time, debating issues we see all too clearly before us now—nationalism, political correctness, isolationism, and the role of the individual in the modern state. For the far-seeing editor in peacetime, the divide between private and beyond, "life" and "non-life," as O'Faolain had once called it, became too great to bridge through the medium of *The Bell*.

—*Harvard University*

59 Julia O'Faolain, 23.
60 Julia O'Faolain, 23.

TUARASCÁIL AR THEANGA: LANGUAGE REPORT

IRISH IN EDUCATION AND THE MEDIA, 1994

JAMES J. BLAKE

THE CURRENT parlous state of the Irish language is illustrated by events—and often by nonevents—in education and in the media, including print. The primary difficulty impeding a healthy revival of Irish-language usage or, at the very least, stemming the decline of its use, directly results from negative attitudes toward the language. Yet, despite the accumulating force of the Irish people's negative reaction generally against the language, professional sociological surveys of present-day attitudes toward the language have revealed, oddly enough, that seventy-five percent of the people are sympathetic to Irish as a school subject for children. In order to be as objective as possible, the sociolinguist Joshua Fishman of Yeshiva University in New York was hired in the 1970s in order to lead a research team which discovered that some latent sympathies for the language persisted.

The latest survey (1994) by Pádraig Ó Riagáin and Mícheál Ó Gliasáin has been issued by the Linguistic Institute of Ireland, and it reveals similar findings, including the fact that none of the English-speaking majority registering sympathetic attitudes about teaching Irish would ever entertain the notion of actually speaking the language. The language is simply not perceived by them as a means of normal communication. Instead, it is sensed as a disembodied school subject comparable to mathematics and geography. Consequently, the editors of *Comhar* (March, 1994) wonder out loud whether the various Irish language organizations need training in reality testing. Are they figuratively on another planet in relation to the actual status of the language now? If the vast majority of Irish people—seventy to eighty percent—do not use Irish, and only about ten percent can conduct conversations in Irish, what plans have these largely government-sponsored organizations developed to reverse this trend? And, then, are these seventy to eighty percent surveyed the same seventy-five percent who are in favor of keeping Irish as a subject in the schools? The signals quite obviously conflict.

Over the past thirty years, the statistics from these periodic surveys reveal a consistent ten percent of the population who customarily speak Irish. Unfortunately, however, all reports indicate that the use of the Irish language in the *Gaeltachtaí* continues to decline precipitously. There may no longer be any monoglot Irish speakers alive today, although no documented evidence has been published to support such a claim. The children in the *Gaeltachtaí* are universally bilingual and are now adopting English under pressure from the media and from the overwhelming dominance of the English language in all aspects of social, institutional, church, and state life in contemporary Ireland. Furthermore, claims have recently been made in the weekly newspaper *Anois* that the Department of Education is trying to undermine the study of Irish in primary and secondary schools by instituting a system of easily obtainable exemptions from the requirement to study Irish as part of the mandatory curriculum.

The emphasis on teaching Irish was curtailed in the late 1970s when Irish was removed as a "compulsory" subject in the schools. Groups with names like the "Language Freedom Movement" successfully launched campaigns claiming, remarkably, that English speakers, not Irish speakers, were oppressed in Ireland—an Alice-in-Wonderland claim that led to undermining the limited public recognition that the language had previously achieved. The argument put forward then was that young children in the English-speaking areas of Ireland, which is most of the country, should be given the option to study Irish voluntarily, with the presumed enthusiastic encouragement of their parents. It was hypocritically asserted that, as a result of their heartfelt love of the language, they would soon master it.

Another major blow to the language was the closing by the government in the late 1960s of the all-Irish teacher training colleges. Since that time, the quality of teaching as well as student mastery of Irish has further eroded. These activities, interpreted in Irish-speaking districts as the height of public cynicism, effectively ended the process of language education that had begun in 1923 whereby at least a quarter of the population of the country left school feeling that they were "fluent" in the language—a success story. The present developments seem to predict that Ireland will eventually lose any vestiges of Irish as a community language and become an entirely monoglot, English-speaking country. Yet, the Irish language is still called the first official language in the Republic of Ireland. In practice, this becomes mere verbal chicanery. Even when one considers the new community of Irish speakers that has been established in Belfast, the political ramifications of what this gesture means may outweigh its simply human and communicative aspects.

Conversely, a particularly striking phenomenon has been the development over roughly the past twenty years of the movement to establish *Gaelscoileanna*—schools that teach all subjects, except other languages, through the medium of Irish. The parents who worked to establish *Gaelscoileanna* for their children receive little official support, and some might claim that they, in fact, are thwarted by government opposition and "benign neglect." Nevertheless, the number of schools has grown significantly since the program began early in the 1970s. The success rate of the *Gaelscoil* students has been considerable. Originally hostile, parents outside the *Gaelscoileanna* now seem to want their children to attend these schools because of the quality of the educational experience the students receive there. However, the fear still exists that the English-speaking majority in Ireland will undermine the Irish-language emphasis of these schools by altering their goals to focus on training to ensure that their sons and daughters "get ahead" by attending such effective schools. Many clamoring for their children's admission to the *Gaelscoileanna* have no intention that their children use the language outside of school.

The *Gaelscoileanna* today also include some secondary schools where students may continue their education through the medium of Irish. In addition, there still remain some unrelated non-voluntary "A" schools within the regular governmental system which teach all subjects through the medium of Irish. The secondary schools in this system may be counted on the fingers of one's hands. The experience of all bilingual schools has been that the students drift toward English, especially outside the classroom. This pattern underlies the perceived necessity for schools that are all Irish-speaking.

In general, most of the students exiting the primary and secondary schools in Ireland demonstrate minimal mastery of the language. This is obviously not a result of an absence of language-learning guides. Today, the necessary materials have long been available, such as proven bilingual methodologies, English-Irish and Irish-English dictionaries and a short Irish-Irish dictionary. The grammar and spelling of the language was standardized in the 1960s. The vocabulary has been modernized by the Dáil translation staff, developing scientific, technological and information-processing terms necessary to work in the 1990s. What is missing is a favorable attitude in regard to the language on the part of most teachers and of the vast majority of the population.

IRISH IN EDUCATION AND THE MEDIA, 1994

At the university level, Irish is offered as a subject in nearly all of the constituent bodies of the National University of Ireland. There were intentions to create University College, Galway, as an all-Irish language institution but that has never become a reality. Instead, University College, Galway, now has a Gaelic Language Center. University College, Cork, has a section of its dormitories specifically reserved for students who wish to speak Irish. In addition, both Queens University, Belfast, and the University of Ulster at Coleraine have Irish-language sections. The new University of Limerick came in for some adverse criticism when it attempted to de-emphasize Irish. Now it offers a credit course for non-Irish students who wish to start studying the language. University College, Dublin, has recently been conducting in-service courses through the medium of Irish for secondary teachers who teach the language. *Comhar na Múinteoirí Gaeilge* is an organization formed by primary and secondary teachers of Irish who wish to implement changes in the instruction of Irish so that they might see greater success teaching students the language.

One of the most interesting new developments in recent times has been the new bachelor of science degree in Finance, Computing and Enterprise, taught entirely through the medium of the Irish language. This four-year program has already been launched at Dublin City University under the direction of Fionnbarra Ó Brolcháin, professor of finance. It specifically counteracts the traditional marginalization of the language as suitable only as a "cultural" pursuit. The refreshing implication of this new degree program is that Irish is perfectly suitable to function centrally in the practical areas of Irish life in the twentieth century. It counters the prevailing negative belief, already sufficiently noted above, that English is the "go-ahead" language and that Irish must necessarily be backward, by its very nature and not because of specific historical circumstances.

In the United States, Irish is offered at a few institutions as part of the credit-bearing curriculum. Irish continues to be offered with a medieval emphasis in the Celtic Studies program at Harvard, in a wide spectrum of periods at the University of California at Berkeley, with a more Modern Irish focus at Boston College, as well as at other institutions. A new credit-bearing course, entitled "Introduction to Modern Irish Gaelic," will be inaugurated by me in the Graduate School of Arts and Science at New York University during the Spring, 1995, semester. In general, Modern Irish has usually been offered at American colleges outside the regular curriculum as a course in continuing education or simply on an ad-hoc basis.

IRISH IN EDUCATION AND THE MEDIA, 1994

Significant scholarship in the Irish language continues to be published. One area of study using Irish has consistently been strong: the Irish language itself and its literature. Though highly specialized in scope, Irish-language scholarship sets a trend counter to the continuing decline in the use of the spoken language.

Three of the major publishing houses that emphasize scholarly, literary, or creative works in the Irish language are particularly notable. Clóchomhar is the most learned and long-lived of the Irish-language publishers. In addition to its other publications in Irish, over eighty volumes have been published by Clóchomhar's series called *Leabhair Thaighde* ["*Research Volumes*"] including the recently issued important reference work in three volumes *1882–1982: Beathaisnéis*—and volume four is soon to be issued—containing thorough accounts, in dictionary format, of the major figures in Gaelic Ireland during the Revival period. Under the direction of Pádraig Ó Snodaigh, past member of the history faculty at University College, Dublin, Coscéim occasionally publishes scholarly works along with creative writing and other popular works. Cló Iar-Chonnachta, under the direction of Mícheál Ó Conghaile, occasionally publishes serious studies along with more popular fare, including an extensive series of compact discs and cassettes of poetry and prose readings, but mainly producing music audios. All books in Irish are available from a central distribution agent: ÁIS, 31 Sráid na bhFiníní, Baile Átha Cliath 2, Éire.

Along with the book publishers, two notable scholarly publications are produced annually from St. Patrick's College, Maynooth. *Irisleabhar Mhá Nuad* is a journal of literary and religious studies. However, the most significant scholarly serial publication in Irish that is frequently accessible to the educated reader is *Léachtai Cholm Cille*. This annual series of lectures was inaugurated in 1970 and is now in its twenty-third volume. It prints the lectures presented at Maynooth in expanded format. The titles of the last three volumes offer a flavor of the variety of subject matters undertaken: Volume 23 *Maigh Nuad agus an Ghaeilge* [*Maynooth and the Irish Language*] (1993), Volume 22 *Oidhreacht na nOileán* [*The Heritage of the Islands*] (1992), and Volume 21 *An tÚrscéal sa Ghaeilge* [*The Novel in Irish*] (1991).

Scholarly work in the Irish language is reported by the two major annual international bibliographical reference sources for studies in language and literature. These are *The Year's Work in Language Study* from The Modern Humanities Research Association of Great Britain, and the annual international *MLA Bibliography* of the Modern Language Association of America. As Celtic Studies section head, I keep coverage as comprehensive as possible so that undergraduate and graduate students as well as language and literary researchers are kept aware that Irish is still enthusiastically employed in scholarly communications.

A comprehensive survey of scholarly activities in Irish over the past hundred years has been published by the folklorist Seán O Súillealbháin. It appeared in a special issue of the monthly magazine *Comhar* (August, 1993) devoted to the Gaelic League's one hundredth anniversary—a near nonevent in 1993. All of the Celtic languages are the subject of careful sociolinguistic and linguistic surveys in Donald Macauley's *The Celtic Languages* (Cambridge University Press, 1992), including a lucid and comprehensive report on "The Irish Language" by Cathair Ó Dochartaigh. For those interested specifically in language *per se* and sociolinguistics, *Teangeolas* is published bilingually twice yearly by Institiúid Teangeolaíochta Éireann, The Linguistic Institute of Ireland.

The major monthly periodical directed at an intellectual readership is *Comhar*, already mentioned above. Of the various monthlies addressing current topics of interest in Irish, *Comhar* is clearly the most impressive. Other monthly periodicals for the general reader include *Feasta* and *An tUltach*. Two weekly newspapers are also published in Irish. *Anois*, one weekly, has come under attack for the insipidity of its coverage of actual news and its emphasis on Dublin and on a putative "teen" readership. The flaws criticized in *Anois* appear particularly bothersome, because it receives government funding. *Lá* is a weekly newspaper published in Belfast and has recently been reorganized. The quality of its journalism has improved and a new marketing effort to expand its readership is underway. The *Irish Times* includes a half-page in Irish entitled "Tuarascáil" ["Report"] appearing in every Wednesday's issue. However, it is clear that it would be difficult to be a full-time journalist working solely in the Irish language.

Despite this, written Irish is undergoing and impressive flowering in various forms of creative expression—particularly poetry, short stories, and novels. As positive as this seems, its negative side is the sad fact that the Irish language is often considered to be merely a cultural and intellectual curiosity rather than a living means of communication. For example, in the last few years, the initial publication of poetry has been in a bilingual format. This points to a perception that it may be unnecessary or even useless to write in the Irish language and that it is necessary to present English along with Irish, as if the only readership worth targeting were a monoglot English-language one.

IRISH IN EDUCATION AND THE MEDIA, 1994

A major disturbance over censorship occurred with the publication of two Irish-language books recently. One is a memoir that included controversial passages favorable to Germany during World War II entitled *Cé hí Seo Amuigh: Cuimhní Cinn,* by Róisín Ní Mheara. Another is a novel concerned with corruption in politics and business entitled *Ardfhear,* by Diarmuid Ó Donnchadha. This novel reverberates with echoes of widely reported, current unethical carryings-on and has elicited comments that a stricter censorship should be imposed. Such responses are a far cry from the days when it was felt that more freedom with regard to subject matter, particularly sexual, was available to the Irish-language writer because his audience was considered limited and essentially confined to Ireland.

Modern Irish continues to be a modest presence in the electronic media. Raidió na Gaeltachta broadcasts about 45 hours a week with studios in the three major Irish-speaking regions: west Kerry, Connemara, and west Donegal. A new Irish-language station called Raidió na Life (102 FM) was inaugurated in Dublin in October, 1993. It relies mainly on amateur volunteers. The station broadcasts Monday through Friday evenings and from 11:00 AM to 10:00 PM on Saturdays and Sundays in Dublin from a studio at Bord na Gaeilge, the government-appointed body responsible for overseeing language activities.

A major controversy has developed over the proposed Telefís na Gaeilge, a television service in the Irish language. Four years of failed government promises to establish one has led to Irish-speakers' distrust, and the extremely powerful anti-Irish lobby has been blamed for the delays. The delays have become almost farcically predictable. In fact, one more year and—even more recently (May, 1994)—a second additional year of delay have been announced. It has been claimed that a staff with sufficient technical expertise as well as fluency in the Irish language is not to be found in Ireland. The proposed television service in Ireland has now been postponed for a total of six years to 1996.

In New York City, my weekly radio program, "Míle Fáilte" on WFUV (90.7 FM), the Fordham University station, emphasizes the Irish language. These broadcasts teaching Irish-Gaelic on the station have continued for fifteen years. Last summer, the program was expanded to a full hour on Saturday mornings, and it receives warm responses from the listening audience as witnessed by their generous financial contributions to the four fund-raisers held each year. Also in New York City, Barra Ó Donnabháin writes a column in the Irish language that appears regularly in the *Irish Echo,* one of three Irish-American newspapers published in the city each week.

IRISH IN EDUCATION AND THE MEDIA, 1994

In general, public life in Ireland is English-speaking. Increasingly, Irish speakers complain that it is becoming more and more difficult to conduct business in the Irish language with the public agencies. Unfortunately, this is true even in the *Gaeltacht* areas. When industries were brought into Irish-speaking regions, they were supposed to maintain and promote the local language and culture. However, the managerial staff and their families usually were English-speaking, again pushing Irish speakers into second-class status on their own home ground. Such a pattern of behavior provides the context for the bitterness with which Irish speakers evaluate the government's lack of progress with Telefís na Gaeilge. Again, government delay and the threat of English-speakers managing the media will simply prove to be another factor serving to further diminish the status of the language and its speakers. Negative attitudes toward the language again come into play here. English speakers in Ireland do not view Irish as a "mother tongue," as the language of home and neighbors. Since speaking Irish has not been the experience of the English-language majority, they generalize their experience to expunge the validity of the actual, felt experience of Irish speakers in the *Gaeltacht*. On the other hand, the threat of language loss leaves the Irish speaker tongue-tied, erasing his or her connectedness with the intimate behaviors and communal traditions of the Irish people.

—*Nassau Community College*

IRISH IN EDUCATION AND THE MEDIA, 1994

GEORGE BRANDON SAUL, 1901–1986:
AN APPRECIATION AND A
SELECTED CHECKLIST

M. KELLY LYNCH

WHEN GEORGE Brandon Saul, poet, writer of fiction, musician, and scholar in Anglo-Irish literature died, he left a large and singularly impressive *oeuvre* behind. Between 1922, when *Cup of Sand*, his first book of verse, was published, and 1986, Saul had written enough poetry to fill thirteen collections. He had also produced fifteen works of fiction and drama; three published children's books; four scholarly editions in Anglo-Irish letters; sixty-two scholarly articles; two anthologies; eighteen critical studies of Anglo-Irish writers; more than a hundred book reviews; and one hundred and twenty compositions for piano and piano and voice. For all this, George Saul had, and still has, no more than a quiet reputation in the United States. The reason for this relative obscurity is a complex matter— a combination of his personality, his aesthetic preference, and the way he chose to position himself in the world. On the odd byway he chose to travel—one deviating significantly from the thoroughfare and moving ever further away as this century moved along—Saul might be considered remarkable, talented—perhaps a genius. Equally capable of inventing a no-slip automatic jack and composing an impromptu for piano, his mathematical ability and draftsmanship were of the highest quality and his mind almost equally balanced between the quantitative and the verbal abilities.

Born in Shoemakersville, Pennsylvania, Saul came from modest beginnings, the eldest of three male children born to Mary and Daniel Brandon Saul, a clerk on the mail trains. Entering Pennsylvania State College, Saul originally planned to study mathematics and engineering. This choice was not his, but his father's, who presumably simply wanted to insure for his son a lucrative position. Loath to tell his father that he wanted to be a poet, Saul acceded to his wishes. However, in the pandemic of 1918, Saul contracted influenza and nearly died. His convalescence of one year was spent in writing poetry and, when he had fully recovered, he enrolled at the University of Pennsylvania as a student of English literature. Daniel Saul, who was dying of cancer—he succumbed in George's first year—was presumably not able to exert the influence he once had over his son. Saul was free to pursue his inclinations and by the time he graduated had published his first book of poetry.

Saul's academic career at the University of Connecticut—then Connecticut Agricultural College—began by chance over dinner at a boarding house in Philadelphia where he was living while clerking for the Indemnity Insurance Company of North America, hating it, and applying for teaching positions in Manhattan. He met Professor Henry Dedlinger of the History Department at Connecticut "Aggie" who urged him to apply for an opening in the English Department there. Saul secured the job immediately.

There is a sumptuous irony in the fact that the twenty-four-year-old six-foot, fair-haired, blue-eyed young blade, who had set his sights on living the poetic life in the Manhattan of the 1920s, ended up in the "barest hole in the hills,"[1] in rural Storrs, Connecticut, slogging from his lodgings past the sheep barns to class. After that experience, he could never bring himself to eat lamb. Sixty-two years later, a professor emeritus, Saul had the distinction of the longest tenure in the university's ninety-five-year history. From 1924 to his death, Saul's life was uneventful, except in the most ordinary and domestic ways: a wife, Dorothy Ayers; a child, George, Jr.; the tragic early death of his wife; a marriage to Eileen Lewis; two more children, Michael Brandon and Barbara Brigid Brandon; a rented house; assorted dogs, cats, automobiles, illnesses, sadnesses, joys, responsibilities; a baby grand piano; a vegetable garden; five grandchildren; two trips to Ireland rather late in his life; a house and mortgage of his own at seventy; building a stone wall; an eleven-month battle with death; a finality.

When George Saul settled in Storrs, he settled for life, and step-by-step succeeded in disengaging himself from the turmoil of the twentieth century. Perhaps his date of birth, 1901, accounts, at least in part, for this disengagement. Too young to serve in World War I and too old for World War II—except as an air raid warden for Storrs, Connecticut—Saul, unlike many born before or after him, avoided being swept like-it-or-not into the mainstream of this century. This charmed life, however, took its toll: Saul lived outside the exigencies and demands of the world and the world recipro-

---

1 Conversations with George Brandon Saul.

GEORGE BRANDON SAUL, 1907–1986

cated. His disconnectedness had much to do with his need for control, and this is eminently clear in the poems. As long as he felt in charge, he was devoted, caring, loving—a perfectly reasonable human being. When the larger world intruded, however, and Saul was incapable of controlling the sweep of events, he took on an extremely unpleasant, irrational, and vitriolic public persona which grew out of fear more than anything else. Nowhere is this more amply illustrated than in his professional career.

The first years at Connecticut went well enough. When he first began teaching, he was one of four members of an English Department in a school with a total enrollment of 484. In 1924 he was promoted to assistant professor; in 1932 to associate; and in 1942 to full professor. During these years, as Connecticut Agricultural College evolved into the University of Connecticut, Saul *was* the English Graduate Program.

In 1949 however, Leonard ("Pete") Dean, a Shakespeare scholar from competitive and political New York University, was offered the chair of the department. It was a position Saul had believed he would be offered. Over the next decade and more, Dean called anathema into Saul's comfortable life. Dean's ambition was to put the English Department "on the map," and the first task toward this goal was to catapult it into the mid-twentieth century by methods that seemed, to the old guard, Machiavellian. He began to nip and worry at the heels of the tenured and entrenched by hiring bright young instructors who brought with them new ideas, new pedagogy, a new canon, and the New Criticism. He began reworking and updating the curriculum and his principle target was George Saul.

It is immeasurably sad that Saul's career as a teacher began to plummet when he was only fifty. When the acrimony and vituperation began, he was already considered "old guard," not because he had been teaching at Storrs for twenty-four years, but because he refused to rethink or re-evaluate his critical criteria for reading text. For him the New Criticism was "hogwash." He made no secret about his feelings about it and Pete Dean. More, however, was afoot. The New Criticism challenged Saul's aesthetic principles and ways of reading and teaching that he had brought with him from the University of Pennsylvania in the 1920s, and those were essentially nineteenth-century models. The New Criticism introduced "relative" reading, tolerance for ambiguity, buried meaning, and unconscious composition. Since Saul's very identity depended on what he could, authoritatively, impart as knowledge to students whose heads were "basically empty," the very idea of having his interpretation challenged was a fearful prospect. It called his entire belief system into question, and this he would not allow.

GEORGE BRANDON SAUL, 1907–1986

On the one hand, therefore, Dean's point of view is easily understood. Notwithstanding his long-range goals, what was he to do with a tenured member of his faculty who seemed hopelessly antiquated in the subject matter he taught and the way he taught it. Here was a man whose course in modern fiction ended with Thomas Hardy and was divided into three sections entitled "The Great," "The Nearly Great," and "The Occasionally Great"; who refused to order texts for his students, but urged them to "soak" themselves in poetry or "read widely" in a particular genre; whose course in modern poetry focused on such obscure writers as Adelaide Crapsey, Hazel Hall, and Ralph Hodgson, but which refused to acknowledge T. S. Eliot, Dylan Thomas, and Anne Sexton except as "coterie poets—second rate, at best"[2] and who rapidly read lectures from note cards, yellowed with age and pipe smoke, focusing on biography, bibliography, and historical background. When Saul did make critical pronouncements, they were arrogant, personal, self-assured, and idiosyncratic.[3] What was Dean to do when the only member of his department teaching Irish literature refused to take James Joyce seriously, or when groups of angry students, as early as 1956, were expressing dissatisfaction and anger at their treatment by Saul?

Yet, Saul's treatment by Dean and the ever-growing number of new members of the department seemed at times to reach depths of systematic cruelty. The titles of Saul's favorite courses were changed from "modern" to "post-Victorian," and then the courses were taken away entirely and assigned to junior faculty. Although he fought valiantly to retain these courses—and his status and his self-esteem—he was unsuccessful. Finally, he was assigned sections of the required introductory courses, which he was ill-equipped to teach, and permitted one graduate course in Anglo-Irish literature from which students were customarily discouraged by their advisors. In fact, with my own advisor's disapproval, I enrolled in the Irish literature course in the Fall of 1963. It had been scheduled to meet for three hours on Friday evenings; there were seven enrolled. By the end of the semester, I was the one student remaining. Although I had become as frustrated as the other six, I "stuck it out," not only because I wished to focus

2   This quotation is from my own memory of Saul's prescriptive pronouncements in a graduate course I took from him. I was even more astonished on the occasion when he told me that "One who has not read Abbie Huston Evans has an undeveloped soul."

3   Again, I quote from recollection, "Ralph Hodgson's *The Bull* is the only epic in the English language."

GEORGE BRANDON SAUL, 1907–1986

on Anglo-Irish literature, but also because in many ways I had come to live with and love this complex and difficult man, who, having missed the train, chose to live at the station.

Saul may have delivered bitter diatribes against the existing power structure, but I believe he understood clearly what was being spoken. This may be best illustrated by the frenzy of "anthologizing" occurring between 1952 and 1964. He painstakingly wrote plans for thirteen anthologies as a response to Dean's hiring of John Malcolm Brinnin—author of *Dylan Thomas in America* and former director of the YM/YWHA Poetry Center in Manhattan—to teach, among other courses, Saul's favorite course in modern poetry. When Saul protested the hiring of Brinnin, who had no Ph.D., Dean pointed out that Brinnin had a recently published anthology: "And where is your anthology, George?"[4]

When I first met Saul, in 1963, he had endured thirteen years of this sort of humiliation, as well as periodic queries, beginning in 1964, about when he "planned to retire." He sat in his office, the stage-professor—tweed jacket with leather patches on the elbows, small round glasses, bow tie—in a pristine environment. There were no books to speak of, no clutter, no papers, and soon, I discovered, no students. Daily he walked the hundred yards from his university-let house to his office, sat there, and stared at the wall. Alienated, isolated, he was trapped financially because of the illnesses of his wife, daughter, and mother who, by 1964, was living with the Sauls. The larger and more interesting question is whether Saul would have made a move had he not been financially strapped. The answer, I think, is no. Saul may have been "in denial" about his teaching competence, but he was not a stupid man, nor unaware of the change and turmoil on university and college campuses across the nation. Nor was he unaware that he was sixty-three years old.

Saul's choice was to stumble through his rituals, refuse to react, and grow more bitter daily, rumbling imprecations in his low, sonorous actor's voice and accruing a reputation for being sarcastic and sour. His salvation was a retreat into his personal world of creativity and scholarship. From 1962 until his death, Saul was more prolific than ever, producing—perhaps in an act of defiance—nine of his thirteen collections of verse, three-quarters of his scholarly articles and half of his scholarly books.

---

4 Saul-Dean Correspondence, Special Collections, Ellen Clarke Bertrand Library, Bucknell University, Lewisburg, PA.

GEORGE BRANDON SAUL, 1907–1986

Without question, Saul's scholarship did much for the cause of Irish literature in the United States when it was a nascent discipline in great need of a scholar trained in the nineteenth-century and early twentieth-century European methods of biographical, bibliographical, and historical research.[5] Saul compiled bibliography upon bibliography, scrupulously sought out arcane documents and sources, unearthed works long lost, and created a canon out of an amorphous and largely forgotten body of text. His work on such Irish writers as Daniel Corkery, Ella Young, Lord Dunsany, and Seumas O'Kelly raised these writers from relative obscurity to respectable critical distinction. Mixed emotions attend, however, his love affair with Yeats.[6] A reading of his own poetry indicates why he "approved"—and "approval" is the word we must use in speaking of Saul's critical judgments—of the early Yeats, for the "Celtic Twilight" of the late nineteenth century expressed many of Saul's own emotions toward the mystical and the magical. Toward the later Yeats, when the Irish poet and playwright got rougher and more sexual, Saul demurred, pronouncing "Leda and the Swan" to be "the finest sonnet in the English language, metrically."

Saul's other contribution to scholarship lay in his absolute devotion to both acknowledged and unacknowledged women writers. Once again, this interest was idiosyncratic, praising such relatively obscure women as Hazel Hall and Adelaide Crapsey, as well as the highly gifted Isak Dinesen and Elizabeth Bowen.[7] Once again, more famous and "modern" women writers, like Virginia Woolf, he would not read.

The bond George Saul felt with the writers he did choose to celebrate is best understood by examining his own creative work. Like the man himself, it is both eclectic and uncompromising. Saul's fiction and poetry are the expressions of a man deeply rooted in Romantic sensibilities, more hair-raisingly Germanic than calmly British.[8] In the fiction, particularly,

5   During his two trips to Ireland, Saul was introduced at many gatherings as "The Great Man of Irish Letters." He took only two trips to Ireland rather late in his life. His explanation was his dread of flying.

6   Trained as a Medieval scholar at the University of Pennsylvania, Saul discovered Yeats by accident while browsing in the modern poetry section of the library. He was so enchanted by *The Wild Swans at Coole* that he abandoned his Medieval studies for the relatively unknown discipline of Irish literature.

7   I recall evenings spent with George and Eileen Saul when he would read from his favorite women poets. Some of the poems were roccoco valentines, and others astonishingly accomplished.

8   Saul was compared to Heinrich Heine upon the publication of *Cup of Sand*. Aside

GEORGE BRANDON SAUL, 1907–1986

his subject matter is drawn from Pennsylvania Dutch folklore and Irish legend and mythology. Both allow him to reach beyond the quotidian and dream dreams of past glories, passions, victories; to embrace and kiss without modern embarrassment; to stride ramparts and fight without modern fears of annihilation. His landscapes are ominous, often pantheistic, and his world of spirits is very much alive.[9]

Of Saul the poet much of the same can be said. Eschewing what he thought to be faddish and popular, he was unabashedly a Romantic. Like the lyric impulse itself, the poetry is introspective, self-nurturing, and quiet—focusing on the changing of the seasons, rather than the changing of the guard; the blooming of the heather, rather than the bombing of Hanoi. Like Saul's handwriting, which was minuscule, elegant, and curvilinear, the poems are metrically perfect, concise—more often "engineered" than written. In blatant confrontation with "obscure" or "modern" poetry, Saul's themes are Romantic as well. He celebrates Nature in all her moods, deplores the passage of time, celebrates love, recalls lost youth, and marvels at the immensity of the world and the minuteness of her temporary human residents.

Except for an increasing preoccupation with death, the poems of Saul's final collection, *Winter's Many Minds* (1982), do not differ markedly from those of *Cup of Sand*, although the world had moved light years between 1923 and 1982. However flawless technically, Saul's poetry is that of a man who was deeply fatalistic and reactionary in his refusal to react. There is fear here, but the source was neither complacency nor political conservatism—for Saul deplored the shift to the Right, Vietnam, the chicanery of Richard Nixon, and the economic plight of minorities. The poems, like those of Poe or the later Coleridge, have nothing to do with the world of "getting and spending," but are an intensely personal testimony of a man who felt hunted and haunted. In the title poem of his collection, *Hound and Unicorn* (1969), Saul undeniably expresses his feelings of entrapment in the "and" of that title. The poem is a testimony to the anguish Saul felt in striving toward mystical vision and epiphany, while being "hounded" by immediate necessity. The inevitable questions arise: can a contempo-

---

from reviews of individual works, the only study of Saul as a writer is Frederick S. Kiley's, "Sun and Snow: The Variety of George Brandon Saul's Literary Art," ÉIRE-IRELAND, V, 2 (Spring, 1972).

9. Eileen Saul recalled George's terror when they returned to his birthplace in the Black Hills of Pennsylvania. Fully believing that "spirits lurked there," he would not venture out after dark.

GEORGE BRANDON SAUL, 1907–1986

rary composer write a "Beethoven" sonata or a contemporary artist recreate the images of Vermeer? What, in fact, draws the line between competent craftsmanship and creativity? The degree to which George Saul's is responsible art can be determined only by one's own belief in the obligation of art to respond to, shape, mythologize, demystify, clarify, change, and make permanent the world in and for which it is created.

The checklist which follows is divided into two parts: A—Scholarly Works, subdivided into Scholarly Books, Scholarly Editions, and Scholarly Articles and arranged chronologically; and B—Creative Works, subdivided by genre into works of Poetry, Fiction, Drama, and Children's Literature, also arranged chronologically. A complete collection of the Saul papers and a catalogue of his correspondence, book reviews, manuscript notebooks, original typescripts, and musical holographs is housed in the Special Collections of the Ellen Clarke Bertrand Library at Bucknell Library, Lewisburg, Pennsylvania.

A. SCHOLARLY WORKS

BOOKS

1. *A. E. Coppard: His Life and His Poetry.* Philadelphia: University of Pennsylvania Thesis Publications, 1932.
2. *The Wedding of Sir Gawain and Dame Ragnall.* New York: Prentice-Hall, 1934. Translation.
3. *The Elusive Stallion and Related Concerns.* Prairie City, IL: Decker, 1948. Essays on metrics and poetic theory.
4. *Handbook of English Grammar and Writing Conventions.* Harrisburg: Stackpole, 1953.
5. *The Shadow of the Three Queens.* Harrisburg: Stackpole, 1953. Introduction to traditional Irish literature and its backgrounds.
6. *Prolegomena to the Study of Yeats's Poems.* Philadelphia: University of Pennsylvania Press, 1957.
7. *Prolegomena to the Study of Yeats's Plays.* Philadelphia: University of Pennsylvania Press, 1958.
8. *The Age of Yeats.* New York: Dell, 1964. Anthology of Irish literature.
9. *Owl's Watch.* Greenwich CT: Fawcett, 1965. Anthology of tales of horror.

GEORGE BRANDON SAUL, 1907–1986

10. *In . . . Luminous Wind.* Dublin: Dolmen Press, 1965. Collection of previously published essays.

11. *Quintet: Essays on Five American Women Poets.* Philadelphia: Walton Press, 1967.

12. *Concise Introduction to Types of Literature in English.* Philadelphia: Walton Press, 1969.

13. *Rushlight Heritage: Reflections on Selected Short Story Writers of the Yeatsian Era.* Walton Press, 1970. Previously published essays.

14. *Traditional Irish Literature and Its Backgrounds.* Lewisburg, PA: Bucknell University Press, 1970. Revision of *The Shadow of the Three Queens.*

15. *Withdrawn in Gold: Three Commentaries on Genius.* The Hague: Mouton and Co., 1970. Essays on James Stephens, Ralph Hodgson, and Isak Dinesen.

16. *Seumas O'Kelly.* Lewisburg, PA: Bucknell University Press, 1971.

17. *Daniel Corkery.* Lewisburg, PA: Bucknell University Press, 1973.

18. *In Praise of the Half-Forgotten and Other Ruminations.* Lewisburg, PA: Bucknell University Press, 1976. Essays on Stevenson, Henley, de la Mare, Helen Thomas, A. E. Coppard, E. A. Robinson, and James Stephens.

EDITIONS

1. A. E. Coppard, *Cherry Ripe.* Hawthorne House, 1935.

2. Seumas O'Kelly and Constance Markievicz, "Lustre," [a play], ÉIRE-IRELAND, II, 4 (Winter, 1967–68).

3. Seumas O'Kelly, *The Shuiler's Child.* Chicago: DePaul University Press, 1971.

4. Daniel Corkery, *Fohnam, the Sculptor.* Newark: Proscenium Press, 1973.

ARTICLES

1. "A Note on Hazel Hall and Her Poetry," *The General Magazine and Historical Chronicle,* XXXVII (1934).

2. "Cherry Ripe," *London Times Literary Supplement* (February 20, 1936).

3. "In Memoriam: Alfred Edward Housman, 1859–1936," *The General Magazine and Historical Chronicle,* XXXIX (1936).

4. "Literary Parallels: Yeats and Coppard," *Notes and Queries,* CLXVIII (1935).

5. "Brief Observations on Frost and Stephens," College English Association *Newsletter,* IV, 6 (1942).

GEORGE BRANDON SAUL, 1907–1986

6. "The Ellusive Stallion: Notes on Poetry," College English Association *Newsletter*, IV, 5 (1942).

7. "Silver Daughter of the Puritans: Winifred Welles," *Poet Lore*, XLVIII (1942).

8. "On English Metrics—and Certain Absurdities," *College English*, V (1943).

9. "A Literary Coincidence?" College English Association *Newsletter*, VI, 9 (1944).

10. "Suggestions Toward a Revised Program in College English," *College English*, VII (1945).

11. "Yeats's Hare," *London Times Literary Supplement*, January 11, 1947.

12. "Yeats and His Poems," *London Times Literary Supplement*, March 31, 1950.

13. "Yeats, Noyes, and Day-Lewis," *Notes and Queries*, CXCV (1950).

14. "Jeffares On Yeats," *Modern Language Notes*, LXVI (1951).

15. "Merlin's Flight: An Essay on Ralph Hodgson," *Poet Lore*, LVI (1951).

16. "A Poet Without Fame In Her Own State," *Connecticut Circle*, XIV, 6 (June, 1951).

17. "James Stephens' Contributions to *The Irish Review*," *The Papers of the Bibliographic Society of America*, XLVI, 4 (1952).

18. "On Mercury and Reason: The Criticism of James Stephens," *Bulletin of the New York Public Library*, LVII (1953).

19. "On the Verse of Roy Helton," *General Magazine and Historical Chronicle*, LIV, 3 (1952).

20. "A Descriptive Record of James Stephens's Contributions to Sinn Féin," *Bulletin of the New York Public Library*, LVII, 4 (April, 1953).

21. "Withdrawn in Gold," *Arizona Quarterly*, IX (1953).

22. "Crutches Toward Stephens," *Bulletin of the New York Public Library*, LVIII (1954).

23. "Yeatsian Brevities," *Notes and Queries*, I (1954).

24. "Introductory Bibliography in Ancient and Medieval Irish Literature," *Bulletin of the New York Public Library*, LVIII (1954).

25. "A Stone Against Oblivion: On the Prose of Ella Young," *Arizona Quarterly*, X (1954).

26. "Thread to a Labyrinth: A Selective Bibliography in Yeats," *Bulletin of the New York Public Library*, LVIII (1954).

27. "The Winged Image: a Note on Birds in Yeats's Poems," *Bulletin of the New York Public Library*, LVIII (1954).

GEORGE BRANDON SAUL, 1907–1986

28. "Hazel Hall: A Chronological list of Acknowleged Verses in the Periodicals," *Twentieth Century Literature,* I (1955).

29. "'A Delicate Fabric of Birdsong': The Verse of Sara Teasedale," *Arizona Quarterly,* XIII (Spring, 1957).

30. "Flinty Bread: The Verse of Abbie Huston Evans," *Arizona Quarterly,* XIII (Summer, 1957).

31. "Daughter of the Vikings: Isak Dinesen," *Arizona Quarterly,* XV (Autumn, 1959).

32. "W. B. Yeats: Corrigenda," *Notes and Queries,* VII (August, 1960).

33. "Yeats's Verse Before *Responsibilities,*" *Arizona Quarterly,* XVI (Summer, 1960).

34. "Coda: The Verse of Yeats's Last Five Years," *Arizona Quarterly,* XVII (Spring, 1961).

35. "Of Tales Half-forgotten," *Arizona Quarterly,* XVIII (Summer, 1962).

36. "The Short Stories of W. B. Yeats," *Poet Lore,* LIX (1964).

37. "A Consideration of Frank O'Connor's Short Stories," *Colby Library Quarterly,* Series VI (December, 1963).

38. "Note on a Literary Curiosity," *Bulletin of the New York Public Library,* LXVII (September, 1963).

39. "The Short Stories of Seumas O'Kelly," *Bulletin of the New York Public Library,* LXVII (April, 1963).

40. "The Short Stories of Daniel Corkery," *Poet Lore,* LVIII (Summer, 1963).

41. "Strange Gods and Far Places: The Short Stories of Lord Dunsany," *Arizona Quarterly,* XIX, (Autumn, 1963).

42. "A Wild Sowing: The Short Stories of Liam O'Flaherty," *A Review of English Literature,* IV, 3 (July, 1963).

43. "A Frenzy of Concentration: Yeats's Verse from *Responsibilities* to *The King of the Great Clock Tower,*" *Arizona Quarterly,* XX (Summer, 1964).

44. "Minor Irish Miscellany," *Bulletin of the New York Public Library,* LXVIII (May, 1964).

45. "The Poetry of Austin Clarke," *The Celtic Cross,* [Purdue University Studies], 1964.

46 "The Short Stories of George Moore," *Poet Lore,* LIX (1964).

47. "The Brief Fiction of Sean O'Faolain," *Colby Library Quarterly,* Series VII (June, 1965).

48. "'Icy Song': The Verse of Elinor Wylie," *The Bulletin of the New York Public Library,* LXIX (November, 1965).

49. "The Short Stories of Elizabeth Bowen," *Arizona Quarterly,* XXI (Spring, 1965).

GEORGE BRANDON SAUL, 1907–1986

50. "Summary Notes on Yeats's Dramatic Accomplishment," *W. B. Yeats Centenary Essays*, Ibadan University, Iran.

51. "The Verse, Novels, and Drama of Seumas O'Kelly," ÉIRE-IRELAND, I, (Spring, 1967).

52. "Philpott's Use of Classical Subject Matter," *Modern British Literature*, II, 1 (Spring, 1977).

53. "Daniel Corkery," in *The Dictionary of Irish Literature*, The Greenwood Press, 1979.

54. "Seumas O'Kelly," in *The Dictionary of Irish Literature*, The Greenwood Press, 1979.

B. CREATIVE WORKS
POETRY

1. *Cup of Sand.* Boston:Harold Vinal, 1923.

2. *Bronze Woman.* Boston: Bruce Humphries, 1930.

3. *Unimagined Rose.* Windham, CT: Hawthorne House, 1937.

4. *"Only Necessity...."* Privately Printed, 1941.

5. *Selected Lyrics.* Prairie City: Decker, 1947.

6. *Hound and Unicorn.* Philadelphia: Walton Press, 1969. Includes the verse drama "The Fair Eselt."

7. *A Touch of Acid.* Philadelphia: Walton Press, 1971. Satiric verse.

8. *Skeleton's Progress.* Philadelphia: Walton Press, 1971.

9. *The Stroke of Light.* Francestown, NH: Golden Quill Press, 1974.

10. *Adam Unregenerate.* Owings Mills, MD: Stemmer House, 1977.

11. *In Borrowed Light.* Storrs, CT: Parousia Press, 1979.

12. *Vision of Ghostly Horses.* Belfast, ME: Wings Press, 1981.

13. *Winter's Many Minds.* Belfast, ME: Wings Press, 1982.

NOVELS

1. *The Wild Queen.* Winston-Salem: Blair, 1967. Historical novel.

2. *Liadain and Curithir.* Philadelphia: Walton Press, 1970. Historical novel.

3. *In Mountain Shadow.* Philadelphia: Walton Press, 1970.

SHORT STORIES

4. "The Night Beast," *General Magazine and Historical Chronicle*, L, 2 (1950).

GEORGE BRANDON SAUL, 1907–1986

5. "The Vermillion-Headed Man," *General Magazine and Historical Chronicle*, LI, 1 (1951).

6. "Inland Storm," *General Magazine and Historical Chronicle*, LII, 2 (1952).

7. "What Came Of An Argument," *New Mexico Quarterly*, XXIV (Summer, 1954).

8. "What Came Of Taking A Wife's Advice," *General Magazine and Historical Chronicle*, LV, 2 (1955).

9. "Lacrimae Rerum," *General Magazine and Historical Chronicle*, LVIII, 2 (1958).

10. *Carved in Findruine*. Philadelphia: Walton Press, 1969. Irish tales retold.

11. *A Little Book of Strange Tales*. Philadelphia: Walton Press, 1969. Ghost stories.

12. *Advice To the Emotionally Perturbed (Married—Past, Present, Willing, or Doubtful)*. Philadelphia: Walton Press, 1971. Humorous tales.

DRAMA

1. "The Shine on the Waters," in *Junto* [University of Pennsylvania Literary Magazine], 1922.

2. "The Trial By Fable," in *Poet Lore*, L, 2 (Summer, 1944).

3. "The Fair Eselt," in *Hound and Unicorn*. Philadelphia: Walton Press, 1969.

4. *Two Plays*. Privately Printed, 1976.

CHILDREN'S LITERATURE

1. *Candlelight Rhymes For Early-To-Beds*. Philadelphia: Walton Press, 1970.

2. *The Forgotten Birthday*. Philadelphia: Walton Press, 1970.

3. *King Noggin*. Philadelphia: Walton Press, 1971.

—*Babson College*

GEORGE BRANDON SAUL, 1907–1986

BOOK REVIEWS

Free Ireland: Towards a Lasting Peace, by Gerry Adams, pp. 224, Niwot, CO: Roberts Rinehart Publishers, 1994, $11.95.

Gerry Adams's *Free Ireland* is a revision and expansion of his earlier political statements, especially *The Politics of Irish Freedom* (1986), in light of the Sinn Féin and SDLP "Irish Peace Initiative" of 1993. This book provides a survey of Northern Ireland since 1968, combined with occasional references to the hagiography of Irish Republicanism. Certain parts of Adams's narrative are of particular interest. His descriptions of his political coming-of-age, of the ambiguities of Loyalism, "Sinn Fein Today," his remarks concerning the reality that both the Republic and Britain will have to provide compelling reasons to Loyalists in order to gain their assent to a united Ireland, as well as his delineation of the "Irish Peace Initiative" process are all cogent and absorbing.

Most of the various, sometimes contradictory, strands of historic Irish Republican ideology manifest themselves in *Free Ireland*. Adams neatly summarizes these origins, among "republicans and socialists, Irish language enthusiasts, and communists" in describing the individuals attracted to the Wolfe Tone Societies in the 1960s. His survey neglects to include the reactionary exclusionist Gaelic, Catholic, nationalist strain in Irish Republicanism, which is curious given his ready and accurate recognition of the quasi-fascist element among Northern Protestants.

The traditional Republican view of Irish history is once again evoked, beginning with Wolf Tone, the initial purported unifier of Ireland's disparate religious traditions. Adams describes Tone as a Protestant, which is superficially true. In actuality, he had little religion of any kind, other than eighteenth-century republicanism, which is perhaps why modern Republicans find him so appealing. Adams notes that "Republicanism is nothing if it is not resolutely anti-sectarian," which is correct, if by this is meant practical indifference to religion. A certain religious myopia is evident throughout the book. Northern Protestants are not Loyalists simply because the "union has, to date, guaranteed them their privileges and their ascendancy." The union also has protected Protestants from the political and social influence of Irish Catholicism, until recently one of the most rigid manifestations of Roman Catholicism in the world. It is incredible to read Adams's assertion that "Loyalism . . . has nothing to do with the Protestant religion," when one knows that within a fifty kilometer radius of Belfast there is a higher concentration of evangelical churches than anywhere in the world.

The contemporary sympathy of some elements in Sinn Féin for Marxist-Leninism is implicit—Mao and Ché Guevara are evoked—but soft-pedaled. Adams most often speaks in vague terms of a "democratic socialist" republic as his eventual goal.

While Adams is correct in noting the importance of Northern Ireland to Britain as a cold-war outpost, his insistence that Britain somehow has gained something of practical economic substance—either from Northern Ireland or Ireland generally, through "subjugation" of a truncated Ulster—seems strained. The costs of maintaining a military presence in Northern Ireland over the past quarter century, and of supporting a welfare state and depressed economy in the northern statelet since long before that, can hardly be seen as clever capitalist "investments" in nurturing a profitable colonial economic relationship—except, of course, by an ideologue. Adams tacitly admits as much in recounting elsewhere the cost to Britain of its presence in the North. The economy of Ireland, united or not, from the early-modern period onward always has been dependent on, or interrelated with, Britain's, and it probably always will be, unless Ireland at some future point aspires to an "independent" economy like that of contemporary Cuba—perhaps Adams's ultimate goal, despite of his jibe at the "right-wing Tory Monday Club" in this regard.

A significant problem with much of Adams's analysis is his unwillingness to recognize and understand the northern Protestants view of themselves as a separate nation, much like, for instance, the Bosnian Serbs. This is not to say, of course, that different nationalities cannot coexist equitably in the same state, as do, for instance, the Flemings and Walloons of Belgium, or the Germans, French, Italians, and Rheto-Romans of Switzerland. Nor is it to say that a united Ireland is not a desirable possibility. Until quite recently, Northern Catholics have been oppressed primarily by Northern Protestants with only occasional direct help from Britain. Britain's basic attitude toward Northern Ireland since partition is accurately noted by Adams: "Prior to 1968 the British government had basically ignored the problems of structural discrimination and sectarian power in the Six Counties; it had been happy enough to leave the unionists to get on with the business of running the place." The British government was "happy" to do so, of course, only because it potentially was less costly for Britain to placate 1,000,000 northern Protestants, the ethnic residue of its first colony, than 500,000 northern Catholics.

In spite of Adams's protestations that Sinn Féin and the Provisional Irish Republican Army are separate organizations, the fact of the IRA ceasefire of last summer is implicit or anticipated throughout the book. The book's appearance, in the late spring of 1994, would seem to confirm the suspicion that *Free Ireland* was intended to place Adams's views before the public in light of this event.

The Roberts Rinehart firm has done a genuine service in publishing *Free Ireland*. One may not agree with Gerry Adams, but the president of Sinn Féin is an individual whose views, as Jack Van Zandt notes in his introduction, "will have to be taken into account by anyone wishing to formulate an informed view of the

Irish situation." These views should be scrutinized in the future, however. Adams presents them here artfully. As a Marxist-Leninist, the ethic of "revolutionary morality"—saying or doing what one needs to at a given time in order to further the goal of the "democratic socialist" world order—is part and parcel of Adams's political heritage, if not necessarily a part of his personal ideology. The future will determine whether or not this is part of his heritage that Gerry Adams has decided to discard.

—John B. Davenport

Tourism In Ireland: A Critical Analysis, ed. by Barbara O'Connor and Michael Cronin, pp. 271, Cork: Cork University Press, 1993, IR £19.95.

Although a plethora of reports and "white papers" on Irish tourism have appeared in scattered sources, this book is important because it collects for the first time such divergent views in one text. The essays here will benefit both the scholarly community, and the government officials responsible for Irish tourism policy. For the tourist, the holiday experience is a personal one, but to those involved in providing a memorable holiday it is a complex balance of social, cultural, economic, and political factors. The needs of the local community providing the services must be balanced against the expectations of the tourist.

The first section provides excellent case studies of holiday resorts—Kilkee, County Clare, in the West of Ireland, and the east coast town of Bray. The two historical accounts compare and contrast the social class origins and activities of the holiday makers in County Clare with the social geography of Bray. The section "Tourist Images and Representations" includes a discussion of the travel writers' accounts of the Irish and their land after World War II. The impression formed by these travel writers created an "image" that came to represent Ireland and tourism to the outsider. These strong images, Barbara O'Connor argues, have had important, but largely unanalyzed, consequences for the construction of Irish national identity.

Though clearly a successful industry, generating massive economic activity, the tourist industry today finds itself at a crossroads. There are critics who advocate a more structured approach to Irish tourism policy. In the third section of the text, the contributing authors look at tourist policy in this broader perspective. Their examination includes the integration of environmental impacts and long-term concerns. James Deegan and Donal Dineen argue in their chapter on "Irish Tourism Policy" that more tourists may not be desirable for the Irish countryside; they contend that, in the long term, the Irish tourist sector would be better served by concentrating on attracting high-spending, long-staying visitors who would have a more subtle impact on the environment. This section also provides insights

BOOK REVIEWS

into tourism policy in Northern Ireland, including tourism trends and the promotion policies of the Northern Ireland Tourist Board. From this account, it appears that what is good for the Republic is good for the North in the economics of tourism. The changing patterns of tourism in the Republic have had an impact on the North, and there is much evidence that suggests a united tourism policy would benefit both regions.

The fourth section of the text examines the emerging growth areas of heritage, often called "cultural tourism." The authors base their arguments on a theory of heritage that defines "cultural tourism" not as merely "nostalgic," but rather as giving the visitor an immediate confrontation with the past. They caution, however, that where such experiences are highly structured, as in a historical theme park, planners must avoid the creation of pseudo-histories. Similarly cautious, the final section looks closely at the relationship between the development of rural tourism and economically disadvantaged areas of the nation. The authors are quite critical of simplistic views that assume tourism will turn into a development panacea. They urge a cautious approach to rural tourism development, stressing that rural communities may lose much by developing a tourist industry.

The authors of *Tourism in Ireland* discuss the costs of tourism to the long-term cultural identity of the nation. The tourism industry brings a set of images that tourists want to see, which images may or may not be appropriate to the local culture. Many communities abandon their local culture: often, the locals will be tempted to adapt to visitors' expectations because the tourists come from economically and politically more powerful cultures—that is, one North America. These researchers urge a more holistic and communally conscious approach in which individual economic gain is not the only objective. The authors and editors of *Tourism in Ireland* suggest several starting points for future research. We might ask, for instance, for an investigation of the "levels of vertical integration" in the industry. Or, who owns and who controls the heritage industry? And, what long-term effect may tourism have on rural communities?

The future of tourism in Ireland depends partly on the future of tourism itself. If the global growth in tourism predicted for the twenty-first century occurs, then Ireland and its tourism industry will continue to grow and change with the industry. Tourism will play a critical part in where the nation will find itself in the next century. This volume may serve as a seminal work for much needed research to come, which will in turn have an impact on the public policy of tourism in Ireland.

—*Susan Raftery*

George Moore and the Autogenous Self: The Autobiography and the Fiction by Elizabeth Grubgeld, pp. 308, Syracuse, NY: Syracuse University Press, 1994, $49.50

Like wits in a Restoration comedy, the friends of George Moore honored his person with a rodomontade of abusive epithets: Moore was a codfish crossed by a satyr, the gray mullet, a boiled ghost, an overripe gooseberry, the white slug, a large distinguished carp, an aborted egg, a very prosperous Mellon's Food baby, and a cat-mummy from the Egyptian Department of the British Museum. In her important new book on Moore, Elizabeth Grubgeld collates these insults, but characteristically she takes them quite seriously as the starting point for a penetrating analysis of the Edwardian social climate of caricature out of which they come, with its competitive display of wit and what Beerbohm called its lust for bedeviling the unfortunate human body. Previously, there has sometimes been a certain *ad hominem* strain in Moore criticism, not surprising among his contemporaries, who were often trying to give as good as they'd gotten, but peculiar when found among contemporary scholars, What this book by Grubgeld offers instead is a learned, theoretically astute, comprehensive, and sympathetic look at the writings of George Moore.

The author of a study like *George Moore and the Autogenous Self* has clearly set aside a significant part of her lifetime for its preparation. To put the study of George Moore on a serious footing, and to show others the peculiar appropriateness of Moore's work to the questions that animate literary criticism today, Grubgeld has at least mentioned, and often analyzed, thirty-eight different publications by Moore. And her scholarly habits are impeccable: she keeps in mind the chronology of Moore's life, the changes over time in his conception of fiction, the differences between one edition and the next, the letters of Moore to others, the letters others exchanged about Moore, and the history of discussion about each book she herself treats. That is just to list the general categories of Mooriana. In addition, she has some ongoing theoretical interests, which lead her to engage with recent research in genre studies in general, autobiography in particular, letters in one quite original chapter, and, to a smaller extent, gender studies. Her special slant is to treat the characters in novels as their own autobiographers, and the narrator of the autobiographies as if he were a character in a novel, and thus a function of plot, scene, chronology, and narrative voice. What is left out of account? She is not much interested in the history of reception, or, with the exception of her chapter on *Parnell and His Island,* in most of the matters that excite cultural materialists. This is not, obviously, a criticism of her book, which entertains a startling variety of theoretical claims without losing its way or giving up its independence of judgment.

Grubgeld's abiding interest is in what Michel Foucault called "the author function." For some time before this article, literary scholars had been repeating Roland

Barthes's argument about the "death of the author": once a writer entered into making a text, the language he inscribed took on a life of its own, most distinctly a life not the author's, and many meanings of its own, none of them the author's. Foucault put the question in an entirely new light: what are the uses, he asked, to which we put the concept of the author? What is its function especially in ancient literature, where we shelve and publish things under the name of Callimachus or Diodorus? These names mean to us no more than certain grammatical features, genre tendencies, periods and places of activity; about the men, we know nothing. In short, the "author function" becomes a way of naming our conception of the way a group of writings happens to cohere.

What Grubgeld lights upon is the fact that GM, as friends called him, did not just write individual consumption commodities, one novel after another, good or bad, to be ascribed to "George Moore," the name on the title page. He studiously elaborated a complex and developing identity for public consumption, manifested in letters to newspapers, public enactments of a studied role, five autobiographies, autobiographical characters in novels, and imaginary conversations. This "George Moore" was first put into books under other names, like "Harding" in the novels of the early 1880s, or "Landlord M—" in *Parnell and His Island;* but from the second edition of *Confessions of a Young Man,* he appeared always as "George Moore." Oddly, this self-created fictional self was not a wish-fulfillment; indeed, he is consistently, at least in some ways, unattractive, even repellent. He has cold blue eyes, weak shoulders, and a body it is surprising a number of women could have loved; he is vain, sometimes insensitive to the poor, cruel to relatives, and on policy unashamed. And "George Moore" is perpetually interested in, and bewildered by, "George Moore": why should he be as he is?

It is true, as Grubgeld shows, that GM and "George Moore" looked and acted rather alike. Even some of the most discomfiting, embarrassing things "George Moore" does in the books, the record shows GM apparently did before him. To take just one instance of stories about his disgraceful behavior to his family, when telling the story of his mother's final illness, a mother who had always been patient with him, against whom he held no grudge, "George Moore" says that he could not bring himself to hurry to her bedside in Ireland, and instead lingered in London, because just a few weeks earlier his young mistress had broken off their affair and he could think of nothing else. As a matter of fact, not long before Mrs. Mary Moore died, Maud Burke, GM's lover, married Sir Bache Cunard, bringing to an end what was for him his most memorable romance.

GM did not, however, put all of himself into "George Moore." Grubgeld shows, on the basis of his correspondence, that he left out the tact, kindness, and generosity that appear in his letters to Gosse, and the flattery, gentleness, coyness, and absence of irony that show up in his letters to young women. So why did he elaborate a tale upon the fact that he could not mourn his mother? Grubgeld has a number of answers. One is that GM had to repudiate his nation, his religion, and most es-

BOOK REVIEWS

pecially his family to make "George Moore." Another is that he wanted to make sport with the sensibilities of "the bourgeois reader," that *hypocrite lecteur.*

But these are local explanations. Grubgeld's most serious account of what for GM made "George Moore" is his conception of "instinct." In the early 1880s, GM, then a student of Zola, believed that people could be explained in terms of their environment, heredity, and instinctual nature. According to this way of thinking, the self is not really free, and GM can be no more than "Landlord M—" of County Mayo. Then in the mid-1880s, he went to school to Schopenhauer, who explained there was a world of will and a world of idea: in the later, we seemed rational, moral, far-sighted, and apparently free; in the former world, which is the real one, we were simply expressions of an ongoing and impersonal life-force—of a great "instinct" bent on reproducing itself. GM found the pessimism of this view of humans as theorizing animals strangely exciting, but he was restless with its definition of instinct. As he developed his own version of "instinct," according to Grubgeld, he tended to write as if a special sort of transcendental instinct *did* set one free, that one being "George Moore," the autogenous self of the title, and maybe a few others, such as Manet and maybe Wagner. Furthermore, this instinct always led him right, even when it led him to be apparently callous to his dying mother, because it brought him to be himself, "George Moore." The rest of humanity, however, apparently had no such superhuman guiding instinct; they were in the main the dupes of all-too-human instincts, which made them, for all their idealizations, greedy, lustful, and foolish. An unsettled and developing dialectic between GM's conception of humanity as a thing made by its past and its species-being, and his own inward sense of himself as a thing made by himself, basically between determinism and freedom, is traced with considerable depth throughout Moore's work by Grubgeld. For the most part, she remembers that Moore acts sometimes as if his "instinct" were a real entity, and part of a serious rethinking of life from end to end, and at other times as if it were a colossal put-on, meant to make fun of the hopeless human aspiration to understand our existence.

This inquiry into the sources of identity leads Grubgeld to very interesting speculations about the relation between the created self ("George Moore") and the sense of time, as manifested in various genres. In his autobiographical writings, GM was prescient, she says, in his depiction of the one who speaks in the story as different from the one who writes it, both of these from the one who acts in it, and all three from the one who is. In one scene from *Memoirs of My Dead Life,* for instance, GM constructs a situation in which nearly all these split selves are present: his "old self," then impotent, tells a story of his "young self," who reportedly met a woman in Paris who used to tell him about her affairs; once she told him of standing in front of a mirror with her lover, both of them naked, and she said, "My, I did look a little tot beside him!" Here you have old "George Moore" looking at young "George Moore," looking at the image in the eyes of a young woman, who looks at herself suddenly with the eyes of her lover. Grubgeld, with her relish for

BOOK REVIEWS

complexities, points out that the narrator, amused and objectifying, is like the reader: both can watch, neither can be seen; both can enjoy, neither can be touched. But voyeurism for "George Moore" is no shameful perversity; it is the highest form of sex. To the inveterate autobiographer, self-watching is story-telling; and story-telling is self-making.

If *George Moore and the Autogenous Self* has a weak point—and of course, every reader will quibble page-by-page, as with any original book—I suppose one could say that Grubgeld writes best of least-written-about texts—"texts" in the broad sense; some of the best things are about gossip, frontispieces, dedications, and other manifestations of the author-function— and least well of most-written-about texts, such as that great but wearisome novel *Esther Waters*. On the whole, however, this is an excellent example of literary criticism. It appears to have been the ambition of its author not to write the last word on George Moore, but a book that would beget yet other books, by illustrating how stimulating an author Moore is, given the variety of genres in which he worked and the complexities of his authorial personality, as stimulating indeed as the most famous novelists of the period. If there are other studies of Moore forthcoming—and Moore à la Lacan should be on its way—they have here a high standard to meet.

—*Adrian Frazier*

Learning the Trade: Essays on W. B. Yeats and Contemporary Poetry, ed. by Deborah Fleming, pp. 313, West Cornwall, CT: Locust Hill Press, 1993, $32.00.

According to the historian Joseph Lee, Irish economic performance has been "the least impressive in Western Europe . . . in the 20th century." The same country overflows with poets of the first rank. Is there a relationship between these facts? If so, what is it? Yeats would have seen the flowering of poetry after him as a vindication of his belief that Ireland's escape from industrialism and materialism made it fertile ground for poetry. It was this Yeatsian doctrine that was espoused by F. R. Higgins when, in a famous BBC exchange with Louis MacNeice, he maintained that Irish poets benefited from "the spiritual buoyancy of a belief in something . . . [,] a belief emanating from life, from nature, from revealed religion, and from the nation." Is this so? Is it true, as Heaney puts the question, that "poetry might have a desirable . . . relation to the life of a nation . . ."? Heaney suggests that Paul Muldoon's reprinting of the Higgins-MacNeice exchange in his *Faber Book of Contemporary Irish Poetry* implies that answering the question in the affirmative "is at best to commit a literary offense, at worst to promote dubious mystiques involving race memory and the chosen-people complex." Nonetheless, Heaney concedes that "however neatly we want a verdict against hazy romantic notions about the poet's bardic relation to his inheritance," the "troublesome complexities" of "the solidarities and antagonisms of politics" keep "nagging at MacNeice and Muldoon"—as they do at Heaney himself and at every Irish poet.

The reader looks to *Learning the Trade* for some explication of these heart mysteries, both because the volume takes its title from Yeats's injunction to "Irish poets," and because Yeats was, as Heaney observes in *The Field Day Anthology*, "the preeminent theorist, visionary and exemplar of a literature based on the category of nationality."

Paul Muldoon's sparring with Yeats on these issues in "7, Middagh Street" is the subject of the volume's thoughtful opening essay by Jonathan Allison. Muldoon's poem consists of seven monologues by various residents of an artistic colony in Brooklyn Heights in 1940–41. Perhaps liberated by his own relocation to the United States, Muldoon invokes the voice of W. H. Auden, one of the monologists, to argue for a cutting of the cord between Yeats and Irish nationality. Taking aim at Yeats's doctrine that all art is a "rooting of mythology in the earth," Muldoon's Auden insists that: "The roots by which we were once bound / Are severed here, in any case, and we are all now dispossessed[.]" Muldoon then sets his Auden to grapple with the famous Yeatsian question on the revolutionary potential of art, "Did that play of mine send out / Certain men the English shot?" "Certainly not," retorts Muldoon's Auden, true to the real-life Auden's insistence, in "In Memory of W. B. Yeats," that "poetry makes nothing happen." Muldoon's Auden then adds insult to injury. In what, in a related essay, John Engle neatly calls "ventriloquistic disrespect," Muldoon's Auden parodies Yeats with the couplet: "If Yeats had saved his pencil-lead / would certain men have stayed in bed?"

Muldoon clearly finds Auden a powerful ally in his quarrel with Yeats's insistence that poetry can, and should, make something happen. Muldoon even seems willing to accept the assertion in Auden's "The Public v. the Late Mr. W. B. Yeats" that "art is a product of history, not a cause." Muldoon's Auden makes the same claim: "For history's a twisted root / with art its small translucent fruit / and never the other way round." Auden's claim, while consistent with the theory underlying his apostrophe to Yeats that "Mad Ireland hurt you into poetry," is refuted by Irish history itself, in which the bard's idea of nationalism perennially breathes itself into history. Auden's theory, and the Irish history that refutes it, both validate Elizabeth Bowen's wish that "the English kept history in mind more, that the Irish kept it in mind less." Perhaps ultimately pulled by the weight of Irish history, Muldoon draws back from letting Auden dominate "7, Middagh Street." Before the poem ends, the voice of MacNeice clearly insists that "poetry *can* make things happen / not only can, but *must*." Even at the far remove of Brooklyn, neither Auden nor Muldoon can escape the link forged by Yeats between poetry and politics. The destructive power of Muldoon's Yeatsian parody—"two girls in silk kimonos / Both beautiful, one a gazebo"—seems ultimately to be no

BOOK REVIEWS

more than a sign, as Mick Imlah put it in a *TLS* review, "of unconscious Muldoonery on Yeats's part."

William Wilson's "Yeats, Muldoon and Heroic History" valiantly, but unpersuasively, attempts to see Muldoon's *Madoc—A Mystery* as a reworking of Yeats's methods and themes in *A Vision*. In fact, *Madoc* rests so heavily on artifice as to raise the question whether Muldoon's enormous talents will not be fully utilized until he foregoes the safety of distance in favor of direct, Yeats-like engagement with his subject matter. This is not to say that Irish poets must involve themselves or their poetry in issues of Irish nationalism. Even F. R. Higgins's dogma is not so narrowly framed. What Higgins claimed for Irish poets was not merely a legacy of belief emanating, in part, "from the nation," but belief itself—what Pound attributed to Browning when he said, "You had some basis, had some set belief."

In Yeats's case, there was belief in a world of the spirit, belief that his poetry would have consequences in reality for which he was responsible, and belief that the process of making a poem enabled him to gain control over his thought and emotion, and thus enabled him to shape his own experience. Perhaps the central Yeatsian belief was that poetry mattered. Whether Irish nationality has a desirable relation to these beliefs is, regrettably, not pursued further. Nor does the volume assess the influence of Yeats's beliefs on the poets under discussion. Most of the remaining essays content themselves with noting similarities with, or differences from, Yeats, but stop short of assessing Yeatsian influence on the nature or quality of twentieth-century poetry.

John Engle's "A Modest Refusal: Yeats, MacNeice and Irish Poetry" finds in MacNeice a "liberating distance" from the claims of Irish nationalism, and argues that such distance provides a more useful exemplar for Irish poets than Yeatsian immersion. Engle makes his case in a vigorously argued appraisal of MacNeice, Montagu, Mahon, Muldoon and Longley. But is a "modest refusal to think big" a worthy goal? One would not have wished for it in Yeats.

Many of the American poets compared with Yeats suffer unnecessarily from the inherent invidiousness of comparison. For example, Edward Lense's article on Theodore Roethke and Yeats leaves the impression that Roethke's principal achievement was that he was not Yeats. Even this dubious accolade is not convincingly established. Lense's assertion "that Roethke almost never really *sounds* like Yeats" (emphasis in original), cannot be squared with Terrence Diggory's detailed showing to the contrary in *Yeats and American Poetry*, a landmark not acknowledged by Lense. Like Lense's Roethke, Lee Zimmerman's Galway Kinnell never seems to emerge into anything more than non-Yeats. Kinnell fares better in Anthony Libby's provocative "Angels in the Bone Shop," which places Kinnell in a tradition, descendant from "Yeats's apprehension of a world still alive with a 19th-century intimacy with nature," a world of particular utility "now that the angels are dying" and "the obvious and radical otherness of animals, their freedom from human ideas, their blessed wildness," make "them logical symbols of connection

BOOK REVIEWS

with the other world, of some sort of spiritual possibility unknowable in ordinary human terms."

Contemporary poets shine more brightly when considered in a context larger than themselves and Yeats. Erik Reece, for example, fruitfully examines Amiri Baraka's "Crow Jane" poems in light of Baraka's refusal, unlike Yeats and Blake, to see love and hate as two sides of the same coin. While Yeats and Blake could find integrating power in the "adversarial potential" of hatred, Baraka's "Crow Jane" poems cannot get beyond "frustrated sadism." Reece's provocative study nonetheless finds a similarity of poetic enterprise in Crazy and Crow Jane to the extent that the authors of both sequences sought "ignorance free of western science, economics and rationality—an ignorance that, as William Carlos Williams wrote in *Paterson,* 'is a kind of knowledge'."

—*Joseph M. Hassett*